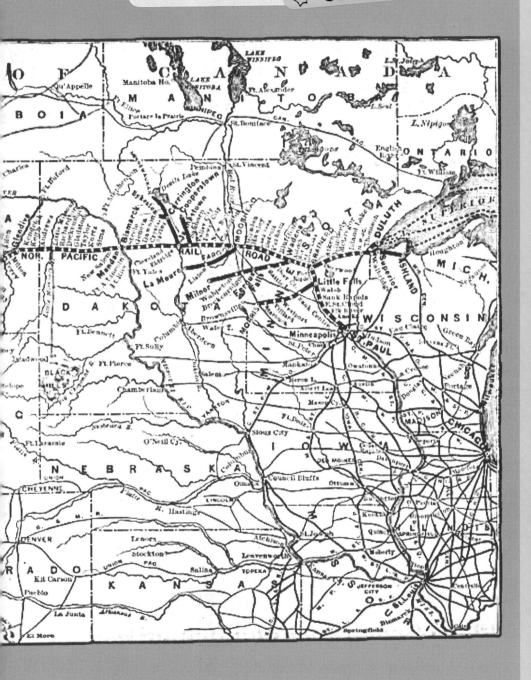

THE MAN WHO FOUND THE MONEY

John Stewart Kennedy

THE MAN WHO FOUND THE MONEY

JOHN STEWART KENNEDY AND THE FINANCING OF THE WESTERN RAILROADS

Saul Engelbourg and Leonard Bushkoff

Michigan State University Press
East Lansing

All Michigan State University Press books are produced on paper which meets the requirements of American national Standard of Information Sciences—Permanence of paper for printed materials ANSI Z39.48-1984.

Michigan State University Press
East Lansing, Michigan 48823-5202

03 02 01 00 99 98 97 96 1 2 3 4 5 6 7 8 9

Library of Congress Cataloging-in-Publication Data

Engelbourg, Saul, 1927-
    The man who found the money : John Stewart Kennedy and the financing of the western railroads / Saul Engelbourg and Leonard Bushkoff.
        p. cm.
    Includes bibliographical references and index.
    ISBN 0-87013-414-0   ⸴
    1. Kennedy, John S. (John Stewart), 1830-1909. 2. Capitalists and financiers—United States—Biography. 3. Philanthropists—United States—Biography.
 4. Railroads—United States—History—19th century. 5. Railroads—Canada—History—19th century. 6. Public libraries—New York (N.Y.)—History. I. Bushkoff, Leonard. II. Title.
HE2754.K46E54   1996
385'.1'092—dc20
[B] 95   41354
                                                                         CIP

To our wives, Charlotte and Kathleen:

Without whom, little is possible;

With whom, everything is possible

CONTENTS

ACKNOWLEDGEMENTS

THIS ACCOUNT OF OBLIGATIONS once owed and now gratefully discharged must begin with our warmest thanks to Albro Martin, whose *James J. Hill and the Opening of the Northwest* (1976), brought John Stewart Kennedy, whose very existence had been virtually unknown, to the fore. Martin not only offered information, counsel and fellowship, but also read an early draft and prevented many an error. Without him, this study would never have been started, much less completed.

Robert V. Bruce, a colleague and friend at Boston University of one of the authors for over thirty years, read the manuscript with his usual attention to detail and readability. We owe him our thanks, as we do to Mansel Blackford, who also read a draft, and the value of whose suggestions, large and small, will be appreciated by all who know his work.

Don L. Hofsommer and the anonymous consultant chosen by the publisher read the penultimate draft, detecting errors of both commission and omission that hitherto had escaped the net.

The research was greatly assisted by numerous American and British scholars and others who responded to inquiries, as did various libraries and other institutions, whose staffs both searched the archives and photocopied various documents. Again, our thanks.

W. Thomas White, the curator of the James J. Hill Reference Library in St. Paul, deserves a special thanks, if only because he offered his great experience as a guide to the invaluable Hill collection, in which our investigations were greatly facilitated by a research grant. John Milnes Baker, a descendant of Kennedy's father-in-law and author of the Baker family history, lent his best efforts to locating any Kennedy material among surviving relatives. In Edinburgh, the Scottish American Investment Company Ltd. photocopied documents, as did Deloitte Haskins & Sells of Glasgow, for records of the City of Glasgow Bank. The Mugar Library of Boston University gave invaluable assistance, as did its Interlibrary Loan Division in particular. Finally, the authors wish to thank the Michigan State University Press for their gracious assistance.

FOREWORD

JOHN STEWART KENNEDY (1830-1909) was a capitalist entrepreneur in an age of economic transformation, a Scots immigrant who excelled in the climb from rags to riches by carving out a fortune—immense for its day—in the railroad building that both conquered the great spaces of America and led its economy to remarkable heights.

Those who harnessed the iron horse during the heroic age of railroad building from the 1850s onward profited enormously, becoming capitalists in an era when that word had no pejorative connotations. The railroads helped rouse the American imagination as they advanced westward from the Eastern seaports, first to the Midwest, ultimately to the Pacific.

Kennedy risked and gained in the great expansion and consolidation of the railroads that still serve as the principal arteries of American commerce. He functioned, to be sure, less as a heroic field marshal than as a senior staff officer, bringing together the capital, supplies and alliances that the great captains—James J. Hill in particular—needed for their campaigns. For each mile of new track required capital, obtained through either short-term loans or by selling stocks and bonds.

Kennedy operated skillfully on either front. As a railroad commission merchant and private banker, he had the information, contacts, prestige and especially the sense of timing required to raise capital at low cost by attracting investors into such new, untried ventures. The railroad operators profited, but so did a nation hungry for efficient transportation. "Merely" a banker and money man, Kennedy played a crucial role in developing the trans-Mississippi transportation and economic system that provided the foundation for the modern American city, for mass production and distribution, and for a truly *United* States.

As railroads grew stronger and more creditworthy, however, they tended to deal directly with their suppliers; Kennedy and other commission merchants no longer were needed. But private bankers remained essential: capital was the lifeblood of any railroad, not least those struggling to maintain their independence in an era of raids, attacks and outright conquests. So Kennedy and others in the know gradually shifted from supplying railroad-related products to providing financial services.

That process also was changing during the 1850s, as private bankers began concentrating in Boston, New York and Philadelphia, while their leaders reached out to potential investors at home and even in Europe, where the lure of a higher rate of return compensated for the risks of investing in the chaotic—but expanding—railroads of a distant, perplexing and sometimes xenophobic land.

▼   ▼   ▼

In all this, private bankers played a crucial—an *indispensable*—role. Not only did they sell securities, but they also led in the reorganizations that saved some railroads during depressions, and they rationalized the industry by consolidating individual lines into regional systems.

These men remain largely unknown, mere names in a vast canvas of economic innovators. What did these private bankers do? How and why did they do it? What were their goals and hopes, skills and methods, problems and difficulties?

Two recent scholarly studies of bankers as entrepreneurs, both based on detailed records, have begun to fill the vacuum: Dolores Greenberg, *Financiers and Railroads, 1869-1889: A Study of Morton, Bliss & Company* (1980); and Vincent Carosso, *The Morgans: Private International Bankers, 1854-1913* (1987).

Greenberg's study, based largely on the George Bliss papers, makes it clear that Morton, Bliss went far beyond merely mobilizing capital. Its partners also owned securities, held directorships and functioned as major decision makers. This extended to railroad consolidations, and even to the actual construction, operation and mergers of such developmental railroads as the Indianapolis, Cincinnati & Lafayette of the early 1870s, and the Canadian Pacific a decade later. Greenberg contends that Morton, Bliss—*not* J. P. Morgan—originated what later became known as "Morganization," i.e., the far-reaching railroad reorganization ventures of the 1890s, which customarily have been attributed to Morgan.

Carosso also argues for the leadership role of the banker. He uses the voluminous Morgan records to present this key private banking enterprise as a true leader, forceful and creative, and not merely a follower, in such security transactions as those involving the New York Central in 1879 and the Northern Pacific in 1880. By portraying Morgan's work as a railroad reorganizer and consolidator in the 1890s—for example, of the Baltimore & Ohio, and the Northern Pacific—Carosso tacitly has aligned himself with Greenberg's interpretation of events.

A more generalized emphasis on the centrality of bankers can be found in Carosso's *Investment Banking: A History* (1970), although it concentrates overwhelmingly on the decades from the 1890s to the 1960s. While both of Carosso's books treat Morton, Bliss & Co., neither mentions J. S. Kennedy & Co., though Kennedy both collaborated and competed with that company, and also with Morgan.

These three books largely exhaust the field. Other private bankers and individual firms have received little scholarly attention, not least because documentation is lacking, company and personal records having been discarded over time. The banker's role in nineteenth-century American economic development is likely, therefore, to remain somewhat unclear, providing more questions than answers, and more speculations than certainties.

These problems arise in any study of Kennedy. His personal papers, and those of J. S. Kennedy & Co., have vanished. He had no children to carry on the company—and perhaps commission a biography of its founder. The extensive James J. Hill archives, and those of the Great Northern (both in St. Paul) do, however, contain substantial correspondence for the thirty years of business dealings between Hill and Kennedy, as well as much other material on Kennedy. He had an equally long relationship with Edinburgh's Scottish American Investment Company, whose archives are helpful. So is Kennedy's testimony and related correspondence in the 1881 trial concerning the liquidation of the City of Glasgow Bank. All these constitute the principal primary sources. None, unfortunately, informs us about Kennedy's early years in Scotland, or of his first steps in American business during the 1850s and 1860s.

About those early years we can only speculate, but it appears that Kennedy was in the classic line of bright, hard-working and upwardly mobile Lowland Scotsmen who benefited from the superior Scottish educational system to vault from the working class into the junior ranks of business. Emigrating permanently to the United States in 1857, he advanced by a partnership with Morris K. Jesup, a commission merchant and private banker, and through a marriage that facilitated entrance into New York financial circles. No doubt he was helped by the booming economy, but he was skilled at exploiting that boom, forming his own banking company at age thirty-eight, in 1868, and suffering remarkably few setbacks in the uncertain financial world of the day.

All this formed the prologue to Kennedy's two-decade climb to a vital niche in railroad finance. During 1868-83, he headed J. S. Kennedy & Co., helped reorganize the Indianapolis, Cincinnati & Lafayette, and then played a key role in transforming the moribund St. Paul & Pacific into the St. Paul, Minneapolis & Manitoba. This coup brought him national recognition, for he became the Manitoba's vice president and a director, standing second only to James J. Hill in leading that line until 1888-89, when Kennedy left it.

After several decades of the most intense and strenuous entrepreneurship, he was then ready—at age fifty-nine—to shift gears downward. Charities and civic activities in New York City always had been important to him; they became vital in his last two decades. And even beyond, for his death in 1909 saw much of his extraordinary fortune distributed to a broad range of charities and philanthropies that were much needed in a growing city of immigrants and social change.

1   THE APPRENTICESHIP OF A FINANCIER

THE RAILROAD BUILDING THAT began in the 1830s with a few tiny lines around the major Eastern seaport cities evolved into major expansion by 1848.

Until the Civil War intervened, railroads built more than a thousand miles of track annually, and more than two thousand in some years; this peaked above three thousand in 1854. In the 1850s, a phenomenal 20,000 miles of track were laid throughout the country, primarily in the South, the Old Northwest, and just across the Mississippi. By then, the Atlantic seaboard had been connected to the Great Lakes and the Ohio River by the Erie, the Pennsylvania, the New York Central, and the Baltimore & Ohio, the great Eastern trunk lines which ultimately controlled this vast territory. In 1847, Chicago had not a single mile of track; by 1860, it had eleven railroads, and was both the national rail center and the fastest growing American city. All this entailed a massive mobilization of private capital by American and British bankers to buy securities and tie lines into east-west through routes which, in turn, gradually sprouted north-south feeders. Consider the result: by 1860, railroad trackage stood at some 30,000 miles, while investment reached about $1 billion, a remarkable figure for the day.

Building intensified after the Civil War. Soon the northern Great Plains were traversed by a handful of powerful lines: the Union Pacific, the Northern Pacific, the Great Northern and the Chicago, Milwaukee & St. Paul. Inevitably, they drove on to the Pacific. The 1880s surpassed other decades in mileage built, and the railroad network was essentially completed by 1890, when capitalization had climbed to $10 billion—though much additional track was built until 1914.

By the 1850s, it was clear that this great transportation revolution required far, far more capital than the sums needed for the new textile mills and iron works that already were transforming economic life. By then, the pattern of railroad finance had been established in Boston, New York and Philadelphia. Capital would have to be mobilized on a grand scale, from investors whose financial horizons barely had exceeded their own vicinity, and who therefore required not merely incentives, but also assurances and guarantees, anything to put the likelihood of gain well ahead of the risk of loss. Here lay opportunities for creativity, innovation, imagination, and a corps of new private bankers stepped forward to fill the breach.

The end of the Civil War brought with it, inevitably, a sharp contraction of Washington's financial needs. The top echelon of private bankers now turned to railroad financing, spurring onward the activity from which there eventually emerged the railroad leaders and financiers who bestrode the continent like so many colossi in the decades after 1865: Jay Gould and Jacob Schiff, James J. Hill and Edward H. Harriman, J. P. Morgan and the Vanderbilts, along with such lesser powers as Morris K. Jesup and George Bliss. These entrepreneurs not only built railroads, but often restructured their capitalization, while consolidating a multitude of short lines into large, self-contained systems.

▼   ▼   ▼

John Stewart Kennedy, first as a migrant from industrial Britain and then as a powerful entrepreneur, added his name to this great industrial movement. This Lowland Scot arrived from the booming Clydeside with skills and business experience rarely held by an immigrant: good schooling and command of English, and a rearing in the homeland of the Industrial Revolution that gave him uncommon insights into its dynamics and possibilities. Kennedy had seen the future—and it worked.

Born in Blantyre, Lanarkshire, Scotland, on 4 January 1830, Kennedy was the fifth son and sixth child of the nine offspring of John Kennedy and Isabella (Stewart) Kennedy. Kennedy's father, a spinner or weaver, was one of those anonymous foot soldiers of the early industrial age, about whom very little is known. Blantyre itself, however, was a major monument to the new era. It was established in 1785 as a self-contained factory village, a model community, with the Clyde River providing power for a cotton spinning mill. There was prosperity and expansion. By 1830, half of the 2,000 inhabitants worked in the mill, with each family occupying a room in the tenements built by management. Crowded though it was, this housing bettered that in the larger towns.[1]

But the Blantyre works were lagging behind others, and this may explain why the elder Kennedy decided to move his family—the infant John Kennedy included—to nearby Glasgow. Here the Industrial Revolution also was in full swing, and on a grand scale. Scotland was much poorer than England until the mid-eighteenth century, but industrialization narrowed the gap.

Migration from the surrounding counties helped Glasgow's population soar from 75,000 in 1800 to 200,000 in 1830, when it ranked as the third largest city in the entire United Kingdom, and formed—along with neighboring Edinburgh—the northern edge of the world's densest consumer market: England, Wales, and lowland Scotland. Cotton textile production dominated Glasgow before 1840, when heavy industry (especially iron and steel, locomotives and rolling stock) began gaining sway. A vigorous export trade—not least, to the United States—and a highly sophisticated banking system nurtured this growth.

One factor in the boom was the remarkable Scots educational system, which fostered literacy and numeracy, providing skills that brought an immediate economic pay-off. Kennedy, for example, acquired sufficient education to write excellent business letters; his later correspondence compares very favorably to that of his peers and associates. He had, in fact, attended school from age six to thirteen, well beyond the usual school-leaving age of eleven, and close to the secondary education of the middle or upper classes. With above-average reading, writing, arithmetic, and possibly bookkeeping, this millhand's son climbed the first rung on the managerial ladder at age thirteen, becoming a clerk in a Glasgow shipping office. He stayed until he was seventeen, in 1847, following both law and custom in receiving formal instruction outside of office hours.[2]

Kennedy then caught the rising tide with his first meaningful position. He became a salesman for the Mossend Iron & Coal Co., one of the large, capital-intensive and vertically integrated firms of a booming iron industry then transforming the Scottish economy while greatly influencing railroad building in the United States and elsewhere.[3] By 1850, Scots and English ironmongers were exporting finished and semi-finished iron products on a large scale. A major force was William Baird & Co., the leading Scots iron manufacturer, which had organized its own marketing system in the United States during the 1840s, with an American as sales agent. While working for Mossend, Kennedy was noticed by Baird & Co., which hired him in 1850, sending him to New York as its first traveling sales representative.[4]

Kennedy stayed for just two years, and undoubtedly visited many of the major commercial and industrial centers: Philadelphia, Boston, Chicago and points between. Americans did not produce iron rails at all until 1844, when the Scranton family and the Lackawanna Iron Co. achieved a breakthrough. So it was British iron producers who fostered the railroad boom of the 1850s—when 200,000 tons of railroad iron were imported *annually* and 20,000 miles of track were laid in all—by selling their rails and other railroad products on credit.

All this activity thrust Kennedy into the thick of things, collecting scattered bits of information as best he could, and dealing with American bankers and commission merchants, as well as with distant railroad companies of uncertain prospects. The responsibility for major decisions was largely his: the trans-Atlantic cable lay in the future. And this brought him close to such major houses as M. K. Jesup & Co.; Winslow, Lanier & Co.; and Duncan, Sherman & Co. They were edging into a banking role, not merely supplying, but also financing railroad expansion.

As a seller of rails, Kennedy very likely contacted Morris Ketchum Jesup, a prominent buyer. Jesup, with whom Kennedy was later to climb the ladder, was well on his way to success. He was the godson of the prominent Morris Ketchum, a leader—for example, as a short-term partner of Junius Morgan—in the railroad expansion of the 1840s and 1850s, and thus a major player in the creation of the Illinois Central. The torch was being passed from one generation to the next, from Ketchum to Jesup, who was exactly Kennedy's age, and who used family and other connections to found Clark & Jesup Co. in 1852. These established men had much to offer Kennedy, the Glasgow millworker's son.

In the every-man-for-himself world of railroading, consolidation already was becoming the watchword. Very few entrepreneurs had realized how much capital the railroads required. The Erie, and also the Baltimore & Ohio, were among the few lines with the resources and vision to define themselves from the outset as long-distance enterprises. Even then, the B & O took two full decades to reach the Ohio River.

But most small, local railroads were financed by small, local capitalists, filled with optimism, and eager to involve their communities—and their own financial interests—in what obviously was the wave of the future, but not always aware of the perils that lay ahead. These lines, lacking substantial capital, were hardly more than stubs, radiating short distances outward from various small cities; connecting links were rare.

This left the way clear for entrepreneurs with vision, who reached out to more distant cities—and markets—by bringing together parallel, connecting and end-to-end railroads. Parallel roads traversed the same territory in the same direction, though at some distance apart; connecting routes provided links, much as a tree's branches join its trunk; and end-to-end railroads united disparate fragments into one entity. The results were impressive: by 1855, three dozen railroads each had over 150 miles of track. The New York Central, for example, was formed by consolidating seven railroads in 1853 to cover some 300 miles from Albany to Buffalo. But long distance construction demanded much capital, and often brought limited returns until far-off destinations had been reached. Only the elite private bankers of Boston, Philadelphia and New York could raise such sums.

Commission merchants, meanwhile, functioned effectively at the low, small-scale end of the railroad spectrum. They served as agents for the new and small railroads which generally lacked the organization to buy the untold number, variety and quantity of products that were needed. In any case, these lines found credit very hard to get during their early, often uncertain years. Clark & Jesup were prepared to help fill these needs, most notably when the Illinois Central was built in the early 1850s. Jesup's godfather, Morris Ketchum, was a founding director of the line, which soon reached Cairo, at the confluence of the Ohio and Mississippi. The contract in this case was not atypical: the firm received $2^1/2$ percent on everything purchased for the rail-road, plus an extra commission of fifteen cents a ton on rails.

Kennedy saw all this at close range until July 1852, when he rose another rung on the ladder, being recalled to Glasgow to head—at age twenty-two—the local office of the Baird company. About the following four years we know virtually nothing, but late 1856 brought a great turning point in Kennedy's career: an invitation from Jesup to join M. K. Jesup & Co. as one of its two junior partners. The term would be ten years, with an option to renew, if mutually agreeable. And Kennedy was to remain in Glasgow, repre-senting the firm there.

Here was a considerable honor for Kennedy, only twenty-six and certainly an outsider on the American business scene. Clearly, he had made a good impression on Jesup and others. But the stipulation that he remain in Glasgow indicates that Jesup was following other investment leaders by estab-lishing a listening post in the British Isles, the very cornerstone of the interna-tional capital market. Kennedy's role would be to play a part in this emerging trans-Atlantic economy by funneling information, contacts and financing to Jesup in New York.

Kennedy accepted the partnership, but not its limitation. He wanted, not a Glasgow where the lines of authority and status were firmly established, but a New York that was the business heart of a booming United States. Kennedy was following the classic Scots trajectory that led the young and ambitious to London, Australia, Canada and throughout the world: moving up meant moving out. And Morris Jesup was wise enough to accept the young Scotsman's proposal. So Kennedy left Baird for Jesup—and New York City—in the spring of 1857. From Blantyre to Glasgow to New York; from clerk to salesman to partner; from minimal responsibilities and income to a say in decisions affecting the most important American industry; and all this by age twenty-seven: the millhand's son indeed had come a very long way.[5]

Now he became an American—and a New Yorker. Immigration, invention and industrialization were rapidly changing the city, much as they had transformed Glasgow, whose population had nearly *tripled* during 1800-30. New York's population of 200,000 in 1830 *quadrupled*—largely through immigration—by 1860, as the traditional artisan class began giving way to a working class, while a burgeoning capitalist class waxed rich on finance, manufacturing, real estate and overseas trade.

Let us consider these capitalists, whom Kennedy was about to join. They numbered some 6,400 in 1855, and included manufacturers, big merchants, bankers and financiers. Not surprisingly, they were overwhelmingly American-born: virtually 5,000 out of the 6,400. The remainder came from Germany and the British Isles: England, Scotland and Ireland. So Kennedy found himself a minority within a minority, part of the Scots fragment within a British/Irish contingent that was far outnumbered by native-born Americans. It is no small irony that this outsider should have spent his life creating the railroads which, more than any other innovation, helped knit these diverse ethnic groups into an American nation.

In little more than a year—on 14 October 1858—Kennedy capped his business success in classic fashion, by marrying a woman of a well-to-do mercantile family. Emma Baker, age twenty-five, of Elizabeth, New Jersey, was the daughter of Cornelius Baker, a substantial coal dealer, who formerly had been a wholesale clothier in New York, and who had helped found New York University. Kennedy had been invited into the family circle in the early 1850s by her brother, Henry Martyn Baker. The connection was tightened by Kennedy's friendship with Matthias Baker Edgar, Emma's uncle and the treasurer of the Illinois Central in the late 1850s. Several of her relatives were prominent in the New York financial world. Her uncle James, for example, was associated with Bank of the Manhattan Company.

Whether the marriage brought Kennedy a dowry or other direct capital is unknown. When Cornelius Baker, a widower, died in 1868, his substantial estate was divided among his six children, with Kennedy himself as one of the two executors. There were stocks and bonds worth some $60,000, plus real estate in New York and elsewhere, as well as the family homestead in Elizabeth. Emma Baker's share certainly helped Kennedy financially, but it hardly was decisive to a man already far wealthier—especially through his partnership in M. K. Jesup & Co.—than his father-in-law.

The marriage nevertheless benefited Kennedy's career (although there were no children), in the access, reputability and standing it provided; all the intangibles that helped smooth this short, stout, Scots immigrant's entrance into the New York financial elite. Kennedy represented that man of the

future, the immigrant with a foreign accent—though muttonchops did provide some protective coloration—who had reinvented himself. All the more
reason for him, lacking the inherited friends or family connections on which
the established elites based their power, to try to integrate himself into
American life by marrying into a family (where he became known as "Uncle
Stewart") which itself had been connected to Peter Stuyvesant in the mid-sev-
enteenth century. And all the more reason for him to cultivate a broad circle
of business associates on which to base his remarkable success in the 1870s
and 1880s.[6]

▼   ▼   ▼

Meanwhile, he plunged into the railroad industry, with all its profits, but
also its risks and complexities. In 1861, there were over 300 separate companies, seven track gauges, and countless unbridged river crossings. Supplies
and financing were vital, and M. K. Jesup & Co. dealt with both. The partners
and their handful of clerks operated in several realms. They imported and
sold rails, locomotives, rolling stock and railroad specialties. They advanced
cash, floated short-term loans, paid interest on bonded debt, and bought and
sold railroad securities, thereby acquiring potentially profitable holdings in
Southern and Western developmental railroads.[7]

The commission merchant greased the wheels of international trade in
various ways. What specific mix of stock, bonds, short-term advances, etc.,
would do the job? For example, the commission merchant might well finance
a deal when an American railroad lacked the cash or credit to buy rails from a
British manufacturer. Or he might speculate by buying a batch of British rails
at a sufficiently low price to turn a pretty profit from a later American buyer.
The merchant bought on commission; sometimes he accepted railroad iron
on consignment and advanced money to the manufacturer. Commission
merchants frequently speculated by selling to the railroad and then purchasing the goods required. In all cases, success depended primarily on knowledge
derived from a wide range of contacts, and on analytical skills born of experience.

Jesup and Kennedy saw Chicago, the nation's pre-eminent railroad center,
as the logical site from which to look South and West. A branch office was
opened in 1859, and Kennedy spent about a year there during 1861-62, reorganizing it to specialize in railroad notes, stocks and bonds. As Jesup's representative, he acquired sufficient prominence to be included among the
hundred or so "incorporators," who lent their names in 1862 to the newly-
organized Union Pacific. The financial downturn of 1857 and the Civil War

slowed construction. But M. K. Jesup & Co. was benefiting from the railroad craze which stirred the towns of the upper Mississippi Valley, whose prosperity seemed certain as the Illinois Central—chartered in 1850 as the very first federal land-grant railroad—pushed southward.

Jesse P. Farley and other prominent citizens of Dubuque, Iowa, for example, had responded by organizing the Dubuque & Pacific, a title richer in hope than reality. But it was one of the many lines dragged into default by the panic of 1857. As the major bondholder, Morris Jesup had it placed in receivership in 1860. It was reorganized—more realistically—as the Dubuque & Sioux City, and its trackage reached Cedar Falls by 1861.[8]

Problems continued, nevertheless: its leaders knew no more about efficient management than did most other small entrepreneurs. It was all very well to lay track, buy rolling stock, and thus create the rudiments of a railroad. Properly managing *and financing* a developmental line was, however, another matter. As an experienced commission merchant, whose livelihood depended on juggling prices and profits, costs and commissions, Kennedy was well placed to reform the Dubuque & Sioux City. Precisely how he and Farley came together is unknown. But that they did so in 1866 or 1867 is clear. This concluded the transfer of authority from local to eastern capitalists, with Jesup becoming the line's president, and James Roosevelt, a New York banker, vice president. The leading stockholders now included Jesup, Kennedy, and D. Willis James, a partner in Phelps, Dodge & Co., a prominent metals dealer and supplier of railroad-related products, for which the line offered a likely customer. James' youth had largely been spent in Scotland, and this doubtless bolstered his close, lifelong business and personal relationship with Kennedy, in which Roosevelt—the uncle of *the* Theodore Roosevelt—also shared.[9]

Here was a classic situation, often repeated in Kennedy's career: a group of small town businessmen, respected locally but invariably under-capitalized, plunge into railroading without fully calculating the odds or the risk of default. The businessmen, fearful of losing their initial investment, turn for money to the eastern capital markets, to New York above all. This means surrendering control to eastern bankers, but the bitter pill is sweetened by the money it brings. And the bankers and investors gain more and more power in the process.

The newly-strengthened Dubuque & Sioux City now was courted by the Illinois Central, which was following other lines in expanding both through construction and by annexing its neighbors. It sought to lease the Dubuque & Sioux City in 1867, but Kennedy bargained hard in acrimonious negotiations; Jesup finally stepped in to achieve a settlement.

Among the properties the line held (and which now passed to the Illinois Central) was a lease on the Cedar Falls & Minnesota Railroad, which ran north from Cedar Falls in Iowa to Mona on the Minnesota border. This railroad under construction had been leased to the east-west Dubuque & Sioux City in 1866, but was not completed until 1868-69. The line had been built cheaply; presumably, improvements would come later. Kennedy was personally involved here, having become the president and dominant voice in 1867 (he remained so for fully twenty years).[10] Now he plunged into yet another battle with the Illinois Central, which was complaining about the low quality of the Cedar Falls line, and was demanding extensive—and expensive—improvements. Kennedy refused, arguing that, having made a deal, the Illinois Central had to accept the consequences. Was the Illinois Central trying, in effect, to nullify the lease?, he complained to Jesup.

The basic issue was not that simple, and it occurred and recurred throughout the railroad age. Capital was the *sine qua non*; it was not unknown for some lines to excavate and grade, but then come a cropper for want of the capital to lay rails. Without government regulation, railroads could build as they pleased, and if Illinois Central trains had to slow down upon reaching the cheaply-constructed Cedar Falls roadbed, this was the price of trying to weld disparate lines into a unified empire. The issue was finally settled in 1869.[11]

All this was part of the learning process for Kennedy during his decade as Jesup's partner. Small railroads had to expand or be swallowed by rivals. Developmental lines—the Dubuque & Sioux City, or the Cedar Falls & Minnesota, for example—could prosper only if "their" territory gained sufficient population and economic activity to increase business. Attracting investors, working with local entrepreneurs, reorganizing capital-starved developmental lines, negotiating with adversaries to protect his interests and those of his allies: all this went into Kennedy's maturation as a businessman, with Morris K. Jesup as a model and James Roosevelt, D. Willis James, and others as associates.[12]

Despite occasional setbacks, the company was profitable and the partners made money. When their ten-year partnership expired in July 1867, Kennedy's net worth of $600,000 placed him, at age thirty-seven, among the richest men in America. Kennedy had made brilliant career choices and had implemented them no less brilliantly: even during a terrible war, there was big money to be made in railroading. The Civil War income tax—which was publicly revealed—presents his earnings for 1863 as an impressive $34,125, not far behind Jesup, who made $44,616 that year. Their partnership expiration offered Kennedy several options: renewal, another partnership, or forming his own firm, which meant risk but also independence.[13]

While considering his future, Kennedy spent much of 1867-68 traveling and visiting in Britain and the Continent. He returned to New York in time to join such other local money men as William E. Dodge of Phelps, Dodge, and also Jay Cooke, in contributing financially to the Republican Grant-Colfax ticket in the election of 1868. Although their low tariff on manufactured goods generally held Kennedy to the Democrats, he responded in this case to Schuyler Colfax's personal solicitations by contributing $1,000, pledging another $1,000 if needed, and offering to solicit funds from other New York businessmen.[14]

By 1868, Kennedy had gone about as far as he could as a subordinate. Was he to become a principal? Was he a risk-taker? Was he satisfied with a small profit, and the small achievements this signified? Or was he driven onward and upward, like the great business potentates of his era? He had acquired the personal wealth, connections and analytical skills to make a powerful mark. His reputation was solid; so was his marriage. There had been no business adventures and no scandals, in an era when "financier" and "buccaneer" too often were linked in the public mind. There were no destructive feuds. Kennedy knew how to get along with his peers, though not always with his subordinates: being in command mattered to him, as we shall see. Finally, the railroad industry was booming, with finance as the key factor on which everything depended. And it was precisely in railroad finance that Kennedy specialized and had succeeded.

NOTES

1. Very little information exists about the first several decades of the life of John Stewart Kennedy. Resort has been made to the sketches in the *National Cyclopedia of American Biography*, 15: 150 and the *Dictionary of American Biography*, 10: 334-35 as well as to the sources cited therein; especially George Austin Morrison, "John Stewart Kennedy," *New York Genealogical and Biographical Record* 41 (July 1910): 163-68; New York Chamber of Commerce, *Fifty-Second Annual Report of the Chamber of Commerce of the State of New York for the Year 1909-1910* (New York Chamber of Commerce, 191), 77-79; A. F. Schauffler, "John S. Kennedy," *Charities Review* 1 (May 1892): 228-31 and obituaries in New York newspapers and periodicals. In addition, John Milnes Baker, *The Baker Family and the Edgar Family of Rahway, N.J. and New York City* (Middletown, N.Y.: Trumbull Publishing, 1972), supplemented other sources by furnishing personal details not otherwise available. On Blantyre, see R.H. Campbell, *Scotland Since 1707* (New York: Barnes & Noble, 1965), 184-85.

2. James Scotland, *The History of Scottish Education* (London: University of London Press, 1969), 1: 183-87; *Biographical Directory of the Railway Officials of America* (Chicago: Railway Age, 1887); *New York Times*, 8 August 1908, 3: 3; Henry Hamilton, *The Industrial Revolution in Scotland* (Oxford: Oxford University Press, 1932), 126; Anthony Slaven, *The Development of the West of Scotland* (London: Routledge & Kegan Paul, 1975), 93; George Seaver, *David Livingstone* (London: Lutterworth Press, 1957), 15-16; Tim Jeal, *Livingstone* (New York: G. P. Putnam's Sons, 1973), 7-8; *Who's Who in America*, 1908-9, 1401; Maurice Walton Thomas, *The Early Factory Legislation* (Leigh-on-Sea, Essex: Thames Bank Publishing, 1948), 209, 213; T. C. Smout, *A History of the Scottish People, 1830-1950* (New Haven: Yale University Press, 1986), 216.

3. Hamilton, *The Industrial Revolution in Scotland*, 187; David Baillie Morrison, ed., *Two Hundredth Anniversary of St. Andrew's Society of the State of New York* (New York: St. Andrew's Society of the State of New York, 1956), 193; Peter L. Payne, *Colvilles and Scottish Steel Industry* (Oxford: Clarendon Press, 1979), 6, 9, 68n.

4. Hamilton, *The Industrial Revolution in Scotland*, 173, 183; Morrison, ed., *Two Hundredth Anniversary*, 193; Payne, *Colvilles*, 48, 54n.16; Alan Birch, *The Economic History of the British Iron and Steel Industry, 1784-1879* (London: Frank Cass and Co., 1967), 174-75; *New York Post*, 6 February 1909; R. D. Corrins, "William Baird & Co. Coal and Iron Masters, 1830-1914," Ph.D. thesis, University of Strathclyde, Glasgow, Scotland, 1974, 1, 14, 32, 84, 90, 93-94, 100, 269, 317.

5. Glenn Porter and Harold Livesay, *Merchants and Manufacturers* (Baltimore: Johns Hopkins University Press, 1971), 85, 103, 106, 106n., 111; R. Gordon Wasson, *The Hall Carbine Affair* (New York: Pandick Press, 1948), 72; Henrietta M. Larson, *Jay Cooke, Private Banker* (Cambridge: Harvard University Press, 1936), 100-1, 104, 163-64; Edward Chase Kirkland, *Men, Cities, and Transportation: A Study in New England History, 1820-1900* (Cambridge: Harvard University Press, 1948), 1: 259; *New York Times*, 3 January 1880, 5: 2; William Adams Brown, *Morris Ketchum Jesup* (New York: Charles Scribner's Sons, 1910), 28, 32-34; Carlton J. Corliss, *Main Line of Mid-America: The Story of the Illinois Central* (New York: Creative Age Press, 1950), 23, 52; Paul Wallace Gates, *The Illinois Central Railroad and Its Colonization Work* (Cambridge: Harvard University Press, 1934), 50, 74, 122; John F. Stover, *History of the Illinois Central Railroad* (New York: Macmillan, 1975), 31; John H. White, Jr., *American Locomotives: An Engineering History, 1830-1880* (Baltimore: Johns Hopkins University Press, 1968), 24; Frank P. Donovan, "The Illinois Central Railroad in Iowa," *Palimpsest* 43 (June 1962): 272; Harold C. Livesay and Glenn Porter, "The Financial Role of Merchants in the Development of U. S. Manufacturing, 1815-1860," *Explorations in Economic History* 9 (Fall 1971): 86; *New York Times*, 20

February 1893; *New York Post,* 6 February 1909; Porter and Livesay, *Merchants and Manufacturers,* 103-4; Brown, *Jesup,* 34-37; Livesay and Porter, "The Financial Role of Merchants," 85n; Dolores Greenberg, *Financiers and Railroads, 1869-1889: A Study of Morton, Bliss & Co.* (Newark: University of Delaware Press, 1980), 45; *Bankers' Magazine* 15 (July 1860): 64; *Commercial & Financial Chronicle* 2 (13 March 1866): 186; 3 (3 November 1866): 545; 3 (10 November 1866): 587; 10 (26 February 1870): 285; Burke Davis, *The Southern Railway* (Chapel Hill: University of North Carolina Press, 1985), 192-93; John F. Stover, *The Railroads of the South, 1865-1900* (Chapel Hill: University of North Carolina Press, 1955), 128.

6. Various legal documents relating to the estate of Cornelius Baker: Accounting; Memorandum of Final Distribution, 1889; Inventory; and Last Will and Testament; *Who's Who in America,* 1908-1909, 1041.

7. *New York Post,* 6 February 1909; *New York Times,* 20 February 1893; Brown, *Jesup,* 35.

8. Donovan, "The Illinois Central Railroad in Iowa," 267, 272; Leland L. Sage, *A History of Iowa* (Ames: Iowa State University Press, 1974), 114; Letter of Thomas Warnock, general manager, Dubuque & Sioux City, to M. K. Jesup, 1 March 1866, Illinois Central Railroad Papers, Newberry Library, Chicago; Stover, *History of the Illinois Central Railroad,* 129, 131-32; Corliss, *Main Line of Mid-America,* 79, 143-44, 146-47; Jesse Kelso Farley, Jr., *Twelve Generations of Farleys* (Evanston, Ill.: Privately Printed, 1943), 137-38.

9. David McCullough, *Mornings on Horseback* (New York: Simon and Schuster, 1981), 26-27; Farley, Jr., *Twelve Generations,* 140.

10. Letter of Charles L. Frost, president, Toledo, Peoria & Western, to Louis Boisot, treasurer, 21 March 1867 and Letter of J. S. Kennedy to M. K. Jesup, president, Dubuque & Sioux City, 25 November 1868, Illinois Central Railroad Papers, Newberry Library, Chicago.

11. Thomas C. Cochran, *Railroad Leaders, 1845-1890* (Cambridge: Harvard University Press, 1953), 47; Notes on Cedar Falls & Minnesota based on Carolyn Curtis Mohr, *Guide to the Illinois Central Archives in the Newberry Library, 1856-1906* (1951); Letters of J. S. Kennedy, president, Cedar Falls & Minnesota, to M. K. Jesup, president, Dubuque & Sioux City, 1 July 1868, 12 November 1869, Illinois Central Railroad Papers, Newberry Library, Chicago; Stover, *History of the Illinois Central Railroad,* 131, 135; Donovan L. Hofsommer, " 'The Grandest Railroad Project of the Age'," *Annals of Iowa* 44 (Fall 1977): 129, 135.

12. *Bankers' Magazine* 15 (July 1860): 64; *Commercial & Financial Chronicle* 3 (3 November 1866): 545.

13. *New York Times,* 8, 11 July 1865.

14. Charles H. Coleman, *The Election of 1868* (New York: Columbia University Press, 1933), 24, 33, 43, 62, 90, 92; Willard H. Smith, *Schuyler Colfax* (Indianapolis: Indiana Historical Bureau, 1952), 1, 282, 286, 307-8; Eric Foner, *Reconstruction: America's Unfinished Revolution, 1863-1877* (New York: Harper & Row, 1988), 338n. 105; Walter T. K. Nugent, *Money and American Society, 1865-1880* (New York: Free Press, 1968), 101; Ellis P. Oberholtzer, *Jay Cooke* (Philadelphia: George W. Jacobs & Co., 1907), 2: 70-71; Larson, *Jay Cooke*, 202; Robert P. Sharkey, *Money, Class, and Party: An Economic Study of the Civil War and Reconstruction* (Baltimore: Johns Hopkins University Press, 1959), 289; Letter of John S. Kennedy, New York, to Schuyler Colfax, 5 June 1869, Heartman Collection, New-York Historical Society, New York.

2 KENNEDY AS AN INDEPENDENT ENTREPRENEUR

IN 1868, KENNEDY TOOK the big plunge by opening J. S. Kennedy & Co., a commission merchant and private banking house that combined credit with trade, and specialized in creating and discounting commercial paper. Such enterprises linked the manufacturers of railroad supplies with the lines themselves, providing market information and purchasing services. This mattered most during the pioneering construction phase, when everything from beans and black powder to rails and rolling stock were vital to the great movable construction camps that inched their way across the landscape from spring to autumn—so long as there was financing.

Commission merchants faced a dark future, however. The cream had been skimmed off the market, as the established lines sought financing on their own, while their purchasing agents negotiated directly with the manufacturers' salesmen. And the small lines were increasingly being gobbled up by the big companies. So the traditional commission merchants were becoming obsolete, facing an uncertain future, without clients.

Kennedy was perceptive enough to recognize this—and to act accordingly. His solution? It was for J. S. Kennedy & Co. to join the forward-looking houses by combining commission merchantry with private banking. Such banks had proliferated after the panic of 1837, and there were several thousand by the 1850s, when they constituted about one-third of all American banks, and held about one-fourth of the banking capital.

Inevitably, the larger private banks were attracted to that booming new industry, the railroad. These banks mobilized short and long-term capital. They invested their own funds, directed the reorganizations needed to rescue defaulting rail lines, and served as officers and directors. The risk could be fearful: some banks hovered at times between ruin and immense profit.

And he had the wealth for private banking: a $600,000 net worth in 1867, plus—we can assume—his wife's share in her father's estate, not including the capital and connections provided by friends and his wife's family. Though

15

J. S. Kennedy & Co. began as a one-man operation, Kennedy clearly intended to bring in partners, presumably drawn from the extended family into which he had married. So a family partnership soon was established, with Kennedy holding half, while his brother-in-law, Henry Martyn Baker, held a quarter after joining in 1868. Baker's brother-in-law, John Sanford Barnes, whose legal knowledge quickly made him invaluable to Kennedy, took the final quarter when he entered in 1870.

Business was good, and the results were impressive. In 1871, for example, Kennedy informed a reporter for R. G. Dun & Co., the credit rating agency, that Baker and Barnes (both were about forty) were each worth between $100,000 and $200,000, while he himself had about a million. Kennedy had nearly *doubled* his wealth in the four years since 1867, and stood among the 115 millionaires in New York as of 1870. He was far ahead of J. P. Morgan, for example, then thirty-four, whose net worth was about $350,000 (though his father, Junius, had over $5,000,000).[1]

Barnes proved very helpful in resolving some problems remaining from the amicable, but complex, dissolution of Kennedy's partnership with Jesup. One such issue related to bonds the partners held in the troubled Texas & New Orleans Railroad, which reached from Beaumont to the nascent regional hub at Houston. Barnes traveled, first to Texas and then to Europe, to find one of the owners, whom he convinced to transfer his bonds from Jesup to Kennedy. The bonds later were sold profitably, and Barnes became president of the line, but its troubles continued. Foreclosure occurred in 1874, and the line stopped in its tracks, though it did reopen in 1876.[2]

Here was painful proof of the desperate need of many Southern lines for capital to rebuild and expand after the Civil War and its destruction. Kennedy became involved in Southwestern railroading through an interest in the Houston & Texas Central Railroad, a north-south line that had been restored since the war. Developmental railroading, meant to service the local economy, was not easy in a state so sparsely populated, with so little capital and not one major city. But beyond Texas was Mexico, with its largely untapped mineral wealth.

So Kennedy found himself among such important New York investors as Moses Taylor, the president of the National City Bank; John J. Cisco, the treasurer of the Union Pacific, and head of the merchant and private banking firm bearing his name; and William E. Dodge of Phelps, Dodge & Co.—who was related to D. Willis James, Kennedy's close friend for some years. Consequently, J. S. Kennedy & Co. began advertising Houston & Texas Central bonds in 1869; the capital raised helped connect Texas railroads with those to the north and east.[3]

Expansion was swift. In 1866, Taylor, Cisco, Dodge and other New York capitalists had chartered yet another line, the Houston & Great Northern, to push north from Houston. Soon thereafter, in 1870, the International Railroad was created, to drive south to the Rio Grande at Laredo: Mexico lay ahead. Barnes, already leading the Texas & New Orleans, served as Kennedy's proxy, first as president and later as vice president, of the International.

Kennedy stepped in personally during 1872, when the International and its various Texas components were reshaped by the New York investors into the International & Great Northern Railroad (which ultimately entered Jay Gould's railroad empire). Kennedy invested substantially in the new line, becoming both its president and a director; in 1878, he was to become chairman of the reorganization committee. The emigrant from industrialized Scotland was putting his mark on the vast empty spaces of the Texas frontier, and was poised to play an international role, an experience that prepared him for bigger tasks.[4]

But an internal dispute was brewing throughout the 1870s between Kennedy and Henry Martyn Baker, his partner and brother-in-law. Kennedy apparently felt that Baker could not handle large and complex matters. They had a falling out after the panic of 1873 subsided, and Baker left in the late 1870s. The firm's standing was not affected, however. Barnes remained as junior partner, and did most of the traveling, while Kennedy handled key policy issues from the New York office.[5]

J. S. Kennedy & Co. followed other commission merchants in turning a profit through the negotiating skill that bought low and sold high. Importing pig and foundry iron, as well as iron and steel rails, it served as the agent for such leading British producers as the Bowling Iron Company of the Glasgow region, and the West Cumberland Hematite Iron Company. On the American side, Kennedy represented western Pennsylvania's Cambria Iron Company and the Edgar Thomson Steel Company, Ltd., a part of Andrew Carnegie's empire.

Much depended on the fluctuations of the business cycle. Prosperous times meant increased rail traffic, hence increased building. The accompanying clamor for railroad material drove prices up, putting the manufacturer in a strong position. Conversely, economic downturns meant less building—and lower prices for his rails, switches, etc. These fluctuations could be rapid, sharp and notably unforgiving to those caught on their wrong side.

One way to lessen the danger was, of course, through such private arrangements as serving simultaneously as the fiscal agent of a railroad and the selling agent of a manufacturer. This we would consider blatant conflict of interest. Not so with Kennedy and his contemporaries, who had no doubts regarding their own probity. In fact, he regarded such arrangements as a point in his favor, worth advertising for all to see.[6]

It was up to the commission merchant to maneuver through these gates and barriers, especially when the panic of 1873 brought turmoil to the market. The key item was rails, with iron giving way in the 1870s to the vastly superior steel version. Different lines used varying types and weights, complicating the merchant's task and making his commission more flexible.

All this could of course mean profits, but banking nevertheless was the real wave of the future. And the Kennedy firm began functioning as a *de facto* private banker, particularly as a conduit for European, and especially English and Scottish capital. Kennedy's agent in London was Robert Benson & Co., an estimable but second-level firm that marketed American railroad securities and also represented the Illinois Central. Kennedy reciprocated by buying American bonds for Benson. Though Benson failed in 1875, this cost Kennedy & Co. only some $3,400.[7]

A new railroad, its future still uncertain, had little chance of reaching investors directly. It needed endorsement from a reputable commercial firm with a good credit rating before either individual or institutional investors would take the plunge. It was this legitimization that Kennedy, with his reputation for probity and wisdom, could provide. But success depended on his ability to assess risks; failure meant being stuck with unsalable securities, notes which had been defaulted, or associates whose losses dragged a firm down—as happened widely during the 1873 panic. Reputation, prestige, credibility were everything.

Although Kennedy had a toe in the waters of railroad management while still a junior partner in M. K. Jesup & Co., he immersed himself more fully after forming his own firm. For example, in 1873, Kennedy himself held top management positions in several railroads: as vice president and director of the Indianapolis, Cincinnati & Lafayette; as president and director of the Cedar Falls & Minnesota; and as a director of both the Cincinnati & Lafayette and the International & Great Northern. He also acted as the trustee of various railroad mortgages.

▼   ▼   ▼

The absence of records makes it impossible to gauge the relative importance of these and other similar positions and ventures. By the early 1870s, however, Kennedy was as one with such private bankers as Morton, Bliss & Co. who were not merely mobilizing capital, but were actively *managing* railroads, especially new and untried lines.

Of course, there were tensions. The aggressive railroaders, far out on the plains, tended to ignore risks as they rushed ahead in the short building season. The cautious money men in New York, always fearful—especially after the panic of 1873—of over-extension and disaster, were apprehensive. Inevitably, it was the financiers who held the high cards and shaped the game; Kennedy was part of the process.[8]

NOTES

1. Vincent P. Carosso, *The Morgans: Private International Bankers, 1854-1913* (Cambridge: Harvard University Press, 1987), 141; R. G. Dun Credit Ledgers, 7 June 1871, 3 July 1873, New York City, v. 348, p. 900, sub-p. A5, Baker Library, Harvard Business School.

2. James J. Heslin, "John Sanford Barnes (1836-1911)," *New-York Historical Society Quarterly* 47 (January 1963): 63; John D. Hayes, "The Battle of Port Royal, S. C. From the Journal of John Sanford Barnes, " *New-York Historical Society Quarterly* 45 (October 1961): 368, 372; John Sanford Barnes, "My Egotistigraphy," Typescript, 1910, New-York Historical Society, 291-96; *American Railroad Manual*, 1873, 374; Charles S. Potts, *Railroad Transportation in Texas*, Bulletin of the University of Texas No. 119 (Austin: University of Texas, 1909), 38; Don L. Hofsommer, *The Southern Pacific, 1901-1985* (College Station: Texas A & M University Press, 1986), 159; *Commercial & Financial Chronicle* 10 (12 February 1870): 208; 21 (4 September 1875): 231; S. G. Reed, *A History of Texas Railroads* (Houston: St. Clair Publishing Co., 1941), 225; James P. Baughman, *Charles Morgan and the Development of Southern Transportation* (Nashville: Vanderbilt University Press, 1968), 195, 217-18, 218n; David G. McComb, *Houston: A History* (Austin: University of Texas Press, 1981), 28-29; "Edwin D. Morgan," *Dictionary of American Biography*, 13: 108-9.

3. *American Railroad Manual*, 1873, 373-74; Lowitt, *A Merchant Prince*, 268; Daniel Hodas, *The Business Career of Moses Taylor: Merchant, Finance Capitalist, and Entrepreneur* (New York: New York University Press, 1976), 254; Maury Klein, *The Life and Legend of Jay Gould* (Baltimore: Johns Hopkins University Press, 1986), 305; Harold van B. Cleveland and Thomas F. Huertas, *Citibank, 1812-1970* (Cambridge: Harvard University Press, 1985), 346n. 17; Potts, *Railroad Transportation in Texas*, 39, 49; *Commercial & Financial Chronicle* 9 (3 July 1869): 4, 13; 9 (31 July 1869): 132; Ira G. Clark, *Then Came the Railroads: The Century from Steam to Diesel in the Southwest* (Norman: University of Oklahoma Press, 1958), 63; Baughman, *Charles Morgan*, 201; McComb, *Houston*, 28; Hofsommer, *Southern Pacific*, 163.

4. Barnes, "My Egotistigraphy," 298, 300; *Biographical Dictionary of American Railway Officials; American Railroad Manual*, 1873, 372-74; Hodas, *Moses Taylor*, 251-52; Lowitt, *A Merchant Prince*, 270; Reed, *A History of Texas Railroads*, 315, 318-19; Potts, *Railroad Transportation in Texas*, 54-55; Clark, *Then Came the Railroads*, 64; Robert E. Caudle, *History of the Missouri Pacific Lines, Gulf Coast Lines, and Subsidiaries International Great Northern* (n.p., 1949), 58-65; Baughman, *Charles Morgan*, 202; *Commercial & Financial Chronicle* 15 (13 July 1872): 44; 15 (14 September 1872): 354.

5. Barnes, "My Egotistigraphy," 296-97, 304.

6. Ibid, 302; *Commercial & Financial Chronicle* 10 (19 March 1870): 384.

7. Stanley D. Chapman, *The Rise of Merchant Banking* (London: George Allen & Unwin, 1984), 44, 129, 133, 153; Barnes, "My Egotistigraphy," 302; R. G. Dun & Co. Collection Credit Ledgers, 17 June, 15 October 1875, New York City, v. 348, p. 900, sub-p. A22; Mira Wilkins, *The History of Foreign Investment in the United States to 1914* (Cambridge: Harvard University Press, 1989), 205, 863.

8. Greenberg, *Financiers and Railroads*, 219-21; *Poor's Manual of the Railroads*, 1873-74, advertisement, 18.

3 KENNEDY AND THE SCOTTISH AMERICAN INVESTMENT COMPANY

FOREIGN INVESTMENT IN THE United States provided billions to an economy that hungered for capital. The railroads, hungering the most, and offering the most, received most by far of this capital formation, and could not have been built without it. The *total* investment in American railroads came to a billion dollars or more in 1867, three billion in 1873, five billion in 1880, and fully ten billion in 1890. The source for some forty percent of this capital before 1914 was Europe, with Britain (including Scotland) far ahead.

The Scottish contribution to all this was vital. Scottish investment, in fact, *doubled* in a mere seventeen years, during 1873-90. And 1873-83 saw Scotland provide perhaps *two-thirds* of total British investment in the American stock market and in mortgages, particularly those of Western grazing lands.

But the absence of political or judicial strictures made international investment inherently risky, as European investors learned throughout the nineteenth century. Witness the bond default by fully *nine* American states in the 1840s, and the occasional cheating of British investors in American cattle ranches, not to mention those injured when the New Haven Railroad issued fraudulent stock in the 1850s. Witness also the easy "writing down"—frequently by as much as a quarter or a third—of capital, so often foreign, during the many railroad reorganizations later in the century.

Foreign investors were fair game to state legislative and judicial attacks, though federal courts, their presidential-appointed judges free from local pressures and more sensitive to the country's need for foreign capital, were much better. Nevertheless, honesty and legality were not invariably respected in the new land. And if the victims were unknown Britons, thousands of miles away, so much the worse for them.

Though British investors were attracted by high rates, they were wary of bonds that seemed to promise too much. There was no way to verify information that was limited and often unreliable, if not downright deceitful.

21

Legal and quasi-legal safeguards for the buyer were almost entirely lacking. Recourse to American courts would hardly help investors in far-off Europe, who were confused in any case by the differences between state and federal jurisdictions. And a vulnerable investor was a fearful one.

How could this fear of the unknown, the unpredictable and unaccountable, be countered? The way lay clear for a third party, with a reputation for trustworthiness and competence in international investment, to step into the breach. And this is precisely what J. S. Kennedy & Co., with its Scots background and its American presence, connections and experience, could do, offering peace of mind to hundreds of small investors who desired the goal but feared the means.

Here was the basis for the winning combination which Kennedy was to pioneer in 1873 with a new force in the Scottish financial world: the Scottish American Investment Company, Ltd., the very first investment company in Scotland (a dozen or so more were to imitate it), and a great success in focusing exclusively on the United States.

In a capital market of individual investors, here was an innovation attuned to the needs of the day: an *institutional* investor, mobilizing small but regular clients—some 500 in 1875—for long-term investing, rather than short-term trading, by satisfying their search for higher returns than the British Isles offered. Capital could, in fact, be obtained in Scotland for about half its cost in the United States. Starting with £1,000,000 in 1873, the firm doubled it by 1875, as new investors flocked to the winner's column. As of 1880, it had invested fully £1,250,000 in the United States, while prudently holding back a substantial reserve with which to snap up any targets of opportunity.[1]

Kennedy devoted much of his effort, and that of J. S. Kennedy & Co., to serving as its New York agent during 1873-83; no other clients were comparable in size and significance. And he remained on Scottish American's Advisory Board for fully twenty-five years. In effect, Kennedy was helping achieve a profitable synthesis between Scots thrift and American opportunity.

He worked in alliance with William John Menzies, the founder and managing director of Scottish American. Menzies had a background in law, finance and investment advising. He knew America from his travels there in 1864, 1867 and 1872, which also strengthened his connections in that tribal brotherhood, the overseas Scottish business community. Of this Kennedy, a member of various Scottish organizations in New York and a frequent traveler to the old country, was very much a part. After the 1872 trip, Menzies decided to form the company, which involved itself in land, mining, ranching, government securities, and land and railroad mortgages.[2]

But first an American agent was needed, a man on the spot who could reach beyond Menzies' limited knowledge to track the latest developments. Menzies initially approached John Paton, who had been very helpful during his 1872 trip. Paton was a junior partner in M. K. Jesup, Paton & Co., and also was the New York representative of the Bank of British North America. But that Canadian bank, perhaps reasoning that no man can serve two masters, opposed his connection with Menzies, and later forced Paton to resign from the Advisory Board of the new enterprise.[3]

Kennedy was the best alternative. He and Menzies conferred regarding the creation of the new company, and Kennedy publicly threw his weight behind it in mid-March 1873, as Menzies convened a meeting of prospective investors. The prospectus he distributed announced that J. S. Kennedy & Co. would act as agent in conjunction with a three-man Advisory Board—of overseas Scotsmen—in New York.

They were chosen, not only for their influence, inside information and analytical skills, but also to counter any impression that Scottish American would depend exclusively on Kennedy's advice—though he, as an *ex officio* member, clearly would be first among equals. Finding appropriate insiders was not easy: the demand in the booming New York financial economy was far greater than the supply. Nevertheless, the Board members at first received only a modest $500 annually, though they benefited indirectly in terms of business and connections.[4]

The first Board comprised Kennedy, William Butler Duncan and John A. Stewart, the elected chairman. Stewart was president of the United States Trust Company of New York, a highly regarded fiduciary institution that he had founded some two decades before. Certainly it was no coincidence that 1874 saw Scottish American deposit funds in Stewart's company.[5]

Duncan was the senior partner in Duncan, Sherman & Co. of New York, a private bank which Scottish American utilized. But this bank ran aground after the panic of 1873, and closed down in July 1875, with a $18,365 deposit from Scottish American on its books. Duncan himself quit the Advisory Board, while J. S. Kennedy & Co. took legal action to retrieve the money. A settlement was not reached until 1880, but Kennedy had demonstrated how important it was to have strong representation on the American side of the water.

Duncan's failure was Kennedy's opportunity. He increasingly became the dominant force on the Advisory Board, where he remained until 1898, long after he had chosen to retire from his own firm. And his partners, first Henry M. Baker, then John S. Barnes, and finally John Kennedy Tod, served successively as secretaries of the Board, which two further "Kennedy men" joined in

1875. One, James Alfred Roosevelt, a senior partner in the private banking firm of Roosevelt & Son, symbolized New York's wealthy old Dutch elite. The other, Robert Lenox Kennedy, was of Scots ancestry though unrelated to John S. Kennedy, and was a private banker and president of the city's National Bank of Commerce; this institution succeeded the failed Duncan, Sherman firm as Scottish American's bank in the United States. J. Kennedy Tod & Co., the successor to J. S. Kennedy & Co. in 1883, continued as Scottish American's agent until 1902.[6]

All this shapes a clear conclusion. For a quarter century, from 1873 to 1898, John Stewart Kennedy would play an important, perhaps a *decisive*, role in the export of Scots capital to the American economy, and particularly to its most dynamic component, the railroads. For Scottish American had an impact beyond its own shareholders, often disposing of American bonds with other Scottish financial institutions. What Scottish American had set in motion thus rippled through the entire Scottish financial system. What part did Kennedy play in this process, how did he play it, and how did he benefit from it?

Before all else, of course, he drew on information from both private and public sources to advise the Scottish American headquarters in Edinburgh on securities transactions. This process was not simple, however. It required constant involvement with his business friends, and a certain skepticism regarding press information, which could be patchy and unreliable in an era when unregulated entrepreneurs often played fast and loose with the facts. So Kennedy had to rely on his own sources, and on his first-hand experience of business men, their capabilities, ambitions and especially their honesty.

Kennedy also had more specific responsibilities, which Menzies defined in May 1873: "Your duties as agent will I suppose be to purchase securities, to transmit them to us, to collect our coupons, and to advise us as to anything going on your side of which we ought to be aware."[7] What was meant by "anything going on your side" soon appeared in that panicky year. A month before, Menzies had urged Kennedy to watch the market carefully, against rumors of an impending panic.[8] It says much for the skill of Menzies and especially Kennedy that the Scottish American not only weathered it, but—as we shall see—actually profited by grabbing some splendid bargains.

His abilities gained investors a return both safer and higher than those available elsewhere. There were clear advantages for them in such centrally-managed pools as Scottish American represented. First, information costs were lower in analyzing both individual enterprises and the economy as a whole. Second, transaction costs were cut, for large-scale purchasing was cheaper than buys by individual investors. Finally, diversified portfolios lessened the risk for such investors. Scottish American proclaimed that it invested no more than one-tenth of its total capital in any single security. There were, to be sure, occasions when the opportunity for profit meant violating the spirit of this doctrine, though the letter might be maintained. But this was rare.[9]

Naturally, Kennedy advised on investments. Immediately after Scottish American's birth, Menzies asked him to prepare an investment plan for about $1,000,000. Later that year, Kennedy was instructed to invest $500,000 in a diversified portfolio, with emphasis on fully eleven railroads.[10] Here he drew on inside information from his long-standing interest in several Texas lines, as well as in the Dubuque & Sioux City, the Cedar Falls & Minnesota, and the Indianapolis, Cincinnati & Lafayette. Menzies was very pleased; in November 1873 he observed that "the best thing we ever did was to appoint Kennedy our agent."[11]

This was an understatement. Kennedy and Menzies, J. S. Kennedy & Co. and the Scottish American Investment Co., were enjoying major successes that autumn, bottom fishing on a panicky market that was dropping precipitously. Rumors of trouble had been circulating in New York financial circles. Kennedy no doubt informed Menzies, who—with impeccable timing—arrived there in September. It was barely four days before Jay Cooke & Co., lacking liquidity as the economy softened, suddenly suspended operations. The stock market plummeted in what was then the worst panic in American history, and the Stock Exchange actually closed for ten days.

Kennedy was a money manager, neither a broker nor a member of the Exchange. But he was in his element, providing the advice on which Menzies acted to grab good, i.e., substantial and inherently valuable, securities at low prices. Menzies' brother, Charles, the secretary of Scottish American, conflated God with Mammon when he gloated in October that "the present crisis was a state of things evidently sent providentially for the Company's interests." He reported William Menzies' remark that "not one security which we have taken through Kennedy is in any way suspicious." And Scottish American's minutes for November reported that "the agents [J. S. Kennedy & Co.], having no anxiety on account of the state of their own affairs had been able to devote their whole time and attention to the affairs of the Company."[12]

Kennedy was indeed buying heavily for the Scots—more than $2,000,000 in all—as security prices dropped further toward the end of 1873. Some older, better-established banking firms were devastated by the panic. But Kennedy, at age forty-three an independent entrepreneur for barely five years, thrived, achieving a great deal for Scottish American as well. From such victories are great reputations made—and with them still greater opportunities for gain.

All this brought Kennedy a substantial income from Scottish American, in fixed fees, expenses and a commission—of half a per cent on the total amount of money invested at any given time—which raised his income with every new investor joining the company. Some fees were for such routine, yet essential, services as ensuring the collection of interest on bond coupons, and therefore were quite small: one-eighth of a percent.[13] After April 1878, Scottish American added a flat $1,000 annually to Kennedy's payments received.

Certainly this income raised Kennedy's already substantial wealth. But there was an indirect gain, incalculable yet enormously important. As a point man in the westward movement of Scottish capital, Kennedy had become a major player in the New York financial world. He had grown up near the bottom in Scotland. Now it was the wealth of Scotland which helped him climb to the top in the new world.[14]

▼   ▼   ▼

The depression of 1873-78 saw a great shake-out of railroad securities. Anticipating demand, optimistic entrepreneurs had built—and overbuilt—thousands of miles of developmental lines during 1865-73. Now business was declining and defaults spread as some lines failed to meet their interest payments. Here was Scottish American's opportunity. Each line's bonds generally were spread among a few hundred buyers, thus ensuring price stability. This was particularly attractive to Scottish American, always concerned about its image of prudence and stability.

In seizing these openings, Kennedy dealt occasionally with the Equitable Trust Company of New London, Connecticut. This was a new, relatively small enterprise which eventually failed in its hopes of becoming an intermediary between the railroads and likely investors. But Kennedy, who ordinarily avoided intermediaries—they added to costs—made an exception here, for the Equitable's board of trustees included James Roosevelt and Robert Lenox Kennedy, men whom he trusted to deal honestly and provide reliable information. Hence the praise which the Scottish American Advisory Board bestowed upon the Equitable: "the high character of the present board of directors [and] the management of the concern."[15]

The question of reputation surfaced again in March 1878, when Kennedy and the Advisory Board discussed some bonds the Equitable hoped Scottish American would buy. He was laudatory, yet hesitant. "[He] expressed a favorable opinion of the Bonds, and of the management, which he believed to be conservative, careful, and responsible." But was that of itself sufficient to clinch a sale? Kennedy "expressed a preference for good railroad first mortgage bonds." Better to save money by buying railroad bonds directly, rather than by buying bonds sold by the Equitable itself. The Advisory Board accepted his judgment—as usual.[16]

The Equitable was simply one of many balls that Kennedy was juggling. There was, for example, an Illinois Central bond issue during January 1875 in which Kennedy—and Scottish American—were to play a big role. The southward expansion of the Illinois Central offered profitable possibilities, with which Kennedy's long involvement in the neighboring Dubuque & Sioux City made him quite familiar. So his offer to Scottish American of a share in the new bond issue carried a certain authority.

But the directors in Edinburgh, worried about the continuing depression, had doubts. They would buy, but only one-fifth of the original offer, i.e., £100,000 rather than £500,000, and then only if other subscribers could be found to share the risk. This Menzies agreed to do; he was, after all, very well connected in the Scottish investment network, and there was a profit, albeit small, to be made in serving as an intermediary. There was also a tiny commission for J. S. Kennedy & Co., as the Scottish American board chose to reward it with a fee of one-eighth of a percent, i.e., $120. This sum was credited, however—perhaps to conceal it from critical stockholders—to a so-called "Insurance Account." (This the independent auditors used later were to criticize as "irregular." Menzies cavalierly told them, in effect, to forget it.)[17]

What do these tiny ripples in a very tiny pool signify? First, that business relations between close associates in a non-regulatory age could bring all sorts of hidden gains. Second, that a chain of intermediaries and connections multiplied Kennedy's influence in funneling Scots capital to American railroads, as individual Scottish investors may have joined Scottish American in buying securities.

And Kennedy benefited personally in many ways. In the summer of 1875, for example, he showed the advantage of good connections at a moment when he was over-extended and short of the cash needed to save the St. Paul & Pacific railroad, with which—as we shall see below—he was deeply involved. Of course he could borrow in New York or London. But the news would most likely leak out. It was vital to maintain a strong image. Otherwise the speculators, smelling blood in the water, might attack and force the price of his securities down.

Menzies and Scottish American offered a solution. In December, Kennedy "sold" them bonds from his longtime holdings in the International

Railroad in east Texas, acquiring $162,000 in return. Scottish American received, not simply collateral, but actual bonds, which Kennedy was obligated to repurchase by a set date, at the original selling price plus interest. Here was a very quiet gentlemen's agreement, with discretion the rule. It was extended for six months in January 1876. In July, Kennedy repaid about $65,000, and Scottish American carried the balance for another six months. Thus, Kennedy got his money, Scottish American made a small profit, and no one was the wiser.[18]

The railroad investment market knew little of boundaries. Scottish American had bought bonds in the Canada Southern Railway, which began operating through southern Ontario in the fateful year of 1873, between Windsor and Niagara Falls. The line was in financial difficulties by September, just as the great panic began: by 1 January 1875, it had missed an interest payment. Should Scottish American sell its holdings? The Advisory Board was opposed, considering how low the market price had sunk. Fortunately for the investors, the Vanderbilt interests brought in new capital, purchasing the line in June 1876 and attaching it to their Michigan Central line from Buffalo to Detroit.

Despite their fluctuations, railroads continued to be highly attractive investments. The Advisory Board favored selling bonds in the mid-1870s from the New York Central & Hudson River, and also the New York Central & Harlem—which the Board assumed had peaked—*if* they achieved a profit of seven per cent. The money then could be applied to other, lower-priced investments. In 1876, Kennedy reported on a bond offering by the Albany & Susquehanna railroad, which connected Albany and Binghamton, New York. The Scottish American directors were favorably inclined. They agreed "to subscribe to the full amount of this loan within the powers of this Company, at the same price as Mr. R[obert] L[enox] Kennedy agrees to pay." Kennedy therefore bought $500,000 of these bonds for Scottish American, plus $200,000 in Cincinnati, Hamilton & Dayton bonds.[19] J. S. Kennedy & Co. became involved during November 1879 in the Nashville, Chattanooga & St. Louis line, of which it bought $100,000 in bonds. It offered $50,000 to Scottish American, which apparently accepted.[20]

In his relentless quest for gain, Menzies proposed one strategy which brought sharp criticism from the normally acquiescent Advisory Board. After the Resumption Act of 1875 ended the threat of inflation through the further issue of greenbacks, he and Kennedy toured the West, seeking to invest in real estate loans and farm mortgages, particularly in large grazing holdings. The Advisory Board and Kennedy as well were dubious. Not only were such investments perceived as "extra hazardous," as compared to railroad ventures, but the information costs involved were greater. In December 1886, the Board again discussed this issue. Roosevelt, Stewart, Thomas Denny (a New York broker), and Kennedy himself all were opposed. That resolved matters: Scottish American did continue land ventures, but on a tiny scale.[21]

So railroads remained the heart of Scottish American's operations. In 1876, Kennedy brought the firm into the complex—and troubled—affairs of the Central Railroad of New Jersey, an anthracite coal carrier in which he had a personal interest. Anthracite production in northeastern Pennsylvania had slumped badly since the 1873 panic; the carriers were suffering as a result. Now the Jersey Central, burdened with an overload of short-term debt, was struggling to survive by reorganizing and issuing $3,000,000 in bonds.

Should Scottish American bet on the railroad's future by taking some of this issue? Or should the Scots get out? There was much disagreement. On the one hand, Robert Lenox Kennedy withdrew in October 1876 from his personal agreement on the Jersey Central with the private bankers, Brown, Shipley & Co. And the Advisory Board recommended that Scottish American, try though it might for the best terms, also sell its investments and get out. The directors hesitated, but finally agreed in January 1877.[22]

On the other hand, John Stewart Kennedy continued his involvement with the Jersey Central, even as it stumbled into receivership; in October 1878, for example, he received a half per cent for collecting its bond coupons. And he submitted its reorganization plan to Scottish American, which still held some bonds.

But anthracite prospects continued poor, and, in December, the Advisory Board proposed that Scottish American rid itself of the anthracite lines by selling all their bonds. The directors agreed, and J. S. Kennedy & Co. followed up by selling $300,000 worth of Jersey Central bonds in January and February of 1879. And the directors accepted Kennedy's suggestion in June 1881 that they sell Jersey Central bonds in the London market. It appeared that Scottish American was now, finally and conclusively, united in withdrawing from Jersey Central.

But Kennedy saw things differently. The industry's serious financial problems spurred the companies to try again in 1886 what they had unsuccessfully attempted earlier: combine to achieve profitability by limiting production and fixing prices. Yet they were unsuccessful, and Kennedy became a receiver of a Jersey Central that was in default. Here he faced a delicate situation, confronting several categories of creditors—including Scottish American—each eager to get as much for itself as possible. As an insider, Kennedy doubtless gained the information that sustained his optimism about the Jersey Central; the Advisory Board accepted his judgment by deciding to defer selling this security.[23]

The International Railroad—now retitled the International & Great Northern Railroad—of eastern Texas was yet another problem child. It long had been a Kennedy interest, but it followed many developmental railroads downward during the 1870s depression, entering receivership in 1878. As president and chairman of its reorganization committee, Kennedy led an attempted revival by dispatching a reorganization plan to Scottish American in October. The directors were satisfied. They gave Menzies the power to approve it, and Scottish American began buying the line's bonds in 1880. J. S. Kennedy & Co. also bought bonds of the Colorado Bridge Company, a subsidiary of the International & Great Northern, which guaranteed them. Kennedy bought still more in June 1881 for Scottish American.

With several such buys, Scottish American had become involved so deeply as to violate its own doctrine about never investing more than one-tenth of its capital in a single enterprise. In April 1884, the Advisory Board, perhaps recognizing this fact, proposed taking advantage of favorable prices to sell $125,000 of the International & Great Northern bonds. But the railroad's future looked bright, and the Board reversed course in November 1887, postponing a sale.

That brightness dimmed, however, and the Advisory Board was considering yet another reorganization by February 1892. By then, the line was in the unfriendly hands of Jay Gould, whose presence transformed the situation—for the worse, Kennedy felt. He criticized the latest plan as unfair to the second mortgage bondholders, Scottish American among them. But there was a deeper criticism as well: "He placed no reliance upon the obligation of Jay Gould to carry out the plan in good faith." Gould's reputation in certain circles, after all, was that of absolute ruthlessness. To rid themselves of Gould, Kennedy favored a foreclosure sale or the replacement of the stockholders as owners by the bondholders. His fellow Board members disagreed. Roosevelt, Stewart and Denny were prepared to tolerate Gould, simply because he was too unscrupulous an opponent to battle. Kennedy, however, felt differently.[24]

He also played a role in the early stages—summer 1874—of a struggle then brewing between the New York Central and the Rome, Watertown & Ogdensburg of northern New York. The latter was essentially blocked in reaching profitable cities by its much more powerful rival, which enjoyed virtually complete freedom in allowing other lines to build across its own, and to use its track or terminals. So the Rome, Watertown & Ogdensburg could only try to build its way out of its isolation. For this, capital was needed, and Kennedy therefore negotiated the sale of $2,000,000 in bonds, evenly split between the United States and London. In August, Scottish American took a full fifth, $400,000, that figure "being the utmost that the Company can hold." Anyone who could dispose of such amounts would have no small influence on Wall Street.

The troubled Rome, Watertown & Ogdensburg reappeared on Kennedy's docket some five years later. Not having reached New York or Buffalo, it still lay within the New York Central's clutches. So Kennedy convened the Advisory Board in May 1879 to discuss getting out altogether by selling the $129,000 in bonds which Scottish American still owned. But how to do so without depressing the price of what was, after all, widely regarded as a serious failure? We have no conclusive answer regarding Kennedy's tactics, but there are hints of how he "made a market." By mixing selling with occasional buying, and by splitting thirteen or so installments of $10,000 each among various brokers, J. S. Kennedy & Co. managed to get rid of all the bonds in a mere three months, by the end of July.[25] And this action was vindicated by events: the Rome, Watertown & Ogdensburg line eventually disappeared, gobbled up by the New York Central.

Kennedy and Scottish American also became inadvertently involved in the Chicago, Milwaukee & St. Paul. This was linked to the collapse in October 1878 of the City of Glasgow Bank, an event which (see Chapter 7) brought broad reforms to the Scottish banking system. The Bank's liquidators appointed J. S. Kennedy & Co. as the agent to save what could be saved by selling its American securities; Scottish American entered the picture by buying liquidator's coupons. There followed a controversy regarding prices, involving Kennedy for the liquidators—and the Chicago, Milwaukee & St. Paul. The City of Glasgow Bank had had holdings of Western Union Railroad bonds; these he exchanged for Chicago, Milwaukee & St. Paul bonds. The liquidators then sold these newly-issued bonds through a syndicate in which Kennedy's firm, Scottish American, and others all participated. So in September 1879, Menzies secured $250,000 of these bonds for Scottish American.[26]

None of these many railroads had a bigger place in Kennedy's career than the St. Paul, Minneapolis & Manitoba, which he and four others—including James J. Hill—organized in 1878-79 (see Chapter 5) from the wreckage of several distressed Minnesota railroads. This road, ultimately renamed the Great Northern, became one of the great trans-Mississippi lines, reaching the Pacific in 1893. And Kennedy was intimately associated with it for a decade.

Inevitably, he brought in Scottish American, to the benefit of both sides: the Manitoba, which soon began pushing across the Great Plains, needed a consistent source of long-term capital. And that the Scotsmen would provide only if they had a shrewd man on the spot to watch over their interests. Kennedy could help in both roles, and the directors of Scottish American agreed in July 1879 to accept his recommendation that they get in on the ground floor by buying $100,000 of a new bond issue, purchasable—thanks to Kennedy's presence on both sides of the transaction—at the very advantageous syndicate price.

This opened a long string of purchases. In September, Scottish American bought $100,000 more first mortgage bonds; in December, yet another $100,000, though in second mortgage bonds. In April 1880, Scottish American's directors instructed Kennedy to sell $50,000 in first mortgage bonds and buy that amount in second mortgage bonds instead; he successfully opposed the sale.

Here was the issue of appearance, image and reality. From his point of view, every buy was a blessing, not only because it provided much-needed cash, but also because it demonstrated to the financial world that the new Manitoba was a likely success, a security-grade investment. Contrarily, every sale damaged the image of success, a setback that might raise doubts among the great, uncommitted investment public.

The buys, quite substantial for their day, continued. In June 1881, J. S. Kennedy & Co. purchased still more second mortgage bonds, of which it soon offered Scottish American a $100,000 portion; Menzies and the Advisory Board accepted. The following January, J. S. Kennedy & Co. bought $100,000 in bonds, and February saw it present to Scottish American $1,500,000 in bonds of the Minneapolis Union Railroad Company, a proprietary of the Manitoba, which guaranteed the principal and interest. The Scottish American directors agreed to subscribe to $500,000 of the issue, and to try to place more with the Dundee Investment Company in Scotland.

In May 1883, Scottish American accepted Kennedy's suggestion that it subscribe $500,000 to a Manitoba bond syndicate, though the men in Edinburgh drew the line there, rejecting the chance to buy another $250,000. Still, Kennedy prevailed upon them to buy $70,000 of these offerings in October. In April 1884, the Advisory Board recommended that $200,000 of Manitoba bonds be sold (nearly a year passed before $170,000 were disposed of). The market price was favorable, and Scottish American's policy against excessive commitment mandated action. This policy, though ordinarily justifiable, lessened the profits that all-out investment in the Manitoba would have brought. No one, of course, could predict how consistently prosperous the Manitoba would become.[27]

Kennedy's successful attempts to bring Scottish American together with the St. Paul, Minneapolis & Manitoba brought him to the very brink of what a later generation might regard as conflict of interest. He was, in effect, representing both buyer and seller, though his actions were quite public; in that sense he never dealt from the bottom of the deck. And he was quite fortunate, for the Manitoba's success was clearly emerging by 1882, so all was well. The question diminished in 1883, when he closed his company, and his connection to Scottish American weakened. Although Kennedy increased his value to both Scottish American and the Manitoba through his multiple roles, the fundamental incompatibility nevertheless remained—as it still does on occasion.

Scottish American was not averse to occasional short-term trading, where buying and selling alternated at some speed. In April 1880, for example, J. S. Kennedy & Co. informed Scottish American about the formation of a $3,000,000 bond issue syndicate for the Chicago & North Western Railroad. Scottish American honored its one-tenth rule by subscribing to $300,000, of which they retained $100,000 and sold $50,000 to clients; $150,000 remained in the bond syndicate, to be sold to outsiders.[28]

Other investments, though nominally intended for a permanent portfolio, sometimes were sold if the price was right. Having bought heavily at the trough of the 1873 depression and gained spectacularly from the rising market of the late 1870s, Scottish American disposed selectively of various securities in 1880, fearing that a market downturn was due. The proceeds would go to short-term investment; better opportunities were expected in the fall. This benefited Kennedy, for the directors agreed to temporarily lend him some uninvested funds. Though he paid interest slightly above the market rate, he avoided having to approach the bankers, with the damage to his image this would entail.[29]

Kennedy continued to represent Scottish American, usually successfully, but sometimes not. One losing battle occurred in August 1880, when he had to fight a former associate, George Bliss of Morton, Bliss & Co., who was linked with Melville Ingalls, head of the Cincinnati, Indianapolis, St. Louis & Chicago railroad, in controlling a line—the Indianapolis, Cincinnati & Lafayette—in which Scottish American held bonds. Predictably, Bliss and Ingalls used their power to favor the bonds which they personally owned, while undervaluing those held by others. This hurt Scottish American, and its Advisory Board naturally backed Kennedy's struggle to get recompense, but to no avail; Bliss and Ingalls prevailed.[30]

To invest in so many railroads inevitably meant risking the occasional failure. Consider, for example, the question of the New York, Chicago & St. Louis—commonly known as the Nickel Plate—which had fallen into default in the early 1880s, after having been built by a speculative syndicate as a "raider road," its purpose being to threaten a profitable neighbor. Perhaps unwisely, Scottish American had obtained some of its bonds, and was understandably upset when the Nickel Plate failed to pay interest. Kennedy became involved through his position as a trustee of the Central Trust Company of New York, which, as the trustee of the Nickel Plate's first mortgage bonds, was the watchdog for the bondholders. The outcome is obscure, but it is clear that the investors whom Kennedy represented lost.[31]

There was also the matter of the New York, Lake Erie & Western—the Erie—in which Scottish American held bonds, and which Kennedy therefore supported in its campaign for primacy during 1886 against the Chicago & Atlantic. As part of this offensive, Kennedy, John Stewart and Robert Lenox Kennedy joined forces to urge the Farmers' Loan and Trust Company of New York to initiate foreclosure proceedings as trustees against the Chicago & Atlantic. The latter ultimately lost, and was swallowed by the Erie.[32]

Kennedy generally had things his own way with his principals in Edinburgh. But not always. He suffered, for example, a rebuff during the war in the early 1880s between the New York Central & Hudson River, and its new competitor, the New York, West Shore & Buffalo, which was building along the Hudson's west bank to undercut the high freight rates of the New York Central. In November 1882, Kennedy and Stewart urged Scottish American to back the new competitors by entering the West Shore bond syndicate. The directors were opposed, however, to what seemed a very risky venture. And they were right. The New York Central was too strong. The West Shore was placed in receivership in June 1884.[33]

But this rebuff constituted an exception. More typical was the situation in May 1883, when Kennedy offered a new Northern Pacific bond issue of $100,000 to Scottish American, which had no objection to taking half of it. And Scottish American, functioning yet again as Kennedy's personal banker, satisfied his request for the loan of $200,000 in Northern Pacific bonds.[34]

Kennedy served Scottish American dutifully and resourcefully from the panic of 1873 to the prosperity of the early 1880s, when, having dissolved J. S. Kennedy & Co. in 1883, he transferred the account to its successor, J. Kennedy Tod & Co. Nevertheless, Kennedy continued to wield much influence in the Advisory Board for another fifteen years. In 1885, for example, his suggestion was accepted regarding the sale of St. Paul & Northern bonds. So was his proposal during November that Scottish American accept an offer for St. Paul Gas Light Company bonds. And so it was in December, when J. Kennedy Tod & Co. offered bonds to Scottish American from the New Brunswick & Canada Railway Company.[35]

▼   ▼   ▼

Kennedy had helped shepherd the Scottish firm through a chaotic financial decade, filled with expansion, setbacks, and reorganization—and aggressive competitors like Jay Gould, George Bliss, William H. Vanderbilt and others. How can his relationship with the men in Edinburgh be assessed? First, it helped enhance *his* fortune. From fees, commissions and payments, he derived an estimated $10,000 annually from Scottish American, whose portfolio stood at about $2,000,000. Perhaps half of his income was indirectly attributable to this relationship. And he had strong additional earnings as a commission merchant, private banker, railroad officer, director and reorganizer. By 1875-76, his net worth was about $500,000, down considerably from the million figure he had put on it in 1870, but nevertheless quite significant in light of the 1873 panic and the depression that followed.

Second, he helped make *their* fortune. By 1882, after a decade of operation, Scottish American had acquired securities in some forty railroads. The smallest holding was only $5,000, the largest almost a hundred times more. By 1885, the combined borrowed capital and paid share capital of the company far outstripped that of any other Scottish investment enterprise.[36]

All this was based on unique inside information regarding a property—its physical and financial condition, its senior management and its prospects—all derived from Kennedy's contacts, for accurate public information hardly existed. In the interaction between agent and principal, Kennedy functioned as an analyst and money manager with substantial discretion, rather than as a broker following specific instructions. He collected and evaluated investment intelligence and offered recommendations, as well as buying and selling investments. He exercised broad latitude, due to his position as agent and his prestigious place in the New York financial community, which provided him with knowledge lacking to Menzies in far-off Edinburgh. And Kennedy bolstered his claim to autonomy with one success after another.[37]

NOTES

1. Ronald B. Weir, "William John Menzies," *Scottish Dictionary of Business Biography, 1860-1960* (Aberdeen: Aberdeen University Press, 1986), 2: 414-15; George Glasgow, *The Scottish Investment Trust Companies* (London: Eyre and Spottiswoode, 1932), 5; W. Turrentine Jackson, *The Enterprising Scot: Investors in the American West after 1873* (Edinburgh: Edinburgh University Press, 1968), 13-14, 16-17, 297-98, 300, 302.

2. Ronald B. Weir, *A History of the Scottish American Investment Company Limited, 1873-1973* (Edinburgh: Scottish American Investment Co., Ltd., 1973), 3-5;

Jackson, *The Enterprising Scot*, 13; William G. Kerr, *Scottish Capital on the American Credit Frontier* (Austin: Texas State Historical Assoc., 1976), 62, 89.

3. Weir, *Scottish American Investment Co.*, 8, 30; William Adams Brown, *Morris Ketchum Jesup* (New York: Charles Scribner's Sons, 1910), 36; W. J. Menzies to J. S. Kennedy, 5 May 1873, extracts, Letter Book No. 1, Scottish American Investment Co. [hereafter cited as extracts, Letter Book No. 1]. I owe these extracts to R. B. Weir who used them in the preparation of his historical brochure on the Scottish American Investment Company; I should like to express my appreciation to the Scottish American Investment Company for furnishing me with a photocopy of the relevant documents; Mira Wilkins, *The History of Foreign Investment in the United States to 1914* (Cambridge: Harvard University Press, 1989), 65, 99, 855n. 92.

4. Minutes, 25 April, 9 May, 14 November 1873; W. J. Menzies to J. S. Kennedy, extracts, Letter Book No. 1.

5. Minutes, 5 March 1873, extracts, Minute Book No. 1, Minutes, 14 November 1873, 6 January, 14 April 1874; Weir, *Scottish American Investment Company*, 7-8; Weir, "Menzies"; Alvin F. Harlow, "John A. Stewart," *Dictionary of American Biography*, 13: 11.

6. Prospectus, 1873; W. J. Menzies to J. S. Kennedy, 5 April 1873, extracts, Letter Book No. 1; *Who's Who in America*, 1912-1913, 605; *New York Times*, 28, 29 July 1875, 21 June 1912; Minutes, 14 November 1873, 31 July, 11, 31 August 1875, 12 January 1880; Weir, *Scottish American Investment Company*, 7.

7. W. J. Menzies to J. S. Kennedy, 10 May 1873, extracts, Letter Book No. 1.

8. W. J. Menzies to J. S. Kennedy, 5 April 1879, extracts, Letter Book No. 1.

9. Prospectus, Scottish American Investment Co. 1873 [hereafter cited as Prospectus].

10. Minutes, 25 April, 9 May 1873; W. J. Menzies to J. S. Kennedy, 10 May 1873, extracts, Letter Book No. 1.

11. Minutes, 23 May, 20, 27 June, 4, 15, 22 July, 1 August, 25 September, 4 October , 14 November 1873.

12. Minutes, 14 November 1873; Weir, *Scottish American Investment Company*, 8-9; C.D. Menzies to W. J. Menzies, 4 October 1873, extracts, Letter Book No. 1; C.D. Menzies to A. R. Duncan, 6 October 1873, extracts, Letter Book No. 1.

13. Weir, *Scottish American Investment Company*, 8; [date **unknown**] November 1873, extracts, Letter Book No. 1; Minutes, 14 November 1873, 3 June 1884.

14. "J. S. Kennedy & Co.," 15 October 1875, New York City, v. 348, p. 900 sub-p. A22. R. G. Dun & Co. Collection, Baker Library, Harvard Graduate School of Business Administration; W. J. Menzies to J. S. Kennedy, 3 May 1873, extracts, Letter Book No. 1; Minutes, 30 April, 27 August 1878.

15. Minutes, 18 August 1874.

16. Minutes, 19 January 1875; 5 March, 30 April 1878; Alvin F. Harlow, *The Road of the Century* (New York: Creative Age Press, 1947), 237; *Commercial & Financial Chronicle* 16 (1 March 1873): 292; 17 (6 September 1873): 324; 17 (20 September 1873): 387; 19 (25 July 1874): 103; 22 (1 January 1876): 16; 22 (10 June 1876): 567; R. Carlyle Buley, *Equitable Life Assurance Society of the United States, 1859-1964* (New York: Appleton-Century-Crofts, 1967), 1: 123, 207n, 208-9.

17. Prospectus, 1873; Minutes, 11, 26 January, 25 May 1875.

18. Minutes, 29 June, 9 July, 14 December 1875, 11 January, 4 July 1876.

19. Minutes, 4, 25 January, 7 March 1876.

20. Minutes, 18 November 1879.

21. Jackson, *Enterprising Scot*, 16; Weir, *Scottish American Investment Company*, 8, 12; Minutes, 5 November 1875, 1 March 1876; 24 June 1879, [undated 1886].

22. Minutes, 4 July, 17 October 1876, 30 January 1877.

23. Minutes, 11 May, 13 November 1877, 15 October, 31 December 1878, 21 January, 4, 18 February 1879, 28 June 1881, [undated 1887].

24. Minutes, 15 October 1878, 15 June, 23 August 1880, 28 June 1881, [undated 1884] 3 June 1884, [undated 1887], [undated 1892].

25. Minutes, 3, 24 June, 1, 15, 29 July 1879.

26. Minutes, 30 September 1879.

27. Minutes, 9 April, 8, 9 July, 16 September, 16 December 1879, 27 April, 11 May, 15 June 1880, 28 June, 19 July 1881, 17 January, 21 February 1882, 1, 23 May, 16 October 1883, [undated 1884], 3 June 1884, [undated 1885], 5 March 1885.

28. Minutes, 27 April 1880.

29. Jackson, *Enterprising Scot*, 46; Minutes, 11 May, 15 June 1880.

30. Minutes, 23 August 1880; Dolores Greenberg, *Financiers and Railroads, 1869-1889: A Study of Morton, Bliss & Company* (Newark: University of Delaware Press, 1980), 94, 179.

31. Minutes, 11 March, 3 June 1884, [undated 1885], 21 December 1885, 29 January 1886.

32. Minutes, [undated 1885], [undated 1886].

33. Minutes, 30 November 1882; Albro Martin, "Crisis of Rugged Individualism: The West Shore-South Pennsylvania Railroad Affair, 1880-1885," *Pennsylvania Magazine of History and Biography* 93 (April 1969): 218-43.

34. Minutes, 1, 23 May 1883.

35. Minutes, 30 September, 12 November, 7, 21 December 1885.

36. Minutes, 3 January 1882.

37. Kerr, *Scottish Capital on the American Credit Frontier*, 91; Jackson, *Enterprising Scot*, 46, 298.

4 DECLINE AND STAGNATION: THE ST. PAUL & PACIFIC IN THE 1870s

THE 1870S DEMONSTRATED THE truth of the old adage that timely insights can help the able financier prosper in bad times as well as good. Railroad freight revenues declined drastically after the 1873 panic, with that year's peak returning only in 1879. Trackage built, predictably, also slumped. In 1875, it reached less than a quarter of the 1873 total, and a solid recovery lagged until 1880.

So Kennedy shifted his focus to those troubled, often defaulting, lines in whose future he nevertheless saw potential. The constraints of Scottish American, with its host of small and conservative investors, did not inhibit him: he invested, and persuaded others to follow him.

Railroad investment was indeed increasing by the late 1870s, involving Morton, Bliss & Co. as one of two dozen leading private bankers. So was J. P. Morgan, who had the power—through his priceless British connections—to marshall the capital needed to strengthen established rail lines, those which had successfully passed the entrepreneurial stage.

Reorganization, stemming from either success or failure, was the watchword. Competition was fierce, survival uncertain, merger or consolidation constant possibilities. Railroad building demanded enormous capital, brought unpredictable returns, and was prey to political and economic vicissitudes. Many lines were swallowed by larger, better managed and more soundly financed systems that spread the influence of Eastern capitalists, with major access to resources, throughout the land. If all went well, costs would decline and viability increase.

Mergers typically involved two or more neighboring roads, often rivals, whose blending into a harmonious entity involved difficulties that only such strong—and neutral—referees as Kennedy could overcome. It was essential to establish the relative worth of each line's securities, and also to determine who would command whom. Despite its imperfections, the market offered a point of departure. But much depended on the relative strength of each line's financial backers. A reasonably just agreement was their objective, tempered not by mercy but by suasion based on power.

Kennedy commanded the experience, prestige and temperament to moderate the blood-letting. But mediating between opposing groups, each stubbornly defending its interests, was never simple; mediators had, in fact, been known to walk away from the table in frustration. And financing a newly-reorganized, yet still shaky line, had its own perils. There was a positive side, however. Kennedy and his fellow private bankers, having bought a faltering line's stock at nominal cost—or even received it free—would make a killing if they succeeded in reviving the line, and its stock then rose. So they would also if the line, borrowing from them in desperation at the high interest dictated by its own weakness, then rebounded. In effect, Kennedy was betting that he could transform today's loser into tomorrow's winner, with himself in on the ground floor. And, more often than not, the bet succeeded.

For these lions, the private bankers, investing in defaulted railroads also could be lucrative. However, vulture investors scavenged among defaulted railroads for bargains. Betting on a turnaround, they invested and became a thorn in the side of bankers, managers, and creditors, thus increasing the hazards for private bankers.

Receivership, following on default and leading to reorganization, was, despite its hazards, a more drastic instrument than merger. A court-appointed receiver would replace the management and try to nurse the failing line back to health. Eliminating interest payments to bondholders enabled lines in receivership to slash their freight rates, thereby drawing business away from competitors. Preventing this practice from becoming excessively prolonged through accounting chicanery or other manipulations—at the bondholders' expense—was up to the courts.

Kennedy's experience with receivership ranged from the relatively simple to the most complex, from creditors who wanted nothing so much as to sell out swiftly, to those who sought delay in the hope that tomorrow might be better. And the entire reorganization process culminated when Kennedy or another private banker issued new securities to replace the old.

Though some railroads never entered receivership, others—such as the Erie—did so constantly, see-sawing back and forth between loss and gain. But virtually none physically disappeared in their entirety. Tracks, roadbed and other facilities were fixed in place, while a citizenry whose well-being required transportation assured a political outcry if "its" line were to vanish. With rationalization essentially precluded, excess capacity therefore was a constant problem.

▼   ▼   ▼

Such were the rules of the game; how did Kennedy play it? During his years as a junior partner in M. K. Jesup & Co., and later as the leader of his own firm, Kennedy had garnered experience, but neither the contacts nor the resources to play in the majors. He had had only a minor role in several reorganizations: the Dubuque & Sioux City in Iowa, and also the International & Great Northern in Texas. He moved upward in the 1870s, participating in the reorganizations of the Central Railroad of New Jersey, and of the Indianapolis, Cincinnati & Lafayette. The latter line resulted from the merger in 1866 of two end-to-end (abutting) lines, the Cincinnati & Indianapolis, and the Indianapolis & Lafayette.

But this particular consolidation soon fell into financial difficulties. The banker-shareholders from New York—who controlled access to further capital—took action, despite opposition from the local, i.e., Ohio and Indiana, stockholders. Among the New Yorkers was George Bliss of Morton, Bliss & Co., a long-time business acquaintance of Kennedy, who himself had been a director of the line since 1868. A committee was formed to investigate and overhaul the property, with Kennedy overseeing finances, while Melville E. Ingalls, a young and promising railroad man, probed into operations. They deposed the entrenched local management, and a receiver took over in 1870.

With 1871 came default, as the bankers refused to keep the line afloat with further loans. Kennedy now was free to reorganize the line, which was sold to its bondholders, the stockholders having lost their equity. Nevertheless, he remained optimistic regarding its future. As one of the three stockholder trustees in 1873 (he also served as vice president during 1872-74), he personally furnished short-term capital for continued operations. The receivership ended that July, and the railroad fulfilled his expectations, repaying him by buying the unsecured short-term debt. Not only did Kennedy turn a tidy profit with all this, earning interest on the loan, and fees for his services as a trustee, but he also enlarged his stake in the line.[1]

Even as Kennedy worked with the Indianapolis, Cincinnati & Lafayette, he was involved in a decade of reorganizing the problematic Central Railroad of New Jersey, one of five lines that dominated—but also depended on—anthracite mining. Primarily carrying anthracite, and often owning the mines as well, their fixed costs were high, and they were inordinately vulnerable to fluctuations in demand, as prices, shipping rates and—inevitably—net income all fell during the depression of the 1870s.[2]

In June 1876, John Taylor Johnston, the Jersey Central's president, was forced to acknowledge openly that only half the current dividend came from earnings, with the remainder coming from surplus. Despite this disturbing news, Scottish American accepted Kennedy's advice in July, and bought $700,000 of a $3,000,000 Jersey Central bond issue. Having staked his reputation, Kennedy tried vigorously to make the line profitable, and it was hardly surprising that Johnston felt compelled to resign after a dividend suspension.

Kennedy, whose father-in-law lived in northern New Jersey and had been a substantial Jersey Central stockholder, was instrumental in bringing in Robert Weeks de Forest to reorganize its legal department. Though de Forest was Johnston's son-in-law, he also was Kennedy's personal attorney, and may be seen as the latter's trouble-shooter. De Forest served as general attorney and general counsel, as vice president, and as a director for many years.

There were serious financial disputes—and shifting alliances—among three factions: the stockholders; the short-term, unsecured creditors; and the bondholding, secured lenders. The latter elected a protective committee, including Kennedy, Robert Lenox Kennedy (then president of the National Bank of Commerce), and three others. Kennedy gained further support through his partner, John S. Barnes, who, as his proxy, served on still another committee. Finally, a compromise was reached in the dispute over control and the relative value of the holdings of each of the three factions. Reorganization came in 1878: Kennedy became one of the three trustees of the new bonds, while several trustees resigned, to be replaced by Barnes and others.[3]

But new leadership alone could not solve the problems of high fixed costs and excess capacity. These remained to plague the Jersey Central, and default resulted—again. In February 1886, Kennedy and two other trustees brought suit and asked that a receiver be appointed. Unless bonded interest was cut, default remained a constant danger. In October 1886, the court accepted the trustees' application and appointed both Kennedy and the line's previous general manager as receivers. And the court granted precedence to this new receivership over one established in 1876.

Kennedy faced a new problem in 1887: a strike. The successful strike against Jay Gould's railroad empire in 1885 prompted similar action against the Jersey Central and other lines. Kennedy fought back vigorously. Witness his statement that: "We have had a great many officious people offering their services as arbiters, but I have told them there is nothing to arbitrate and have declined to have anything to do with them. I am determined to fight this thing out, and have refused to take any of the strikers back . . . if we succeed as we certainly must." Kennedy reflected the attitudes of his time and class in rebuffing the workers' challenge. He saw them as nothing more than hired hands, to be treated accordingly.[4]

The Jersey Central soon prospered sufficiently to pay interest on its bonds, the receivers having convinced the bondholders to take a cut in the rate in return for an increase in total indebtedness. This problem resolved, the receivership finally ended in January 1888, and Kennedy received public kudos—which doubtless raised his reputation. The *Commercial & Financial Chronicle* editorialized: "The receivership of Kennedy . . . has been most satisfactory."[5]

▼   ▼   ▼

Kennedy's experience and talents were stretched to their limits during the 1870s in a new and ultimately very important enterprise: a large-scale drive north and west by the St. Paul & Pacific Railroad. No longer was it a question merely of reorganizing or refinancing a troubled line, nor of assisting bondholders in their struggles. Rather, Kennedy was to join in true empire building, the opening up of Minnesota and the Dakotas as a potential world breadbasket.

For some two decades, the settlers there had hoped, prayed and worked for a major railroad which would amalgamate and expand their embryonic railroad system, bringing wealth and population by carrying their wheat and lumber to the great Eastern markets. Potential builders faced a complex situation; mistakes could be disastrous. Transportation costs per ton mile could vary significantly from one line to another. A line with extensive track and low freight haulage would have high costs, for unused capacity brought higher unit costs. Hence the constant quest for additional freight, and for the settlers who both produced and consumed it.

Settlers were attracted to regions with an existing line. But railroads, requiring immediate business to generate revenue, needed settlers already *in place*, and feared over-reaching themselves by advancing into empty regions. By contrast, the Union Pacific, that great, federally-subsidized line of mythic proportions, surged ahead without regard for settlers. If sufficient bonds could be sold, however, a line might decide to break the customary barrier, even without a land grant. Making those sales was of course up to Kennedy and all those who could tap the great capital markets.

In 1856, the state of Minnesota had chartered the Minnesota & Pacific as a land grant railroad. It would link St. Paul, the capital and economic heart of the region, with the Red River Valley to the west, a potentially rich wheat granary that also provided a complex and expensive outlet—by rail and river steamship—through American territory for Canadian wheat.

But the railroad, a classic local, predictably undercapitalized venture, went downhill rapidly after the 1857 depression. In 1862, a new corporate entity was created, the St. Paul & Pacific, whose influential trustees offered a glimmer of hope. Not only were Minnesota businessmen involved, but so were two important New York railroad financiers: Russell Sage and Samuel Tilden, Sage's lawyer (and the Democratic presidential candidate in 1876). Both men were experienced in railroad development in the upper Midwest. A contract to extend the line was given in 1862 to two outsiders, the brothers E. Darwin Litchfield, a London financier, and Edwin C. Litchfield, a Brooklyn, New York, lawyer and railroad financier; their payment was to be in the line's stocks and bonds.

Financing came hard. There was little success in tapping the London market in 1862 by selling bonds—whose high yield practically proclaimed their high risk—through Robert Benson & Co., a British private banker with some experience in marketing securities for the Illinois Central during the 1850s. Yet Benson was a secondary player; the very fact that none of the major houses (the Barings, for example) were interested raised doubts among potential investors.

The bond issue was now taken to a subsidiary market. The Netherlands had been placing about a third of its substantial foreign investment in the United States, often in railroads. These included the Illinois Central, the Louisville & Nashville, the Chicago & North Western, and the Chicago, Milwaukee & St. Paul.

Such Dutch private bankers as Oyens & Co., Adolph Boissevain & Co., and Lippmann, Rosenthal & Co. did not stop with investment alone, but represented Dutch clients in reorganization and related matters. Lippmann, Rosenthal had enjoyed a strong reputation since its founding in 1859 by Leo Lippmann and George Rosenthal. It had connections to both the Amsterdam Exchange and the Amsterdamsche Bank, and was to join with Jay Cooke & Co. in 1871 to market a United States government bond issue.

So most, if not all, of the St. Paul & Pacific issue was taken by Dutch private bankers, possibly as early as 1862, certainly by 1864. But construction was too diffuse, moving too slowly in too many directions, to attract investors. Hence the decision in 1864 to focus on the Red River drive by creating the First Division of the St. Paul & Pacific as a separate legal entity, owned by the Litchfields, and taking over the charter rights of the St. Paul & Pacific main line. This separation was legal, not actual: the lines formed a kind of jigsaw puzzle, with pieces interlocking, making unity essential if traffic was to proceed.

The Litchfields now engaged their elder brother, Electus Backus Litchfield, an Eastern railroad contractor, to do the building. He completed the lines to Breckenridge and to St. Cloud by the mid-1860s. He too was paid in stock, thereby obtaining control of the best, i.e., most heavily trafficked, parts of the route. The Litchfields bore no responsibility for the line's future. They simply were one of many American railroad builders, who, having no intention of running the line, probably soon sold their stock in their search for immediate profits.

The St. Paul & Pacific companies (including the First Division) were in difficulties by the late 1860s. Traffic remained insufficient. Acquiring capital was expensive. The great post-Civil War railroad construction boom was, after all, well underway. In any case, investors had little confidence in the line, not least because mismanagement raised suspicions of inefficient construction.

Even the Litchfield brothers apparently had no long-term interest in the St. Paul & Pacific: Electus sold it to E. Darwin in 1868. He in turn sold it in 1870 to Jay Cooke's highly speculative Northern Pacific, the region's dominant railroad as it moved westward through northern Wisconsin and Minnesota. Cooke's likely purpose was controlling, not strengthening, this potential competitor.[6]

The St. Paul & Pacific could survive only if it continued building, yet building entailed borrowing. It had done so on a moderate scale while the Northern Pacific was in control. It did so again in 1871 with the remarkably large bond issue of $15 million brought in by Lippmann, Rosenthal & Co. The line paid heavily, however, for its reputation as a high risk venture. Even with the extremely high interest rate of 10 percent, the Dutch sold only $10.7 million of the bonds, retaining the remainder as security against various advances.[7]

In September 1872, Lippmann, Rosenthal stopped lending to the St. Paul & Pacific, whose position was sinking rapidly. The Northern Pacific, its nominal parent, was itself facing difficulties and also refused to lend. Construction ground to a halt, and the line defaulted in October, largely because of insufficient traffic, and mismanagement, i.e., the high cost of construction. The Dutch bondholders now faced a classic dilemma. Should they try to keep their investment afloat, safeguarding their options, while spending as little as possible? Or should they simply sell out quickly, and take the losses this would inevitably bring?[8]

They chose the first path, and, with it, the services of John Stewart Kennedy, who became involved in the summer of 1873, in return for commissions and other fees. By then, Lippmann, Rosenthal had organized the Amsterdam or Dutch Committee as the voice of the bondholders; it selected J. S. Kennedy & Co. as its agent. The reasons can be found in personal contacts. First, London's Robert Benson & Co., which had been Kennedy's agent there for years, also represented the Dutch. Second, Kennedy had a long business relationship with Samuel J. Tilden, who was both a railroad attorney and a trustee for the St. Paul & Pacific bondholders. These men, either separately or jointly, brought Kennedy into the affairs of this defaulted railroad. His task essentially was to nurse the line along on the cheap, hoping that a rising economy would increase business and eventually attract a buyer. For by now the Dutch wanted to get out—while avoiding a fire sale.

John S. Barnes, Kennedy's partner, then visited St. Paul to evaluate the railroad, its management, finances and prospects. The First Division—which defaulted that year—and the St. Paul & Pacific, legally separate yet functionally related, had total mortgages with a *face* value of no less than $28 million. The construction cost was doubtless closer to $20 million, but so much spending had produced all too little.[9]

A friendly receivership was essential to protect the bondholders' interests. So Kennedy and his partners, Barnes and Henry Martyn Baker, joined Lipmann, Rosenthal in July to bring suit through the trustees to foreclose the mortgages and obtain a receiver. In August, the prestigious John F. Dillon, the federal judge for Minnesota, backed Kennedy's request by appointing as receiver Jesse P. Farley, the superintendent of the Iowa division of the Illinois Central. And Kennedy made him the chief resident operating officer.

Farley was in his sixties, very much a local railroad operations specialist, who was known to Kennedy—as we have seen—from the latter's ventures with the Dubuque & Sioux City line in the mid-1860s. Farley received a salary in the $10,000 range, and eventually owned $30,000 of First Division bonds. He also was president and general manager of the Dubuque & Southwestern Railroad (which Kennedy controlled), and secretary and treasurer of the much larger Dubuque & Sioux City Railroad; he held investments in both lines. Kennedy was concerned lest these commitments, which tied Farley and his family to Dubuque, some 225 miles from St. Paul, would divert him from the St. Paul & Pacific. Farley also understood the problem. In October, he wrote to Kennedy—with characteristic grammatical confusion—that, "From the situation I have given Judge Dillon, he will naturally infer the extension lines of the St. Paul & Pacific have not received that attention that should have been bestowed upon them."[10]

Kennedy fought for the Dutch bondholders, primarily against the Litchfields, and secondarily against the xenophobia of many Minnesotans, and their opposition to the transfer of both their railroad and the land itself to Dutch hands. The Northern Pacific, a major federal land grant line with access to strong financing even after it defaulted in 1873, also had to be watched. Finally, there was the intense panic of 1873, followed by a depression whose length, depth and damage to business drove freight revenues downward, exacerbating the task of meeting fixed interest payments.

E. D. Litchfield (acting for his brothers as well) also faced a complex situation. The default of the Northern Pacific in 1873 gave him possession of controlling St. Paul & Pacific stock. His equity in the First Division had value *only* if he could prevent the Dutch bondholders—who were seeking the interest owed them—from obtaining foreclosure. His strategy rested on the legal tactics of postponement and delay, stalling for time while hoping that circumstances would improve.[11]

Initially, Kennedy tried to reconcile the opposing interests of stockholders, bondholders and short-term creditors, but a settlement proved elusive. Following a dog in the manger policy, the Northern Pacific managed for a time to delay foreclosure, which would require the transfer of ownership to the Dutch bondholders. With his majority of the St. Paul & Pacific stock, Litchfield attempted a reorganization in 1875, but was defeated by Kennedy and the Dutch bondholders.

Then both sides came together—to a degree—in the so-called Litchfield Agreement of August 1875. This was not entirely surprising, for they had a mutual interest in preventing foreclosure, and thus the appointment of a receiver, who basically would be free to do as he pleased. Since he might very well be a local man, that likely would benefit the public and hurt both the bondholders and Litchfield. And this these two players desperately wanted to avoid.

Hence the Litchfield Agreement, in which he turned over control of the board of directors to the bondholders, and they agreed not to foreclose. That is, *a minority* of them agreed. For there was, in far-off Holland, a split among the bondholders, with enough of them refusing to accept the Agreement to prevent its legal enactment. The pro-Agreement faction simply ignored these dissidents, and acted as though the Agreement had legal standing during the year in which it was to run. So the board appointed new managers to the First Division, particularly Barnes, a Kennedy partner, as president. Yet he would be an absentee, tied to New York by his business commitments.

Disagreement over control nevertheless began anew between Litchfield and the bondholders. This see-saw battle for power continued during autumn 1876, when Tilden's resignation—to run for the presidency—brought Kennedy forward as trustee of three First Division mortgages. Formerly only the agent for the Dutch, Kennedy was increasing his involvement—and his influence—having become their trustee as well. But business remained bad, revenues were low, and the First Division still could not pay interest. Therefore Kennedy, as president of the board of trustees and representative of the bondholders, stepped in to maneuver the railroad into the hands of the bondholders.[12]

He also confronted major political problems. In a general way, Americans welcomed foreign bondholders, who brought much-needed capital, and expected nothing more than periodic interest payments. But many Minnesotans resented their state's aid to a St. Paul & Pacific railroad which had signed a contract and received land, yet had produced so little despite some two decades of plans, projects, promises—and wasted resources. So there was anger regarding the Dutch bondholders, who would benefit through foreclosure from a state land grant to take over a broad swath of Minnesota land, improve it with a railroad, and then profit substantially by selling parcels to new settlers.

And high risks for the bondholders translated into high interest rates, which necessitated high freight rates that further angered a citizenry which refused to recognize its own culpability. Only after Minnesotans were strongly represented in the ownership and management of the St. Paul & Pacific did public opinion begin supporting the line. As Farley later put it, "In the absence of . . . home influence . . . foreign stock and bondholders can get no sympathy from the people of these western states." Hard times made everything worse. It was hardly surprising that, early in 1875, the Minnesota House of Representatives would consider a bill to transfer the St. Paul & Pacific's land grant to a local contractor company, which still was owed payment for its construction work.

Kennedy defended his foreign clients in a letter to the chairman of the Minnesota House Committee on Railroads:

> To all intents and purposes, the enterprise was abandoned, and its affairs in utter confusion. There was no one in the country who had any pecuniary interest in the property, or who would acknowledge any responsibility for or on account of it. The only hope that existed in regard to it lived in the minds of the creditors of the Company and of the Northern Pacific railroad managers, that the bondholders could be induced to satisfy their claims in making an effort to recover losses which were inevitable, and in comparison with which all other losses were insignificant.

Kennedy was, in effect, pointing out that a railroad required capital, that the Dutch would provide it, that Minnesotans would benefit from it, and that everyone should bury the past and go forward.[13]

He ended with a promise that also held an implied threat:

> We beg, in conclusion, to say in direct response to your inquiry, that as soon as the St. Paul & Pacific Railroad company can be reorganized by foreclosure

and sale under the mortgage, the purchasers, should they be the bondholders, will undoubtedly proceed, without delay, with the work of construction, *if they are satisfied of a friendly, liberal and just disposition towards them* [italics in original].[14]

Kennedy's efforts to make an authoritative impression in Minnesota, while tightening his control over the First Division of the St. Paul & Pacific, were complicated by his difficulties with Jesse Farley, who moved in February 1876 from being receiver to also becoming general manager of the First Division. Kennedy and his partners, John Barnes and Henry Baker, were of course bankers in New York who had no desire to run the line themselves, much less move to St. Paul. Farley, an experienced and trustworthy man on the spot, would be in charge, especially since the receivership was expected— like most—to be short-lived. "This executive committee will reside here [New York]," Barnes informed Farley, "and the actual management will be left to you in St. Paul."[15]

The depression that opened in 1873 changed things, however. "It is clear," Barnes informed Farley in February 1877, "that we shall continue for some years to come to manage the St. Paul & Pacific interests." The ultimate goal remained as before: to find a buyer and sell out—on favorable terms. The likeliest prospect would be another railroad, possibly a neighboring line seeking to expand. But such a line would have to have deep pockets indeed to accept the burden of the St. Paul & Pacific at a time when income was low. A less likely prospect would be outside investors seeking to enter the railroad business. Only a real bargain would probably attract them, however, and this was precisely what Kennedy and the Dutch bondholders wanted to avoid. The old strategy had been passive, a holding operation until the economy rebounded; the new one was to aggressively improve the line's value—and thus its appeal to potential buyers—by pulling together its disconnected pieces.[16]

In his ungrammatical and sometimes dangerously confusing way, Farley wrote constantly to his superiors in New York during 1873-79, about local information, routine railroad matters, and the difficulties of nursemaiding the line while scavengers tried to pick up pieces on the cheap.[17] Barnes and Kennedy, who retained tight control, told Farley little regarding major issues, while maintaining good relations and feeding him advice on personnel matters, iron and steel rails, and prices and price forecasts.[18]

Farley had difficulties with his tasks, not least because he sidestepped his intended role as "the man on the spot" by coming to St. Paul from his Dubuque home only as needed. And the constant squabbling for control of the St. Paul & Pacific made difficult tasks even more so. Farley was expected to hold costs down through efficient management and to increase revenue, while keeping the local public and political personages happy, *and* also squeezing the utmost construction out of the short fair-weather season. Barnes issued a blunt reminder when writing Farley during January 1877: "The parties [the bondholders] interested in the property have learned to *look to you and Kennedy for all sorts of results.*"[19]

For a deadline loomed in late 1878. Unless the St. Paul & Pacific tracks reached the Canadian border, fully 500 miles to the north, it was virtually certain to lose its state land grant and thus its future prosperity. Could Farley do it? Lippmann, Rosenthal found him wanting, while Kennedy, who could be tight-fisted about paying the bills that Farley submitted, found him tactless. Nevertheless, Farley kept his job, in part because dismissing him required convincing the court that had appointed him. And *that* sort of publicity Kennedy and the troubled line wanted to avoid.

So it was a question of build—or lose everything. Building of course meant borrowing. There already had been a serious setback in 1875, when Farley, as the receiver, had obtained court approval for borrowing $5 million to finish several track extensions. But lenders were willing to risk only a pittance, a mere $100,000, in a loan using such tenuous collateral as unsold bonds; the skeptical Dutch, having invested so much in a losing cause, lent nothing whatever.

Kennedy, Farley and the others were not put off. They scrambled for construction dollars, and Kennedy even risked some of his own—while not, however, ignoring a chance for personal profit. There was the question of rails, which were the cornerstone of construction. Economies could be achieved in labor, in building roadbeds, and even in buying and using locomotives, but there was no way to avoid purchasing a fixed number of rails per mile—though these could be in cheaper iron, not expensive steel.

In this Kennedy had his own interests to consider. In April 1876, for example, Barnes told Farley to get a price quotation for rails from the North Chicago Rolling Mill Company. "Then I will see what can be done with Cambria, whose rails I much prefer, if they will deliver at same price and terms." The Cambria mill, of Johnstown, Pennsylvania, certainly was an innovator in high quality rails. More to the point, J. S. Kennedy & Co. was its agent. Not surprisingly, Farley did buy some 500 tons of steel rails from Cambria in November. Kennedy had represented both buyer and seller, using his own money to clinch the deal. Was this conflict of interest? Few people cared in that unregulated era.[20]

A certain discretion nevertheless was prudent. When another buy was conducted in 1877, for instance, Barnes told Farley that "We should like to have the Cambria Co. take the [steel rail] order, but K[ennedy] does not want himself to buy them [as a commission merchant] and prefers you should do so, getting your bids in without references to him, beyond informing him of what you have done or propose to do." No doubt Barnes was right in proclaiming the superiority of the Cambria rails, but his advice on how best to cover Kennedy's tracks says something about that era's ambiguous sense of business morality.

With the land grant deadline coming closer, Kennedy and his associates had to show progress. They organized the Red River & Manitoba Railroad in August 1877, with Barnes as president, Kennedy as vice president and Farley, that universal factotum, as general manager. Its purpose was to compensate for a widespread anomaly in railroading: the building of small, isolated stretches of track, which required connections to make through traffic possible.

How did such situations, which seem to defy all common sense, come about? The answer lay in the opportunism forced by the incessant search for capital. Citizens of small towns might well invest, offer tax benefits and free land for terminals, etc., *if* the line built some trackage in their vicinity. To bridge the gaps lying between, Kennedy relied on the confidence he enjoyed with the Dutch investors. They provided the small sum of $500,000 to connect Breckenridge on the Red River with Barnesville in Minnesota, thus providing the St. Paul & Pacific with greater coherence and viability.[21]

Kennedy's long-term strategy always had been to find a buyer and get out, though little could be done until he gained firm control by vanquishing the Litchfield interests in 1876. Barnes' occasional trips to St. Paul were spent in evaluating the line for that purpose. The prospects looked bleak, however. None of the regional lines—the Northern Pacific, Chicago & North Western, or Chicago, Milwaukee & St. Paul—was interested. They had no desire to buy, but only to block competitors from doing so. In any case, the depression left them without resources. Kennedy also sounded out various businessmen, but unsuccessfully. Why should they respond when his bargaining position was weak and the asking price might sink even lower? All he could do was hold on—and hope.

NOTES

1. Alvin F. Harlow, *The Road of the Century: The Story of the New York Central* (New York: Creative Age Press, 1947), 381-89; Dolores Greenberg, "A Study of Capital Alliances: The St. Paul & Pacific," *Canadian Historical Review* 57

(March 1976): 29; Dolores Greenberg, *Financiers and Railroads, 1869-1889: A Study of Morton, Bliss & Company* (Newark: University of Delaware Press, 1980), 83-88, 150, 179, 233n. 25; *Railroad Gazette* 1 (12 November 1870): 153; 5 (21 June 1873): 256; *Commercial & Financial Chronicle* 13 (11 November 1871): 635; 13 (16 December 1871): 800; 16 (14 June 1873): 796; 16 (21 June 1873): 828; "Melville E. Ingalls," Dictionary of American Biography, 9: 464; Edward Hungerford, *Men and Iron: The Story of the New York Central* (New York: Thomas Y. Crowell Co., 1938), 349-52; Ared Maurice Murphy, "Big Four Railroad in Indiana," *Indiana Magazine of History* 21 (June and September 1925): 109-273; *Commercial & Financial Chronicle* 11 (5 November 1870): 594; 19 (24 October): 422; George S. Cottman, *Centennial History and Handbook of Indiana* (Indianapolis: Max R. Hyman, 1915), 128-30.

2. Jules I. Bogen, *The Anthracite Railroads* (New York: Ronald Press, 1927), 147-48, 151, 156; Wheaton J. Lane, *From Indian Trail to Iron Horse: Travel and Transportation in New Jersey, 1620-1860* (Princeton: Princeton University Press, 1939), 384-85; George Rogers Taylor, *The Transportation Revolution, 1815-1860* (New York: Holt, Rinehart and Winston, 1951) 99; Richard Lowitt, *A Merchant Prince of the Nineteenth Century: William E. Dodge* (New York: Columbia University Press, 1954), 163-64, 173; "William E. Dodge," *Dictionary of American Biography*, 5: 352-53; Daniel Hodas, *The Business Career of Moses Taylor* (New York: New York University Press, 1976), 138; "Sidney Dillon," *Dictionary of American Biography*, 5: 312; *American Railroad Manual*, 1873, 170; J. L. Ringwalt, *Development of Transportation Systems in the United States* (1888; reprint, New York: Johnson Reprint Corporation, 1968), 273.

3. Bogen, *Anthracite Railroads*, 164, 171; "John Taylor Johnston," *Dictionary of American Biography*, 21: 236-37; "Robert Weeks de Forest," *National Cyclopedia of American Biography*, 42: 15, B: 61; Stanley Mallach, " Robert Weeks de Forest," in Walter Trattner, ed., *Biographical Dictionary of Social Welfare in America* (Westport, Conn.: Greenwood Press, 1986), 220; *Commercial & Financial Chronicle* 22 (1 April 1876): 326; 22 (24 June 1876): 613; 23 (7 October 1876): 353; 24 (24 March 1877): 274; 24 (26 May): 494; 26 (19 January 1878): 66; 26 (8 June 1878): 574.

4. Bogen, *Anthracite Railroads*, 67, 174-76; *Who Was Who in America*, 1: 525, 1352; *Commercial & Financial Chronicle* 42 (13 February 1886): 214; 42 (10 April 1886): 462; 42 (8 May 1886): 574; 43 (16 October 1886): 458; 44 (1 January 1887): 21; 44 (4 June 1887): 712; 21 (18 June 1887): 781; 45 (2 July 1887): 25; 46 (7 January 1888): 3, 37; Kennedy to Hill, 4 February 1887, Hill Papers.

5. Farley v Hill, 39 *Federal Reporter*, 519; Arthur H. Moehlman, "The Red River of the North," Ph.D. diss., University of Michigan, 1932, 216, 267-68, 270, 277.

6. Dorothy R. Adler, *British Investments in American Railways*, edited by Muriel E. Hidy (Charlottesville: University Press of Virginia, 1970), 147n, 187n, 203-5; Augustus J. Veenendaal, Jr., to SE, 23 September 1988.

7. Joseph Gilpin Pyle, *The Life of James J. Hill* (Garden City: Doubleday, Page & Co., 1917), 1: 159, 161; Richard S. Prosser, *Rails to the North Star* (Minneapolis: Dillon Press, 1960), 160; George B. Abdill, *Rails West* (Seattle: Superior Publishing Co., 1960) 12; Augustus J. Veenendaal, Jr., "The Kansas City Southern Railway and the Dutch Connection," *Business History Review* 61 (Summer 1987): 291, 293-94; John L. Harnsberger, *Jay Cooke and Minnesota: the Formative Years of the Northern Pacific Railroad, 1868-1873* (New York: Arno Press, 1981), 175-76, 187n. 29, 189, 192; Greenberg, "A Study of Capital Alliances," 33; Eugene V. Smalley, *History of the Northern Pacific Railroad* (1883, reprint; New York: Arno Press, 1975), 185, 296-97; John B. Rae, "The Great Northern Land Grant," *Journal of Economic History* 12 (Spring 1952): 141-43, 145; Paul Sarnoff, *Russell Sage* (New York: Ivan Obolensky, 1965), 116, 124, 271; Ralph W. and Muriel E. Hidy, "Great Northern History" manuscript, undated, Archives, Baker Library, Harvard Business School, 4n. 6, 9; Mira Wilkins, *The History of Foreign Investment in the United States to 1914* (Cambridge: Harvard University Press, 1989), 117, 205, 210, 484, 684; Augustus J. Veenendaal, Jr., "An Example of 'Other People's Money': Dutch Capital in American Railroads," *Business and Economic History* 21 (1992): 148-49, 153-54, 157.

8. Veenendaal to SE, 23 September 1988; Wilkins, *History of Foreign Investment*, 681; Robin Winks, *Frederick Billings* (New York: Oxford University Press, 1991), 204.

9. Farley v Hill, 39 *Federal Reporter*, 515, 519; John Harnsberger and Robert P. Wilkins, "Transportation on the Northern Plains," *North Dakota Quarterly* 29 (Summer 1961): 86-87; Henrietta M. Larson, *Jay Cooke* (Cambridge: Harvard University Press, 1936), 370; Hidy and Hidy, "Great Northern," 7n. 4; Harnsberger, *Jay Cooke in Minnesota*, 313-15; John Sanford Barnes, "My Egotistigraphy," New-York Historical Society, 1910, 306; William Watts Folwell, *A History of Minnesota* (1926, reprint; St. Paul: Minnesota Historical Society, 1969), 3: 446; Greenberg, "A Study of Capital Alliances," 30n. 17; Pyle, *James J. Hill*, 1: 185, 2: 432; Wilkins, *History of Foreign Investment*, 212; *American Railroad Journal* 32 (1859): 120; 34 (1861): 646, 666; 35 (1862): 939.

10. Barnes, "My Egotistigraphy," 307-8; Folwell, *A History of Minnesota*, 3: 446; J. P. Farley to J. S. Kennedy & Co., 18 October 1873, Farley v Hill, Transcript of the Record, 1: 180.

11. Barnes, "My Egotistigraphy," 307; Harnsberger, *Jay Cooke and Minnesota*, 374.

12. Farley v Hill, 39 *Federal Reporter*, 515; Folwell, *A History of Minnesota*, 2: 450; J. S. Barnes to J. P. Farley, 17 March, 6 October 1876, Farley v Hill, Transcript of

the Record, 1: 241; Barnes, "My Egotistigraphy," 309-10; *Commercial & Financial Chronicle* 21 (6 November 1875): 442; 23 (14 October 1876): 376.

13. J. S. Kennedy & Co. to T. B. Clements, 3 February 1875, Farley v Hill, Transcript of the Record, 2: 1298-99.

14. Ibid., 2: 1300.

15. J. S. Barnes to J. P. Farley, 14 February 1876, Farley v Hill, Transcript of the Record, 1: 236-37; *Railroad Gazette* 8 (10 March 1876): 112.

16. J. S. Barnes to J. P. Farley, private, 6 February 1877, Farley v Hill, Transcript of the Record, 1: 277; *Commercial & Financial Chronicle* 25 (8 August 1877): 154; Prosser, *Rails to the North Star*, 156-57; J. P. Farley to J. S. Kennedy & Co., 4, 11 August 1877, Farley v Hill, Transcript of the Record, 1: 230, 232; J. P. Farley to J. S. Kennedy & Co., 19 November 1877, Hill Papers; Greenberg, *Financiers and Railroads*, 157.

17. Hidy and Hidy, "Great Northern," 175n. 11; Farley v Hill, 39 *Federal Reporter*, 516; Poor's *Manual of Railroads*, 1869-1870, 187; 1870-1871, 112; 1873-1874, 656; *American Railroad Manual* (New York: American Railroad Manual, 1873) 527-28.

18. J. S. Barnes to J. P. Farley, 13 May 1876, 5 June 1876, Farley v Hill, Transcript of the Record, 1: 248, 251.

19. J. S. Barnes to J. P. Farley, 23 January 1877, Farley v Hill, Transcript of the Record, 1: 269; J. P. Farley to J. S. Kennedy, trustee, 22 June 1877, Hill Papers.

20. J. S. Barnes to J. P. Farley, 27 April 1876, 13 May 1876, 18 May 1876, Farley v Hill, Transcript of the Record, 1: 243-44, 248, 249; J. P. Farley to J. S. Kennedy & Co., 18 November 1876, Farley v Hill, Transcript of the Record, 1: 277.

21. J. S. Barnes to J. P. Farley, Private, 6 February 1877, Farley v Hill, Transcript of the Record, 1: 277.

5 DISCORD AND REBIRTH: THE ST. PAUL & PACIFIC UNDER NEW LEADERSHIP

A GLIMMER OF HOPE SUDDENLY emerged for Kennedy in late 1876, with the appearance of four potential buyers, later known as the "George Stephen Associates." As we shall see, they had little capital and less experience, but good local connections and plenty of tenacity and optimism. And these, ultimately, helped tip the scales in their favor.[1]

The most substantial of the quartet was George Stephen himself, who had interests in Canadian textiles, railway rolling stock, iron and steel processing, and, most significantly, in the Bank of Montreal, a dominant force in the Canadian capital market. Donald A. Smith, Chief Commissioner and a major investor in the Hudson's Bay Company, also was a large stockholder and director of the bank. These Scots-Canadian second cousins had migrated separately to Canada, where they met in 1866; they fully understood Canadian needs and aspirations.

There also was Norman W. Kittson, a major fur trader, agent of the Hudson's Bay Company, and former mayor of St. Paul, where he remained influential. Finally, there was James J. Hill, a commission merchant, freight handler and forwarder, and the agent in that city of the St. Paul & Pacific. As a highly innovative former coal dealer, Hill understood railroad freight charges and procedures. He was Kittson's partner in the Red River Transportation Company, which operated steamboats between Winnipeg and Fisher's Landing, Minnesota, then the terminus of the St. Paul & Pacific. The partners, both American citizens of Canadian origin, had much commercial experience on both sides of the border.[2]

Stephen and Smith were personally close, as were Hill and Kittson. All four had knowledge and connections. They were not typical investors, picking and choosing between various opportunities, but regional builders, strong in their insights and commitment to a particular area, and eager to make their mark. They bridged three different countries: Scotland, Canada, and the United States, much as Kennedy himself linked several financial worlds. Each perceived the key to unlocking the wheat treasures of the

Canadian-American borderland as an all-rail connection, a first step to the European market. The problem was similar to that further south: how could there be a railroad without settlers in place?; yet how could there be settlers in place without a railroad? But a solution could not simply follow American models: Canada stood far behind the United States in the population and economic development needed to generate capital.

Manitoba wheat always had been exported via a costly and circuitous combination of rail and steamboats that depended on a river which froze early, thawed late, and sank low during the arid summers. Stephen and Smith offered a solution in 1871 by joining others in seeking a charter from the Canadian government to build a railroad south from Fort Garry (Winnipeg) to the international border.

Stephen, the wealthiest of the four Associates, had become a director in 1871, vice president in 1873, and president in 1876 of the Bank of Montreal, which—in association with a New York agency—was influential in foreign trade and exchange. Even so, the depression after 1873 hurt Stephen's attempts to finance this Winnipeg-St. Paul railroad: the reaction of the bank's stockholders had to be considered. Nevertheless, he was quite ready to benefit personally from his influence on its lending, and his connections with the British capital market as well. Stephen therefore was absolutely indispensable if capital were to be found to buy the St. Paul & Pacific.[3]

By contrast, Hill was a strictly local figure in 1878, worth only about $150,000, including personal property and real estate. But he was very knowledgeable regarding the St. Paul & Pacific, and its relationship to the transportation needs of the Northwest. He was close to both Smith and Kittson, whose name was famous on the Red River for his courageous support of the American "free traders" south of the amorphous border. Hill prepared a meticulous prospectus on the St. Paul & Pacific; Stephen was impressed.

Despite their solid knowledge of local conditions, the Associates' position had some obvious weaknesses. None of them had a large personal fortune, let alone any direct experience with railroads, which were, after all, the largest, most demanding enterprises of their day. While operational experience could be hired, that was no substitute for experienced policy-making at the top, where none of the Associates had ever stood. Finally, the public mood was pessimistic—though hindsight reveals that the depression was abating by 1877-78. Where could the money be raised for a venture with a grim past and leaders with little capital to contribute?

Nevertheless, a long campaign of negotiation and maneuver that led to the sale—and the rebirth—of the line began in 1876, when Hill asked Barnes, then on one of his periodic trips to St. Paul, if J. S. Kennedy & Co. could state a price for the St. Paul & Pacific bonds. Barnes apparently took this in stride. Hill, after all, was merely a rising businessman in a bustling but hardly wealthy provincial town. Though Kittson also entered the talks, Barnes continued hedging: he could, he assured them, name no asking price. But the situation might change, and they certainly should keep in touch. Barnes informed Farley in June 1876 that these talks had made a deep impression, and that Kennedy had been informed.

The Litchfield Agreement, which in some ways had inhibited action by the bondholders, expired in August. Hill and Kittson followed up by reminding Barnes of their hopes. Would the Dutch committee, they inquired, wish to set a price on the bonds it controlled? To Barnes, knowing by now where they stood financially, all this must have seemed grossly unrealistic.[4]

The mating dance continued nevertheless, with the Associates inquiring regarding an asking price so that serious negotiations could begin. Kennedy remained evasive, even into the following May. The Associates persisted, trying to outflank him by presenting an offer directly to the Dutch, who sought his advice. He thought the price was too low, but worth considering. The Dutch rejected this price, while holding the door open for the future.[5]

Kennedy was becoming concerned. His remark to Farley in June 1877 that "it would be rather hard to lose this property," certainly was an understatement. The St. Paul & Pacific's land grant with the state of Minnesota would expire on 31 December 1878, and there were no buyers in sight except the Associates, who had very little capital. Though a failed sale might not cost Kennedy much financially, his reputation would suffer—and with it his influence and thus his prosperity. He had survived the panic of 1873; was J. S. Kennedy & Co. to drown in the wake of the St. Paul & Pacific?[6]

He also faced difficulties with some of the Dutch Committee bondholders—represented by Johan Carp—who were jostling each other and striving to get higher prices for their particular bond issues by approaching the Associates. There had been five such issues during 1862-71, with much variation in price and interest. In bargaining with Kittson and Hill, Carp, who had made the arduous trip to St. Paul, got their consent to changes in the prices paid for the various issues, though the total remained the same. Carp and his followers were merely an irritant that could not block a sale. But they could delay it, hinder it, and create obstacles which would weaken Kennedy's bargaining position by bringing the land grant deadline ever closer. "We fear the delays," Kennedy informed Farley, "and recognize fully the weakness of the Dutchmen's position, and have said and done all we could to bring the matter to a favorable conclusion."[7]

Barnes conferred with the Associates in Montreal during mid-September, 1877. Though Hill and Kittson knew the St. Paul & Pacific at close range, Stephen and Smith, the two Canadians, did not. So Stephen traveled to Minnesota late that month to inspect the line; clearly, matters were becoming more serious.

Yet Stephen remained excessively skeptical, even suspicious, of Kennedy's intentions, believing that J. S. Kennedy & Co. was over-eager to retain the commissions and other sums it received from the Dutch bondholders. A decade later, Stephen in fact testified in court "that Kennedy & Co. thought they had a good thing in representing the Dutch bondholders and would not likely be willing to give it up. In short that they would be unfavorable to the Committee [i.e., the Dutch bondholders] accepting the offer that had been made to them."

First Minnesota, then Europe. Stephen traveled there late in September to begin the very difficult task of personally searching for the venture capital on which everything depended. For only if the Associates could make the St. Paul & Pacific profitable would that capital acquire value.

Desperation impelled them to be generous. Years later, Stephen offered a rambling explanation of their reasoning: "It was generally understood that it [the venture capital] might probably take a share in the profits that it was supposed might be realized of one fifth to secure the financial aid necessary to carry the thing through. . . . Each would have one fifth, leaving one fifth to be disposed of to secure the money necessary to buy the Company's bonds. It was understood in a general way that I was in a position to concede any reasonable terms that might be exacted in order to attain our objective."[8]

In London, Stephen relied heavily on his friend and former attorney, Sir John Rose, a prominent Canadian financial and political figure with high-level British and American banking contacts. Rose was a partner in Morton, Rose & Co., an important Anglo-American private banking firm, whose head was Levi P. Morton, a future American vice president. Stephen offered Morton, Rose "an equal interest with us in the outcome," that is: one fifth of the stock, plus five per cent interest on the loan of any cash advanced to complete the agreement.

How much money was being sought? We do not know: the records are entirely lacking. It may well be that even Stephen didn't have a precise figure in mind, that the variables and intangibles made it difficult to reach one. No matter the amount, the money could not be found. The venture apparently fell between two stools. It was both too small and too risky to attract the most powerful London financiers, say, Baring Brothers or J. S. Morgan & Co., yet it was too big for the smaller bankers.

Morton, Rose & Co. turned for information and advice to its American affiliate, Morton, Bliss & Co., which was given the opportunity to buy at a virtually nominal price. Yet it declined: why? George Bliss, of Morton, Bliss, relied heavily for advice on a consultant, Edward F. Winslow, an Iowa railroad executive, who focused on the likely revenue from selling off parcels of the Minnesota land grant. That was, after all, the principal asset of the St. Paul & Pacific, but selling entailed competition with other lines, which also were selling land, and even with the federal government, which was both selling and giving it away through the Homestead Act. With so much competition, Winslow was pessimistic about the immediate future of the St. Paul & Pacific.

After several months of fruitless negotiations, during which Morton, Bliss & Co. hesitated but never actually refused, Stephen had to accept failure. So it was with the other soundings he made in London. In December 1877, Stephen therefore returned to Montreal, where he joined the other three Associates in choosing the unusual strategy of trying to buy the bonds on credit.[9]

The Associates proposed paying for the bonds with which the Dutch had been saddled for so many years with the new bonds of a successor company. In effect, this meant trading in one set of I.O.U.s for another set with presumably greater security; the cash changing hands was negligible. Several hundred Dutch bondholders were, instead, being asked to rely on new and untried managers in distant Minnesota who would make the St. Paul & Pacific a profitable venture after some twenty years of dispute, disappointment and outright failure. Yet what could the Dutch do but accept? And that they did.

Kennedy played a central role in all this. Anxious to keep the deal alive, he held his first meeting with Stephen in New York during January 1878. The Dutch bondholders, relying heavily on Kennedy's judgments and his day-to-day actions, apparently thought the deal was already settled; a majority of them had accepted, Kennedy informed Hill. "We are still negotiating with Stephen," Kennedy wrote to Farley late that month, "in regard to the sale of the Dutch interest and we are in hopes that the transaction will be completed satisfactorily—and our opinion is that it will be although the details are very intricate and difficult of arrangement."[10]

There was, however, a problem: Jesse Farley. Any hope he might have had of striking it rich in some way or another was dashed with the arrival of the new management team. He complained about being slighted by the Associates. They in turn believed he was building far too slowly. Stephen urged Kennedy to prod Farley into accelerating construction to Pembina, on the border with Manitoba. Kennedy already had criticized Farley for completing the construction to Sauk Center, Minnesota, with only two days to spare. He nevertheless tried hard to placate Farley, even as he had to ask him in late January 1878 to give the firm's cypher code to Hill or Kittson, who did show more tact as time went on.[11]

Kennedy always had been thoughtful about supplying Farley with information; the Associates were not. They even withheld the terms of the offer, leaving it to Kennedy to write Farley in February that: "Stephen and his associates have accepted the amounts [the prices of the bonds] and extended the time for two weeks for other bondholders to come in. So that the transaction is virtually closed and they [the Associates] are the owners of a good large majority of each issue. We believe that they will get in, the full amounts as the minimum—and probably if they want them, nearly all the outstanding issues." Kennedy was referring to the stipulation requiring that a majority of the bonds held by the owners for each of the five issues accept the agreement for it to become valid; their rights vis-à-vis the other bondolders were protected, which provided substantial justice. He felt it wise to ask Farley to keep this vital data to himself.[12]

The Associates made their second offer late in January 1878 (the first, a year earlier, had been rejected). They and Lippmann, Rosenthal & Co., the representative of the Dutch Committee, signed it on 13 March 1878. The projected scenario mandated foreclosure (which in fact didn't occur for about a year), and then the creation of a new company to operate the line. Success seemed assured—at long last.

Kennedy was satisfied; the work of some five years was beginning to pay off. "I presume you have seen Kittson and Hill since their return to St. Paul," he wrote confidentially to Farley in April, "and learned from them how matters stand between them and the Dutch Committee. They are now the virtual owners of the property, and with their friends in Canada [Stephen and Smith], must go on and complete it as early as possible, and this is quite as much for the interests of the Dutch bondholders whom we continue to represent. As for Kittson and Hill and their associates, we hope you will do everything in your power to aid them." Kennedy was, in effect, urging Farley to hurry in laying down more track during the coming summer, for the Minnesota land grant expired just eight months away, on 31 December.[13]

The sale reflected the complex and unprofitable history of the St. Paul & Pacific. The Dutch bondholders sold their approximately $28,000,000 in bonds to the Associates at roughly the market price, with a spread ranging downward from 75 cents to $13^{3}/_{4}$ cents on the dollar. The early bonds had retained most of their value, presumably because their trackage was favorably placed, close to St. Paul, where there was sufficient business to provide enough revenue to cover much of the cost.

The Associates paid 75 cents for each dollar comprising the $1,200,000 Branch Line issue of 2 June 1862. And so it went: 30 cents on the dollar for the $3,000,000 Main Line issue of 1 March 1864; 28 cents for each dollar of the $2,800,000 Branch Line issue of 1 October 1865; 35 cents for the $6,000,000 Main Line issue of 1 July 1868; and 13³/₄ cents for the $15,000,000 Extension issue of 1 April 1871. Thus, the largest issue received the paltry payback of 13³/₄ cents on the dollar. The entire package, comprising the St. Paul & Pacific and the First Division, plus other miscellaneous property, sold for $4,380,000. The Associates paid for this with receiver's debentures, thirty-year bonds in an as-yet-unformed company, and a small amount of cash to cover the Dutch Committee's outlays for the costs of receivership, the foreclosure suits and similar expenses.[14]

With so many qualifying factors to consider, the concept of "fair market value" hardly applies. Valuation is the key to resolving default cases. How much is the defaulted company worth? The more valuable it is, the more available to distribute among creditors, who are paid according to their level of seniority; i. e., the priority of the claims, as determined by their agreements and collateralization.

Specifically, what were the defaulted bonds of the railroad then worth, and to whom? What likelihood was there that interest and principal ever would be paid? What about external circumstances and, above all, the question of management? In hindsight, it is clear that the property passed into stronger hands, and that good timing helped the Associates gain a remarkable bargain. For recovery from the depression of the 1870s, plus the advent of the sod-breaking steel plow, spurred settlement in the great triangle, St. Paul-Winnipeg-Fargo. In 1870-80, for example, Minnesota's population of more than 400,000 soared to nearly 800,000, while that of the Dakota Territory rose even more steeply. This meant more freight, especially wheat. Sheer good luck, bolstered by insight and courage, had put the Associates in the right place at the right time to benefit from the upsurge in traffic.

Paradoxically, however, all this might create huge problems. It seemed for a time that the Litchfield interests might profit, possibly even regaining control of the line. For more traffic meant higher revenues and therefore the ability to pay interest on the bonds. This, in turn, would end default, thus averting foreclosure, and of necessity would restore Litchfield's control. A prompt foreclosure—it came in spring 1878—would forestall this possibility and protect the Associates.

They recognized, nevertheless, the need to deal with the threat that the Litchfield interests posed; Kennedy and the Dutch bondholders backed this decision. After considerable bickering, the Associates bought the First

Division securities in January 1879 from E. C. and E. D. Litchfield for $500,000. Then, and only then, could the Associates consider with Kennedy the transfer of the physical properties represented by the securities.[15]

The Litchfields represented a loose end; now it had been secured. Kennedy's fee for his work since he became involved in 1873 was yet another. He had, in fact, been buying St. Paul & Pacific bonds from various Dutch bondholders all along, at prices which, though steeply discounted, were quite consistent with those paid by the Associates. In addition, he had continued to function as a commission merchant and private banker, purchasing and financing iron rails, for example, thus becoming an unsecured creditor. So Kennedy, who had begun in 1873 as an agent for the Dutch Committee, gradually had enlarged his position, becoming a player in the game—though on a scale which cannot be determined. All this was later to trigger a lawsuit against him.

Now the bondholders had taken new securities—thirty-year bonds— instead of cash. Ultimately, these bonds proved a great benefit, consistently paying interest. The Associates' offer to buy was accepted by Lippmann, Rosenthal & Co., as representatives of the Dutch Committee, but was contingent on approval by J. S. Kennedy & Co.; in effect, Kennedy morally guaranteed the contract. For all these services, he wanted $100,000 from the Dutch Committee, though he settled for $80,000, a considerable but hardly unreasonable sum for a half dozen years of intense activity.[16]

In June 1878, Kennedy and Barnes conferred with Stephen and Hill in New York: how were the remaining bonds to be acquired? For it was important to placate the dissident bondholders, who might, after all, cause difficulties, either by floating rumors hurtful to Kennedy and the Associates, or by bringing a lawsuit which the financial press doubtless would publicize. The task fell to Barnes, who sailed for the Netherlands—while Kennedy and Stephen left for salmon fishing in Canada. Lippmann, Rosenthal had indeed signed with the Associates on 13 March. But the Dutch Committee had yet to formally agree. And the individual bondholders retained the option of selling or not. But Barnes triumphed, gaining the assent of all parties.

Nonetheless, the Associates still had to find the money to complete the transaction and proceed into construction as quickly as possible. The deadline for their land grant, after all, was only months away. And the line was still in receivership, which inhibited their freedom of action.

Kennedy provided some funding; his reputation attracted other investors. And Stephen, as president of the Bank of Montreal, proved invaluable, for his bank advanced the substantial sum of $700,000 to the Associates in mid-1878 on nothing but their personal security. Stephen papered over complaints of a conflict of interest that arose at a stockholders' meeting a year later.[17]

The Associates tried for substantial borrowing by selling "receiver's debentures," which were based on trackage yet to be built. Kennedy was optimistic. But the judge of the Circuit Court of Appeals in St. Paul, John Forrest Dillon—who had no railroad experience—hesitated to authorize the issuance of so many. Dillon rightly "said it was an extraordinary and unusual thing he was asked to do." Hill had advised Kennedy in April 1878 that, "The court did not like to undertake the construction of great lines of railroads." But the argument undoubtedly was presented that, without such construction, the land grant would be revoked, the entire venture would suffer, and so would the investors and the citizens of Minnesota. Judge Dillon approved the request in May. "The letter killeth, but the spirit giveth life."

The next question was to find buyers. Who would put up the money that would help turn the 13 March agreement into an economic reality? Kennedy devised a plan based on his position as the agent of the Cambria Iron Company. It sold steel rails to the St. Paul & Pacific, and accepted receiver's debentures in partial payment. Kennedy advanced money to the railroad, which in turn paid part of its rail bill with Cambria. Kennedy then bought the receiver's debentures from Cambria at a discount, and sold them to investors.[18] This credit bridge stretched the limited amount of cash. "If we are willing to come forward with the money," Kennedy explained to Farley in July, "under these extraordinary circumstances, taking the debentures from the contractors whoever they may be we should have a reasonable margin." Stephen, expecting to get receiver's debentures, also put himself at risk by providing personal funds. Like ordinary railroad bonds, the debentures could be issued only after construction had created the trackage involved.[19]

Tension increased as November passed and the 31 December land grant deadline neared. But the new managers—especially Hill—of the St. Paul & Pacific were doing what their predecessors had failed to do for two decades: reach the Canadian border from St. Paul. Fully 105 miles had been added that year, completing links to St. Vincent and Alexandria, Minnesota, thereby ending the danger of expiration. The Canadians soon finished their line, south from Winnipeg to the border. At long last, an all-rail connection had been forged between Winnipeg and St. Paul.[20]

Inevitably, there still were difficulties, particularly for Kennedy. He had to travel to Texas early in 1879 to deal with his railroad investments there. There was the nagging question of Jesse Farley, self-important yet eminently fallible, and an obstacle to the attempts by Stephen and Hill to revitalize the line, especially in construction. The Associates were undercutting Farley's authority, and Kennedy himself was gradually withdrawing his support.

Finally, Judge Dillon's decision had left Kennedy financially vulnerable. The receiver's debentures that Dillon had authorized to cover the St. Paul & Pacific's most recent construction would not be issued until well into December, after building had been completed. Even then, their negotiability would be clouded by Dillon's last-minute refusal to rule them an absolute lien on the entire railroad. This ruling excluded them from the line's most valuable trackage, that in the St. Paul area where traffic was densest, confining them instead to newly-built, lightly-settled areas of low traffic density. This was reasonable, because the money for the receiver's debentures had been used to build some of that new track. Nevertheless, Dillon's decision left J. S. Kennedy & Co. seriously extended for months to come.[21]

▼   ▼   ▼

Despite these difficulties, Kennedy could look back with satisfaction over his early years with the St. Paul & Pacific. First had come a holding action, an attempt to stave off a disaster in the terrible times after 1873. The advent of the Associates not only enabled the Dutch bondholders to extricate themselves from their plight, but also helped Kennedy to recoup the money he had placed at risk. The sale to the Associates brought on a remarkable attempt to make bricks without straw, a drive into the unknown, based on enterprise and resourcefulness rather than cash, and on dreams of the future rather than bankable assets in the present. Was Kennedy's support decisive in legitimizing their audacious—almost presumptuous—venture? Clearly, he saw in them the hope of at last putting the line on a sound footing.

The outcome remained unclear in late 1878. But there were hints of success: witness the 105 miles of track built in a few months. At last the people of Minnesota received what they had long wanted; the state land grant had been justified after all. All this was to bring opportunities to Kennedy, as he neared fifty, that he had never known before.

Notes

1. John Sanford Barnes, "My Egotistigraphy," Typescript, 1910, New-York Historical Society, 310.
2. Heather Gilbert, *The Life of Lord Mount Stephen* (Aberdeen: Aberdeen University Press, 1976), 1: 27; Merrill Denison, *Canada's First Bank: A History of the Bank of Montreal* (Toronto: McClelland & Stewart, 1967), 2: 205.
3. Mira Wilkins, *The History of Foreign Investment in the United States to 1914* (Cambridge: Harvard University Press, 1989), 213, 467.

4. J. S. Barnes to J. P. Farley, 15 December 1876; J. S. Barnes to J. P. Farley, Private, 6 February 1877; N. W. Kittson to J. S. Barnes, 4 August 1876, Farley v Hill, Transcript of the Record, 1: 267, 277, 2: 992.

5. J. J. Hill to J. S. Kennedy, 8 May 1877, Farley v Hill, Transcript of the Record, 1: 2, 604-5, Hill testimony.

6. J. S. Kennedy to J. P. Farley, 19 June 1877; J. S. Kennedy & Co. to J. P. Farley, Confidential, 22 June 1877; J. P. Farley to J. S. Kennedy & Co., 30 June 1877; Johan Carp, Utrecht, to J. P. Farley, 30 July 1877, Farley v Hill, Transcript of the Record, 1: 289, 289-90, 2: 1015, 1: 295.

7. J. P. Farley to J. S. Kennedy & Co., 26 September 1877; J. P. Farley to J. S. Barnes, 28 September 1877; J. S. Kennedy & Co. to J. P. Farley, Private, 29 September 1877; J. S. Kennedy & Co. to J. P. Farley, Private and Confidential, 2 October 1877; J. S. Kennedy & Co. to J. P. Farley, 10 October 1877, Farley v Hill, Transcript of the Record, 2:1017-18, 1018, 1: 310-11, 313.

8. George Stephen testimony, Farley v. Hill, Transcript of the Record, 2: 1231, 1233-35; Hill to Stephen, 29 June 1878, George Stephen testimony, Farley v Hill, Transcript of the Record, 2: 1236.

9. George Stephen testimony, Farley v Hill, Transcript of the Record, 1: 1237, 1237-38, 1239-40; James J. Hill testimony, Farley v Hill, Transcript of the Record, 1: 617-18; Dolores Greenberg, *Financiers and Railroads, 1869-1889: A Study of Morton, Bliss & Company* (Newark: University of Delaware Press, 1980), 152, 155-56, 243n. 53; "John Rose," *Dictionary of Canadian Biography*, 11: 767-71; "Edward F. Winslow," *Dictionary of American Biography*, 20: 395-96.

10. J. S. Kennedy to J. P. Farley, Private, 7 January 1878; J. S. Kennedy & Co. to J. P. Farley, 26 January 1878; Farley v Hill, Transcript of the Record, 1: 315, 2: 992; Greenberg, *Financiers and Railroads*, 154; Gilbert, *Life of Lord Mount Stephen*, 1: 43.

11. J. S. Kennedy & Co. to J. P. Farley, Receiver, 26 January 1878; J. S. Kennedy & Co. to J. P. Farley, Confidential, 19 February 1878, Farley v Hill, Transcript of the Record, 2: 993.

12. G. Stephen and D. A. Smith to J. S. Kennedy & Co., 29 January 1878, Hill Papers, James Jerome Hill Reference Library, St. Paul, Minnesota; J. S. Kennedy & Co. to J. P. Farley, Confidential, 19 February 1878; J. S. Kennedy & Co. to J. P. Farley, Private, 27 February 1878, Farley v Hill, Transcript of the Record, 2: 994.

13. J. S. Kennedy to J. P. Farley, Confidential, 4 April 1878, Farley v Hill, Transcript of the Record, 2: 998-99.

14. Augustus J. Veenendaal, Jr., "The Kansas City Southern Railway and the Dutch Connection," *Business History Review* 61 (Summer 1987): 295; Charles Edward Russell, *Stories of the Great Railroads* (Chicago: Charles H. Kerr & Co., 1912), 21-22.

15. J. S. Kennedy & Co. to J. J. Hill, 27 December 1878, James J. Hill Correspondence, President's Office, Great Northern Railway Company Records, Minnesota Historical Society, St. Paul, Minnesota; J. J. Hill to J. S. Kennedy, 19 June 1878; G. Stephen to J. J. Hill, 10 July, 21 August 1878, 17 January 1879, Hill Papers; Gilbert, *Life of Lord Mount Stephen*, 1: 45-46.

16. Testimony of J. S. Kennedy, Sahlgaard v J. S. Kennedy (1881); G. Stephen to J. S. Kennedy & Co., 26 July 1878, Farley v Hill, Transcript of the Record, 2: 1755, 1764; 2: 1026.

17. Barnes, "My Egotistigraphy," 318; J. J. Hill to G. Stephen, 23 June 1878; G. Stephen to J. J. Hill, 26 June 1878; J. J. Hill to G. Stephen, 29 June 1878; G. Stephen to J. S. Kennedy & Co., 25 July 1878; G. Stephen to J. J. Hill, 21 August 1878, Hill Papers.

18. J. P. Farley to J. S. Kennedy, 13 June 1878, Farley v Hill, Transcript of the Record, 2: 1019; Gilbert, *Life of Lord Mount Stephen*, 1: 30-33; Denison, *Canada's First Bank*, 2: 201; Maury Klein, *The Life and Legend of Jay Gould* (Baltimore: Johns Hopkins University Press, 1986), 166, 263, 287; J. J. Hill to J. S. Kennedy & Co., 21 April 1878, Hill Papers; J. S. Kennedy & Co. to J. P. Farley, 8 July 1878, Farley v Hill, Transcript of the Record, 2: 1495.

19. J S. Kennedy & Co. to J. P. Farley, 8 July 1878; J. S. Kennedy to J. P. Farley, Private, 10 July 1878; G. Stephen to J. P. Farley, 24 September 1878, Farley v Hill, Transcript of the Record, 2: 1495-96, 2: 1000, 2: 1711.

20. J. J. Hill to J. S. Kennedy, 14 April 1879; G. Stephen to J. J Hill, 26 November 1878, Hill Papers.

21. G. Stephen to J. J. Hill, 17 February 1879; J. S. Kennedy to G. Stephen, 16 April 1879, Hill Papers; G. Stephen to J. P. Farley, 4 January 1879, Farley v Hill, Transcript of the Record, 2: 1496; J. J. Hill to G. Stephen, 25 March 1879; J. S. Barnes, Amsterdam, to J. S. Kennedy, 3 April 1879; J. S. Kennedy to G. Stephen, 17 April, 21 November 1879; G. Stephen to J. S. Kennedy, 4 April 1879, Hill Papers; J. S. Kennedy to J. P. Farley, 30 January 1879, Farley v Hill, Transcript of the Record, 1: 319.

6 THE ST. PAUL, MINNEAPOLIS & MANITOBA—AND THE CANADIAN PACIFIC

KENNEDY AND THE ASSOCIATES HAD made substantial achievements during 1877-79. But the losers counterattacked, with occasional sniping in the courts and elsewhere.

Jesse Farley had had to face disappointment: not only was his receivership soon to expire, but his claim to preferment would be rejected; so he fought back. A few Dutch bondholders—"the outstanders"—tried to gain more for their bonds by alleging fraud in a court suit against Kennedy and the Associates. The defendants defeated them in court, but then offered a shrewd and generous settlement. John Barnes, Kennedy's partner, also tried to gain personally; failing that, he was forced out of J. S. Kennedy & Co.

First, however, came the exploitation of victory. In May 1879, Kennedy informed a credit reporter from R. G. Dun & Co. that he, Stephen and the other Associates now controlled the St. Paul & Pacific, of course including all its components: the First Division, the Red River & Manitoba, and several branches and extensions. It was renamed on the 23rd as the St. Paul, Minneapolis & Manitoba, in recognition of the line's new Canadian orientation, and of Minneapolis' growing importance as the economic capital of the upper Midwest.

This was the first of several steps required to get the new company underway. As mortgage trustee, Kennedy attended in May 1879 to what had become a formality: the foreclosure of the $15,000,000 First Division bond issue. The Associates now took over, and were elected (along with Barnes) as directors, at the Manitoba's organization meeting. Pending distribution of the new company's stock, Barnes—as trustee—temporarily held virtually all the Manitoba stock as collateral for the small sum the Associates owed the bondholders.

Kennedy played a major role in the new company's finances. The trustees under the first mortgage included him, Barnes and James A. Roosevelt, a long-time associate. Under the second mortgage bond issue, the trustees were Kennedy and Samuel Thorne, a New York investor with coal and iron interests; he also was close to Kennedy. And J. S. Kennedy & Co. and Roosevelt & Son became agents for the bonds the new company now issued. To market these bonds more effectively, Kennedy innovated by asking for weekly construction and earnings reports with which to impress prospective investors. The directors responded to his work as fiscal agent by authorizing annual payments totalling $20,000 to J. S. Kennedy & Co. The Associates paid him a further $50,000 as a closing cost for representing the Dutch bondholders. This came out of the $280,000 the Associates had had to put up (which Kennedy held) to assure the bondholders that the cash was indeed available.[1]

Events began to fulfill the promise of the new company. Kennedy was delighted by an operations report for October 1879 which showed rising revenue: "The showing is a grand one almost *too* good." The Associates were benefitting from an unbeatable combination: a business upturn, a tide of settlers, and new, hard-driving management.

There was an irritant, however: Jesse Farley. As a court-appointed receiver, Farley became superfluous once the receivership ended. Kennedy had, in fact, pointed out to him a year before the conflict of interest inherent in being simultaneously a receiver and a director. Farley nevertheless hoped to hang on in one capacity or another.

Farley also had major difficulties with James Hill, a tough, efficient and vigorous entrepreneur of forty-two who had emerged as the general manager of the new railroad and the dominant man on the spot. Stephen was the president, to be sure, but he had major interests to care for in far-off Montreal. Though Kittson was indeed in St. Paul, he had neither direct experience in railroad operations (nor did Hill, for that matter), nor the desire, in his sixties, to take on so gargantuan a task. That left Hill, who began revamping the St. Paul, Minneapolis & Manitoba, firing, promoting and transferring personnel as he went. All the while, Farley remained in Dubuque, coming to St. Paul only for business; Hill later complained about Farley's "*very frequent*" absences. Farley was experienced, but not particularly effective or energetic—and he was sixtyish. He complained often to Kennedy of being tired: "I must look forward to an early day when I must be relieved from this strain of nerve and brain." By the end of the summer of 1878, Hill had rightly concluded that he could build the railroad faster and cheaper than could Farley, whom Stephen occasionally deprecated as "the old man;" Barnes used similar language.

Fearing a public controversy at a delicate time, Kennedy managed to keep the peace. Kittson also was conciliatory, and by early 1879 was considering giving Farley a moderate severance payment, the better to go forward without a public row. Kittson and even Hill may have hinted at payment the year before. Certainly Farley thought so, having informed Kennedy in February 1878 that they had made a vague offer to him. And Kennedy replied quite positively: "We think it will pay you to take an interest with Kittson and Hill, and we are glad that they have offered it to you."

Things began changing, however, once the Associates started tightening their grip on what had become *their* railroad. In February 1879, Kennedy undercut Farley's authority by directing him to clear everything with Stephen and Hill. And Kennedy argued with Farley in March that, just as he, Kennedy, could not be both a director of the new company and also a trustee, so Farley could not be a receiver while also becoming a director. "I regret very much to see the manner in which Farley acts," Kennedy wrote Stephen in April, "and if his vanity and egotism are carried much further, the Trustees may in the interests of the property be compelled to remove him and appoint Hill his successor."

Farley fought back—as best he could. His receivership of course ended with the creation of the St. Paul, Minneapolis & Manitoba in May 1879. Neither a directorship nor a bonus in either cash or stock was offered him. Within weeks, Farley brought a lawsuit in St. Paul. Though Kennedy stated privately that Farley's action "is the most preposterous one that can be imagined," he nevertheless wanted to settle out of court, thus avoiding both legal costs and public scandal.

There was, however, intense anger on both sides, particularly between Farley and Hill. The Associates chose not to settle privately, but to fight. The suit dragged on for well over a decade, from appeal to appeal, with the findings generally against Farley. By 1893, it reached the Supreme Court in Washington, which upheld a lower court decision against him. He died in 1894.[2]

Another lawsuit arose in June 1879 from a few Dutch "outstanders." They, having rejected the settlement of March 1878 with the Dutch Committee, were demanding more. This was no more than a nuisance suit, brought as a bargaining ploy by bondholders who held less than $300,000 out of the First Division's $15,000,000 bond issue of 1871. Their complaint lay in the paltry $13^3/4$ cents on the dollar offered them for their bonds, even as owners of other issues were receiving much more. These payments were of course largely determined by market values, but the outstanders were, in effect, rejecting that measuring rod.

The Associates were disposed to fight, as they had with Farley. "After having given such ample opportunities of adhering," Stephen had asserted to Hill the year before, "I have no compunction in *freezing out* entirely the outstanders when we come to sell the property and both Kennedy and Barnes say that we shall be quite justified in doing so."

The outstanders, as plaintiffs, worked through an American bondholder in similar circumstances to bring suit in St. Paul. They petitioned the court to declare the foreclosure null and void, charging "constructive fraudulent collusion." They spied an opportunity in the property's huge rise in value since the recent foreclosure. Did this stem from facts known to inside buyers, i.e., Kennedy himself, but concealed from the mortgagees? Or did it largely result from the new broom that the Associates were wielding so effectively? Kennedy's image, both public and private, depended heavily on the outcome.

For he was the principal target, with the Associates second. As a trustee, he was legally and morally obligated to protect the bondholders' interests by securing the maximum price for their bonds. The outstanders alleged that he had compromised this trust by colluding with the Associates to artificially depress the price.

Kennedy was deeply upset, suffering painful headaches that no mere legal vindication could assuage. A trustee, a fiduciary for the beneficiaries of the trust, was held to a higher standard of morality than that of commerce. And his success as a private banker rested on his reputation for honesty; to impugn that was to strike at the very roots of his career.

So Kennedy travelled to St. Paul to testify. He was angry, perhaps defensive. In a letter of September 1879 to the Dutch Committee, he averred: "We have no personal pecuniary interest whatever in this venture of Stephen." The damage that a possible compromise might bring to his reputation is hinted at in a letter to Hill: "I hope that you will not settle . . . but fight the case to the end; as Trustee I certainly will not consent to any settlement."

The Associates themselves had counterattacked by buying out some of the outstanders, thus splitting their ranks and weakening their position. Hill tried to ease Kennedy's mind in December by predicting a favorable outcome. He was right: the court ruled for the defendants in June 1880, exactly a year after the trial opened. Kennedy was vindicated, and he printed and had distributed in New York some 200 copies of the decision. He did this again in July 1882—though in the Netherlands—when the appellate court upheld the lower court's judgment.

Having triumphed, the Associates showed magnanimity and wise business sense, settling with the handful of outstanders by buying their bonds at par, plus interest: instead of $13^3/4$ cents, the latter now received a full dollar. Tenacity and risk-taking had, in effect, paid off for a few outstanders, very largely because the Associates had chosen to buy the good opinion of a Dutch investing community whose guilders they might need in the future.[3]

When Kennedy insisted that he had "no pecuniary interest whatever" in the Manitoba, he was being somewhat disingenuous. He was not a stockholder of record, to be sure, yet there was the murky question of stock pledged by the Associates in 1878 to J. S. Kennedy & Co., of the tensions this created between Kennedy and Barnes, and of the dissolution this caused of their partnership.

The key problem for the Associates in late 1877 had been finding capital for what became the St. Paul, Minneapolis & Manitoba. As we have seen, thay had been ready to reward Morton, Bliss & Co., or indeed any major investor who might appear, with a full fifth of the stock in the line. J. S. Kennedy & Co. had stepped into the breach, though of necessity most discreetly, for Kennedy also was a trustee and agent for the bondholders. Was he crossing the invisible, yet potentially dangerous, line separating buyer and seller? Was there a conflict of interest? If so, would this besmirch the reputation on which Kennedy's career had rested?

The facts remain obscure, perhaps deliberately. All interpretations must remain tentative. It is, however, certain that in early 1878, the four Associates had divided ownership in what became the Manitoba into fifths, each to receive one-fifth, while Stephen himself held the "fifth fifth" in trust "for the purpose of securing the cooperation of an associate or associates in said enterprise to enable us to complete such purchase [as] may be obtained."

None of the Associates saw Kennedy as one of them. And, in September 1879, Kennedy himself denied to the Dutch Committee any involvement. In November 1880, Stephen advised John A. Macdonald, the Canadian prime minister, that Kennedy did not own "one dollar of interest" in the Manitoba, whose records support this assertion; Kennedy was not at that time a stock-holder of record.

The evidence, however, suggests another explanation. A stockholders' list of 15 September 1880, makes clear who owned what of the 150,000 shares. There were a very few minor stockholders. Then came Smith, Kittson and Hill, each with approximately one-fifth, or 23,000 shares each. Stephen held—but only temporarily—substantially more: 57,881 in his own name, plus 17,469 *in trust*. This particular trust had been created only a month before, when Smith, Kittson and Hill each transferred 5,823 shares, or a total of 17,469, to Stephen.

There was no mention of Kennedy, and no analysis of what the numbers truly signified. J. S. Kennedy & Co. were, in fact, told in August that, "There would seem to be no occasion for you to go behind the record as it exists in your transfer books in dealing with Stephen's stock." Both sides apparently preferred to avoid leaving a paper trail that might prove potentially embarrassing.

These very large holdings might suggest that major wealth had been created, and that the Associates had made themselves quite rich. This was not so. The Manitoba had not begun to prove itself. The territory it traversed was still largely empty, with few settlers, little freight or much revenue. So its stock was a great unknown, and was easily shuffled around in the inner circle. Some of it, in fact, went to a new member, Richard B. Angus, who had helped greatly with financing while general manager of the Bank of Montreal, i.e., as a lieutenant to Stephen. Angus had become vice president and general manager of the Manitoba for a short time after August 1879, and the four Associates each chipped in to make him an important stockholder.[4]

Clearly, a substantial block of Manitoba stock had been placed in trust. And Kennedy was to emerge some years later as a very large stockholder. Was there a causal connection? Did the stock eventually fall to him? There is no precise documentation, but there is some highly allusive evidence.

One tidbit came from George Stephen, writing thirty years later to Sir Arthur Bigge, then secretary of the Prince of Wales. "When I first knew Kennedy in 1878," Stephen stated, "he considered himself a *very* rich man having by twenty years hard work accumulated *$500,000*. He was agent for the Dutch bondholders . . . Kennedy was very useful to me. To reward him I *gave* him one-fifth interest, making him equal to Hill, Kitson [sic], Smith, and myself and that is how he became the Scotch millionaire." The relationship between Stephen and Kennedy had long since cooled, as Stephen's sardonicism suggests. How much credence can we therefore accord these remarks?[5]

There is more, however, in the unpublished autobiography (1910) by John Barnes, Kennedy's partner during the Manitoba transactions. Barnes alluded to "one-fifth of the two-fifths coming to him [Stephen], for account of J. S. Kennedy & Company, an agreement to that effect having been made by him with us." Barnes certainly had been an insider. But his objectivity is suspect; he and Kennedy had parted unhappily in 1880, and Barnes had achieved little thereafter.[6]

The question nevertheless arises: did Kennedy have an implicit understanding in 1879-80 regarding future disposition of the Manitoba stock? The documentation is inconclusive, but the answer is very likely yes. When questions arose at the time of the outstanders' trial regarding Kennedy's stockholding in the railroad, he could honestly deny it, but just barely. What he apparently did have was a tacit agreement regarding ownership of stock, not in the present but in the future. For the Associates, desperately needing capital in 1878 to buy the St. Paul & Pacific, had seen Kennedy alone support them. They reciprocated by holding shares in trust for him behind a screen that obscured. Thus, Kennedy was by way of founding one of the great American fortunes.

Kennedy did become an important stockholder in the Manitoba during the 1880s, as the line expanded and prospered. In 1881, a year before the

Manitoba began paying dividends, Kittson, who was the oldest of the Associates and had never been more than a passive owner, sold out privately. His stock went—at sixty—to Angus, Hill, Kennedy, Smith and Stephen. In 1883, Kennedy held 6,000 shares out of 200,000; his firm held another 2,800. Hill, Smith and Stephen each owned substantially more than did Kennedy. When active in managing the Manitoba during the mid-1880s, however, Kennedy controlled fully 25,000 shares out of 200,000, either in his own or in street names which concealed ownership. Some150 stockholders (including Hill, Smith and Stephen) held the remainder.[7]

Even after Kennedy sold 10,000 shares of common stock in October 1889, he still owned 15,000 shares out of 200,000, and was second only to Hill; some 750 stockholders owned the rest. J. S. Kennedy Tod & Co.—the successor to J. S. Kennedy & Co.—held another 5,000 shares in its name. And Kennedy owned 20,000—out of 250,000—in preferred stock. What had begun for Kennedy in the early 1870s as a holding operation with a moribund provincial railroad that required constant maneuvers to ensure its survival, progressed in the 1880s into the mainspring of his fortune. And that in turn propelled him into a major venture: financing the Canadian Pacific Railway.[8]

But a minor problem had to be resolved: a falling out between Kennedy and his junior partner, John Barnes. The latter was a distant relative (by marriage), virtually a contemporary of Kennedy's, but always a subordinate, who executed policy without formulating it. Now there was open disagreement between the two, though its cause is uncertain. The issue appears to have been that of the payment which J. S. Kennedy & Co. should receive from the Associates. While Barnes was eager to accept the stock the Associates offered, Kennedy was not, fearing the imputation of conflict of interest inherent in his involvement on both sides. On this the partnership foundered on 28 February 1880, barely two weeks before its agreed expiration date of 13 March. Barnes sold his three-eighths interest in J. S. Kennedy & Co. to Kennedy for cash. Why Kennedy felt called to end early what would have expired in two weeks is unknown, though the always-secretive Kennedy had been expressing suspicions about Barnes for some time.

Now Kennedy informed the Manitoba's Angus in late February 1880 that "I am making my arrangements to close up with Barnes as soon as possible, and hope to have everything concluded by 1 March although he may insist on going on to 13 March when our contract will expire by limitation. It is very evident that he had no idea of separation and he appears to be in a dilemma what to do and I really feel sorry for him, while at [the] same time almost every day furnishes additional evidence that the step I have taken was taken none too soon and it would have been much better for me if it had been taken earlier." Ominous words; what they mean precisely remains unknown.[9]

Behind all this stands the construction of the Canadian Pacific Railway, a huge venture, reaching east and west across the plains both to link Canada's exports with the outside world, and to counteract the centrifugal tendencies that afflicted its scattered communities, ethnic groups and provinces. The British North America Act of 1867 had created the Dominion, but it was vital to put socioeconomic flesh on this political skeleton if it was to become a thriving polity and not merely a name: there was, after all, a booming, expansionist United States at close range. At a purely pragmatic level, Canadian leaders wanted to be able to respond with military reinforcements, rapidly and independently of American railroads, should unrest ever occur in the Western provinces.

What was to be done? The enterprise was as big as anything attempted south of the border, yet Canada lacked major resources. The population was thin and scattered, the construction season short, the financial market weak, and the level of economic activity relatively low. The plan was to create a transcontinental line in one sustained effort, linking existing trackage with new construction into an integrated whole. Much of the land traversed would be virtually empty: freight revenues would be very low for some time to come. Only the Canadian government could promote and oversee a venture far beyond the capabilities of private business.

In 1880, the government sought the necessary private capital and management through a contract with a financial syndicate headed by George Stephen of the Bank of Montreal, whose relationship with Kennedy and the St. Paul, Minneapolis & Manitoba was just beginning to bear fruit. Stephen was bringing together American, British and Continental investors.

Inevitably, this involved Kennedy: his standing with the international investment community was much needed by the Canadians. He accepted Stephen's invitation that autumn to join a nucleus of Manitoba veterans—Stephen himself, Donald Smith, James Hill and Richard Angus—plus the well-known Morton, Rose & Co. of London and New York. J. S. Kennedy & Co. took 5,000 shares, and Stephen designated it as the Canadian Pacific's New York banker and fiscal agent; Kennedy became a director of the line in 1881.

Canadian Pacific financing pivoted on Stephen in Montreal, Kennedy in New York, and Morton, Rose in London. Their combined efforts overcame the difficulties of financing an enterprise so large and so dependent on foreign capital. In 1882, J. S. Kennedy & Co. managed a $10,000,000 bond issue, leading a syndicate that took $7,500,000; the Bank of Montreal under George

Stephen took the remainder. Kennedy confidentially advised Hill in November that "there are so many people who express a desire to be 'counted in' when a stock syndicate is made up." And Kennedy passed on important news to Hill in December regarding a stock issue of no less than $25,000,000: "We have now got, amongst others, Messrs. Drexel, Morgan & Co. and Kuhn, Loeb & Co." For the very first time, Kennedy was touching the top echelon of international finance, the great firms which dealt with the largest and most important ventures, and which doubtless were attracted by the involvement of the Canadian government. Nonetheless, he contended that other investment bankers should be recruited to help place this issue. An even larger Canadian Pacific stock issue, for fully $30,000,000, materialized in 1883.

Kennedy threw himself vigorously into this new enterprise, declaring to Hill in January 1883 that: "I regret that the multitude of my engagements here for the past ten or twelve days has prevented me from writing you as often and as fully as I could wish. I have been under a very heavy pressure, working late and early and mainly over Canadian Pacific matters which, I am happy to be able to advise you, seem to be getting into very good shape indeed. I have large applications to be admitted to the [stock] syndicate from some of the very best people both in this city [New York] and in Amsterdam, London and Scotland." The reference to "the very best people" speaks for itself.

So does Kennedy's mention of "very heavy pressure": this man of fifty-three was indeed close to exhaustion. For several years, he had been operating on different fronts: J. S. Kennedy & Co.; the St. Paul, Minneapolis & Manitoba; and now the Canadian Pacific, as well as some lesser enterprises.[10]

The emergence of the Canadian Pacific created thorny issues for Kennedy and his associates. The Manitoba had reached the Canadian border in 1878. A Canadian line connected it to Winnipeg shortly thereafter, and the St. Paul, Minneapolis & Manitoba profited substantially as Canadian wheat began flowing south to St. Paul, Chicago and points east. But the Canadian Pacific project eventually would create a major competitor, drawing Canadian wheat eastward on Canadian rails, not southward on American trackage.

This threatened the unity of the Manitoba team. Hill and Kennedy were of course Americans. Stephen and Smith were not simply Canadians, but were indeed leaders of the Canadian Pacific. The Americans talked of cost, revenues and the Manitoba's prosperity; the Canadians, of national unity, growth and progress. The division was intensified by geography. Hill was skeptical regarding an all-Canadian route, which could only traverse—at enormous expense—the desolate northern shore of Lake Superior, with its solid granite terrain. Why not use American soil, either the south shore of the lake, or much further south, through Chicago? The Canadians, Hill argued, should open up the potentially rich prairie, west from Winnipeg, and shunt traffic south from there, via the Manitoba, to Chicago.

This of course ignored a basic aspect of the Canadian Pacific project, the felt need of Canadians to be free of American dependency. Stephen and Smith responded to this imperative by choosing the all-Canadian Lake Superior shore route.[11]

As so often, Kennedy was the man in the middle, trying to conciliate and negotiate. For the prosperity of the Manitoba was at risk. Hill complained to Kennedy in October 1882 that Smith and Angus failed to understand the need to safeguard the Manitoba. Kennedy advised him in May 1883 that: "I hope we can get along with the Canadian Pacific. . . . I have spoken about it to Angus who is of course in favor of peace and I think . . . that the matter . . . can be satisfactorily arranged. If not, however, I would let them strike the first blow and only act on the defensive." This aggressive language was matched by Hill, for whom conciliation was not to be equated with appeasement.[12]

The problem was exacerbated because Stephen and Smith, as leaders of the Canadian venture, were helping to finance the new line by gradually selling off their Manitoba stock. They acted cautiously, but the aggregate was substantial and the result was to drive Manitoba prices downward in the long run, which hurt both the company and its investors. In effect, the Canadians were riding two horses simultaneously, stealthily shifting their weight from the Manitoba to the Canadian Pacific—while trying to pretend that nothing was happening. As the Manitoba's stock transfer agent and registrar, Kennedy was distressed by all this, as he informed Hill in December 1882.[13]

Stephen was more forthright in his actions than Smith, who tried to cover his tracks, "but," as Kennedy informed Hill in March 1884, "I have been too long in the Street to be fooled in that way." Yet the Canadians remained substantial stockholders, and had to be handled respectfully. So Kennedy cautioned Hill in July to keep Stephen on the Manitoba board of directors: his departure might accelerate a rupture with the Canadian Pacific, "with all of its uncertain consequences."[14]

Hill himself had been withdrawing from the Canadian Pacific, whose stock he had begun selling a full year earlier, in the spring of 1883. And he resigned from the board of directors that July. His problem was to evacuate the ship without sinking it and all aboard; his solution was to sell privately to insiders who pledged to withhold the stock from the market. Kennedy always contended that having sizable holdings in a company without actually controlling it was unwise, was to be at the mercy of unpredictable forces. Now events were bearing out that dicta.[15]

The growing split between the American and Canadian camps upset Kennedy, who always inclined toward mediation and compromise, though even he was tilting toward the American side. Having been told by Hill that he was leaving the Canadian Pacific board, Kennedy replied in April 1883 that "I am going to see whether they will not let me off also, especially as I am going off to Europe for four months. I should like very much to be relieved [Kennedy had been ill that winter] but fear they will insist on my waiting for the present, especially as my firm are fiscal agents here." Kennedy did in fact leave the board that year, weakening the Canadian Pacific on Wall Street.

His health indeed was becoming a problem. He was over-extended mentally, continuing—as the Canadian Pacific's fiscal agent—to immerse himself in the new line's financing, while trying to soften the conflict between the Manitoba's top men. "The labor over all these things," he reported to Hill in January 1883, "has been immense and I have sat up night after night till midnight correcting and remodeling them. I have never felt more the importance of getting a thing through and seeing that no mistake was made, for we must make it successful and should we fail I don't know where we would be. I spent an hour before a committee of the Stock Exchange . . . explaining everything to some of the brightest . . . men in the city."[16]

The tension intensified from 1883 onward. In November, Kennedy suggested to Hill that they sell their Canadian Pacific stock as soon as the Canadian government completed its plan to guarantee the dividend, which no doubt would attract conservative buyers who would keep values high. Kennedy feared lest a sizable sale by him would hurt Stephen—who was prepared to buy, though slowly and by stages—and the Canadian Pacific, which this experienced financier saw no need to antagonize gratuitously. Using $10,000,000 in unissued Canadian Pacific stock as collateral, Stephen borrowed $5,000,000 via J. S. Kennedy & Co., representing a consortium, to buy much of their stock from Kennedy and Hill. Kennedy sold still more in 1884, though still retaining 10,000 shares.

With the Canadians gradually selling off their Manitoba holdings, October 1886 saw Kennedy finally accept Hill's proposal that Stephen resign from the Manitoba board; both Stephen and Smith did so the following year. Smith continued selling Manitoba stock and buying that of the Canadian Pacific; Kennedy stated to Hill in November 1887 that "it is a mere question of time, and probably a very short time, when he [Smith] and Stephen will cease to hold a share."

This prediction was a worst case scenario; fortunately, matters never reached that pass. Nevertheless, the actions of Stephen and Smith had the effect of damaging the creditworthiness of the Manitoba. But the ties of friendship and interest binding these men, their mutual support during the risky days fighting for what became the Manitoba line, proved far stronger than the transitory tensions which the Canadian Pacific brought in its wake. For that line was a special case, an expression of Canadian nationalism that, as Stephen later wrote to Kennedy, he had to defend no matter what. As head of the Bank of Montreal, he was by far the leading financier in Canada, and this entailed responsibilities as well as advantages. Once this affair was past, however, Stephen easily rejoined Hill and Kennedy during 1887 by investing in the Manitoba/Great Northern's drive to the Pacific, and yet again in acquiring, first the Northern Pacific, and then the Chicago, Burlington & Quincy.[17]

In all this, Kennedy played a quiet yet indispensable role. Skilled at evaluating the stock and debt issues of companies in or near default, he also showed enormous patience and tenacity in guiding such potentially valuable property as the St. Paul & Pacific out of debt and despair and into growth and prosperity. Generally, he was a peacemaker. In such skirmishes as the Farley affair or the Manitoba-Canadian Pacific conflict, Kennedy invariably sought the middle way, that of compromise and settlement. Better a conciliatory settlement, his strategy suggested, than a victory which produced anger and hard feelings among the defeated. But in the case of the Dutch outstanders, whose suit threatened the reputation on which his career hinged, he fought to the end—and won.

NOTES

1. Deposition of J. S. Kennedy in Sahlgaard v Kennedy (1881), Farley v Hill, 2: 1753-58, 1761-62; *Railroad Gazette* 11 (22 August 1879): 457; 11 (14 November 1879): 613; St. Paul, Minneapolis & Manitoba Minutes, 23 May 1879 to 20 December 1879, meetings of 23 May, 21 June 1879, Hill Papers; John S. Barnes, "My Egotistigraphy," Typescript, New-York Historical Society, 1910, 322; J. S. Kennedy to J. J. Hill, Confidential, 3 September 1879, 10 September 1879, James J. Hill Correspondence, President's Office, Great Northern Railway Company Records, Minnesota Historical Society, St. Paul, Minnesota.

2. J. S. Kennedy to J. J. Hill, 9 December 1879, James J. Hill Correspondence, President's Office, Great Northern. J. S. Kennedy to R.B. Angus, 21 January 1880, James J. Hill Correspondence, President's Office, Great Northern; Deposition of J. S. Kennedy in Sahlgaard v Kennedy in Farley v Hill, 2: 1747-48, 1758; J. P. Farley to J. S. Barnes, 22 May 1876; J. P. Farley to J. S. Kennedy, 16 December 1876, 22 February 1878; J. S. Kennedy to J. P. Farley, 25 February 1878; J. J. Hill to J. S. Kennedy & Co., 22 July 1878; G. Stephen to J. S. Kennedy & Co., 25 July 1878; J. J.

Hill to G. Stephen, 23 July 1878; G. Stephen to J. S. Kennedy & Co., 3 September 1878; J. S. Kennedy to J. P. Farley, 27 July 1878; J. P. Farley to J. S. Kennedy, 2 November 1878; G. Stephen to J. S. Kennedy, 24 December 1878; G. Stephen to J. S. Kennedy & Co., 12 February 1879; J. S. Kennedy & Co. to J. P. Farley, 15 February 1879; J. S. Barnes to G. Stephen, 15 February 1879; Farley v Hill, Transcript of the Record, 2: 1747-48, 1758; 2: 1494; 2: 1010; 2: 1009; 1: 317; 2: 1026; 2: 1024-25; 2: 1027-28; 2: 1028; 2: 1019; 1: 939; 1: 320-21; 1: 321; J. J. Hill to J. S. Kennedy, 14 April 1879, Hill Papers; J. S. Kennedy to G. Stephen, 16 April 1879; J. S. Kennedy & Co. to J. J. Hill, 21 July 1879, James J. Hill Correspondence, President's Office, Great Northern; J. S. Kennedy to J. P. Farley, 21 November 1879, enclosure in J. S. Kennedy & Co. to J. J. Hill, 21 November 1879, James J. Hill Correspondence, President's Office, Great Northern; J. S. Kennedy to J. J. Hill, 17 July 1879, James J. Hill Correspondence, President's Office, Great Northern.

3. J. S. Kennedy to J. J. Hill, Confidential, 3 September 1879, James J. Hill Correspondence, President's Office, Great Northern; *Railroad Gazette* 11 (26 September 1879): 517; J. J. Hill to J. S. Kennedy & Co., Telegram, 28 June 1880; J. J. Hill to J. S. Kennedy & Co., 30 June 1880; J. S. Kennedy to G. Stephen, 29 July 1880, James J. Hill Correspondence, President's Office, Great Northern; J. S. Kennedy & Co. to R.B. Angus, 13 August 1881, Farley v Hill, Transcript of the Record, 2: 1743; G. Stephen to J. J. Hill, 21 August 1878; J. S. Kennedy to J. J. Hill, 21 December 1881, 20 July 1882, Hill Papers; J. S. Kennedy to the Dutch Committee, 24 September 1879, Farley v Hill, Transcript of the Record, 2: 1760; Augustus J. Veenendaal, Jr. to SE, 21 January 1988; Deposition of J. S. Kennedy in Sahlgaard v Kennedy, 1881, Farley v Hill, Transcript of the Record, 2: 1742-43; R.G. Dun & Co. Collection, 29 May 1879, New York City, v. 348, p. 900 sub-p. A107; Sahlgard v J. S. Kennedy, et al., Federal Reporter 295 (1880); Sahlgard v J. S. Kennedy, et al., Federal Reporter 242 (1882).

4. Joseph G. Pyle, *The Life of James J. Hill* (Garden City: Doubleday, Page & Co., 1917), Appendix 5A, 427, Preliminary Form of Agreement of 21 January 1878. See also untitled document, 21 January 1878, Hill Papers. Albro Martin, *James J. Hill and the Opening of the Northwest* (New York: Oxford University Press, 1976), 240 quoting G. Stephen to J.A. Macdonald, 13 November 1880, Public Archives of Canada; J. S. Kennedy to Dutch Committee, Farley v Hill, Transcript of the Record, 2: 1760; "Stockholders St P & M M, Sept. 15, 1880," J. S. Kennedy & Co. to R.B. Angus, 23, 30 July, 8 August 1881, James J. Hill Correspondence, President's Office, Great Northern; Stock share certificate book no. 1, 21 June, 22 November 1879; Minutes stockholders meeting, 11 May 1880; Albro Martin to SE, 19 May 1984.

5. George Stephen to Sir Arthur Bigge, 16 October 1908, quoted in Heather Gilbert, "The Unaccountable Fifth: Solution of a Great Northern Enigma," *Minnesota History* 42 (Spring 1971): 176, emphasis in original; George Stephen to Sir Arthur Bigge, 16 October 1908, quoted in Gilbert, *The Life of Lord Mount Stephen*, 1: 237-38; Barnes, "My Egotistigraphy," 329-31.

6. Barnes, "My Egotistigraphy," 327-31.

7. Account of Kittson Purchase of St. Paul, Minneapolis & Manitoba, 1881. In account with J. S. Kennedy & Co., 12 October 1881; St. Paul, Minneapolis & Manitoba Railway (Private Account) in account with J. S. Kennedy & Co.; J. S. Kennedy & Co. to J. J. Hill, 8 April 1882, James J. Hill Correspondence, President's Office, Great Northern; StPM&M minutes, 2 November 1882 to 26 August 1887, Stockholders meeting, 25 August 1883.

8. List of stockholders in St. Paul, Minneapolis & Manitoba Railway Company, Great Northern Railway Company, Secretary's Department.

9. Barnes, "My Egotistigraphy," 327-31; J. S. Kennedy to R.B. Angus, 21 January 1880, James J. Hill Correspondence, President's Office, Great Northern; J. S. Kennedy to R.B. Angus, 28 February 1880, James J. Hill Correspondence, President's Office, Great Northern; R.G. Dun Collection, 1 March 1880, New York City, v. 348, p. 900, sub-p. A107; J. S. Kennedy to R.B. Angus, Private, 6, 11, 13 March 1880; R.B. Angus to J. S. Kennedy, 10 March, 18 May 1880, Hill Papers; James J. Heslin, "John Sanford Barnes (1836-1911): Naval Officer, Financier, Collector," *New-York Historical Society Quarterly* 47 (January 1963): 63; John D. Hayes, "The Battle of Port Royal, S.C. From the Journal of John Sanford Barnes," *New-York Historical Society Quarterly* 45 (October 1961): 374; Barnes, "My Egotistigraphy," 329-31.

10. Harold A. Innis, *A History of the Canadian Pacific Railway* (London: P.S. King, 1923), 102n. 5, 104, 110, 113; W. Kaye Lamb, *History of the Canadian Pacific Railway* (New York: Macmillan, 1977), 71, 93, 108, 112; Denison, *Canada's First Bank*, 2: 100, 204-5, 208, 217; George P. de T. Glazebrook, *History of Transportation in Canada* (New Haven: Yale University Press, 1938), 266-67; Pierre Berton, *The Impossible Railway: The Building of the Canadian Pacific* (New York: Alfred A. Knopf, 1972), 325, 407; John Harnsberger and Robert P. Wilkins, "Transportation on the Northern Plains," *North Dakota Quarterly* 29 (Autumn 1961): 104, 107; Gilbert, "The Unaccountable Fifth," 176; Gilbert, *Life of Lord Mount Stephen*, 1: 70, 84; Greenberg, "A Study of Capital Alliances," 38; Greenberg, *Financiers and Railroads*, 194, 207-8, 198-99, 251n. 19, 252n. 25; Vincent P. Carosso, *The Morgans: Private International Bankers 1854-1913* (Cambridge: Harvard University Press), 249, 723 n. 125; John Milnes Baker, *The Baker Family and the Edgar Family of Rahway, N.J. and New York City* (Middletown, N.Y.: Trumbull Publishing, 1972), 73, 401; J. S. Kennedy to J. J.

Hill, Private, 4 March, 21, 28 December 1881; J. S. Kennedy to J. J. Hill, Private, 4 November, 13 December 1882; J. S. Kennedy to J. J. Hill, Private, 9 January 1883, 16 January 1883; J. J. Hill to J. S. Kennedy & Co., 10 March 1881; J. J. Hill to J. S. Kennedy, 4 January 1882, Hill Papers; J. S. Kennedy to J. J. Hill, 18 March 1881, James J. Hill Correspondence, President's Office, Great Northern; J. S. Kennedy Deposition, Farley v Hill, Transcript of the Record, 2: 1609-10.

11. William J. Wilgus, *The Railway Interrelations of the United States and Canada* (New Haven: Yale University Press, 1937), 113, 129; Richard Pomfret, *Economic Development of Canada* (Toronto: Methuen, 1981), 106-7.

12. J. J. Hill to J. S. Kennedy, 5 October 1882, 15 May 1883; J. S. Kennedy to J. J. Hill, 7 May 1883, Hill Papers.

13. J. S. Kennedy to J. J. Hill, Confidential, 20 December 1882, Hill Papers.

14. J. S. Kennedy to J. J. Hill, Personal, 16 January 1883, 1 March, 9 July 1884; Lamb, *History of the Canadian Pacific Railway*, 112; Innis, *History of the Canadian Pacific Railway*, 113.

15. J. S. Kennedy to J. J. Hill, 30 April, 5 November 1883, Hill Papers; Berton, *The Impossible Railway*, 407, 457; Innis, *History of the Canadian Pacific Railway*, 276; J. Lorne MacDougall, *Canadian Pacific* (Montreal: McGill University Press, 1968), 55.

16. J. S. Kennedy to J. J. Hill, Personal, 16 January 1883, Hill Papers; Robert A. Sobel, *The Big Board: A History of the New York Stock Exchange* (New York: Free Press, 1965), 85-86.

17. J. S. Kennedy to J. J. Hill, 3 July 1885, 27 May, 5, 9, 16 October 1886, 11 February, 23 May, 19 November 1887, Hill Papers; Wilkins, *History of Foreign Investment*, 225-26, 747n. 292.

7 PREVENTING "A WRECKING LIQUIDATION": KENNEDY AND THE CITY OF GLASGOW BANK

WITH 133 BRANCHES, 1,800 SHAREHOLDERS, and over $8 million in deposits, the City of Glasgow Bank was a key factor in the Scottish banking and investment system until October 1878. Then the bank collapsed disastrously, the result of grossly imprudent investments and negligent directors, as magnified by the outright criminal behavior involved in circulating false balance sheets.

Rumors of difficulties had led to demands by depositors on the bank, which suspended operations, triggering an investigation that uncovered falsified books. Criminal charges were brought against the directors, and the whole ramshackle structure disintegrated. The shareholders and depositors ultimately lost fully $6 million.

This precipitated a major financial crisis in Britain, and much upset among international bankers and investors generally, which the press fully reported. *The New York Times*, for example, covered the scandal prominently for days. The bank directors were tried and imprisoned for falsifying the books. And Scottish banking regulations were fundamentally revamped.

The banking community stepped in to restore confidence by policing itself, with Kennedy and others striving for nearly two years to establish order, even as he pursued his normal schedule. Though not heavily paid for this complex clean-up, he enhanced his prestige among his peers. This incident bore out J. P. Morgan's famous remark to the Pujo Committee in 1912 that "character," i.e., trustworthiness, was the decisive ingredient for credit.

There was an enormous gap between the ambitious, yet prudent enterprises in which Kennedy had been so deeply involved, and the well-meaning but ultimately catastrophic policies that the City of Glasgow directors had followed. Diversification had been Scottish American's watchword: not too many eggs in too few baskets!

The bank directors had committed some calamitous blunders. The worst was their acquisition in the 1850s of the Western Union Railroad Company (quite different from the Western Union *Telegraph* Company), which connected Racine, Wisconsin, on Lake Michigan, with Rock Island, Illinois, on the Mississippi. This meant direct operation of a line some 4,000 miles from Glasgow and without effective local representatives, violating that wise dictum: don't invest in what you don't understand. To be sure, the Glasgow bankers had tried to partially withdraw in 1869 by selling fifty-one percent of their stock to Alexander Mitchell, a prominent Midwestern financier of Scots origin, who bought it as a personal venture, having invoked their common ethnic heritage with the Glasgow men.

But this sale hardly solved the problem. The bank essentially had ceded control, to an outsider, of an enterprise in which it still held large and illiquid investments. And Mitchell now profited by selling the stock to the neighboring Chicago, Milwaukee & St. Paul Railway Company, which he headed. Later, Kennedy was among those critical of a deal that, even in those freewheeling days, smacked of conflict of interest.

Four liquidators were appointed when the bank collapsed. They very quickly recruited Kennedy, who took over in November as the American agent. He was one of several trustworthy experts needed to sell the remaining assets, the Western Union line above all, and to satisfy the depositors' claims as best they could. For the City of Glasgow Bank adhered to Scottish practice, which permitted unlimited liability banks. The shareholders therefore were responsible to the last penny, and could be sued accordingly. Kennedy eventually received about $50,000 for very demanding work in two stages over a year and a half: first, in an intense battle with Alexander Mitchell that lasted until June 1879; and then in a prolonged campaign to sell several million in railroad bonds. A brief postscript in 1881 involved Kennedy's testimony in a law suit brought by the liquidators to obtain additional funds from those responsible.[1]

Kennedy was chosen for background, connections and experience. His frequent visits to the Glasgow in which he had grown up had given him excellent contacts there, and he was known personally to two of the four liquidators: John Cameron, of Glasgow's Clydesdale Bank, and George Auldjo Jamieson, a chartered accountant and auditor for Scottish American. And Kennedy had much experience in Mississippi Valley railroading. This had begun with M. K. Jesup & Co., which had been the fiscal agent for the Western Union line, and had continued with the St. Paul, Minneapolis & Manitoba, which did business with the Chicago, Milwaukee & St. Paul, whose expansion-minded Alexander Mitchell was seen as the likely buyer of the Western Union and its associated holdings.[2]

Kennedy's task was to realize the maximum on the Bank's American securities, whose nominal or par value of some $5 million was, given the grim circumstances, woefully unrealistic. So his first concern was obtaining reliable information regarding the current value. There were some substantial figures to consider: $300,000 worth of stock in the Racine Warehouse and Dock, plus $44,810 owed it by the Western Union Railway; $407,300 in Chicago, Milwaukee & St. Paul stock; and an impressive $1,992,340 in stock and $2,926,000 in bonds of the Western Union railroad.

Of all these issues, that concerning the Racine Warehouse and Dock was settled most readily. The Western Union line had previously contracted to buy it at a valuation—set by arbitrators—of $44,933. Kennedy believed this was insufficient, but the arbitration was binding, and he advised the liquidators to accept. In addition, the Western Union paid them its $44,810 debt.[3]

Disposing of the 4,073 shares of Chicago, Milwaukee & St. Paul stock—estimated at thirty-one percent of par—was equally straightforward, but revealed some differences in judgment between a pessimistic Kennedy and the more hopeful liquidators.

Fearing the market might fall, he wanted to sell quickly, and did indeed receive forty while selling 500 shares in April 1879. Kennedy made his case in a letter of the 30th to the liquidators: "We propose to continue making further sales of the Chicago, Milwaukee & St. Paul . . . stock, without unduly pressing it on the market. The stock is not only one that is speculative in itself, but the property is managed mainly by men who are notoriously speculative, and it is impossible to arrive at any intelligent conclusion from the facts that can be obtained, as to what its intrinsic value may be." Here was another fear, that Alexander Mitchell and his lieutenants in the line could not be trusted: it was wiser to get out—and fast.[4]

Kennedy also was apprehensive lest bad weather diminish the wheat crop, and with it the traffic—and the stock prices—of such grain carriers as the Chicago, Milwaukee & St. Paul. In a letter of early May to Cameron, his contact with the liquidators, Kennedy concluded that "we are rather disposed as favorable opportunities seem to offer to dispose of a considerable holding of your stock."[5] Kennedy had indeed exploited an unexpected price rise to sell 200 shares at forty-four. He used the New York agency of the Bank of Montreal, with his ally George Stephen at its head, to transfer funds from the sale to Glasgow.

The liquidators there were much more optimistic about the New York market, which they perceived as rising. Hence Kennedy should delay selling and await higher prices. His letters recognized the rise, but he persisted in selling, though in small amounts. With five years of a crushing depression behind him, Kennedy contended that the price rises might be mere temporary fluctuations, and that it was safer to sell out. As he put it in early May,

"The tendency still being upward, we have made no further sales for your account, but are watching the market closely."[6]

By mid-May, a more optimistic but still cautious Kennedy reported more sales at slightly higher prices. "The market for this stock," he announced, "has been improving the last day or two, owing to favorable accounts regarding the growing crop in the West, which . . . now promises to be very large. We do not propose to press any more upon the market, but simply to sell, if at all, small amounts at a time as the market keeps advancing."[7]

The market continued bullish, with Chicago, Milwaukee & St. Paul stock reaching 51 late in May. But Kennedy continued misinterpreting the trend, selling a mere 100 shares. "We shall continue to act under the best advice possible," he announced, "and we hope to take advantage of the present speculative movement so as to realize the most possible from this holding."[8] What he dismissed as merely "the present speculative movement" was, in fact, the early, tentative sign of an incipient bull market, which had moved upwards from his first sales of railroad stock at forty in April, until a final remnant of seventy-three shares was disposed of in September at sixty-seven. By then, Kennedy began accepting the bullish reality. "We had decided," he wrote Cameron, "to sell this stock at seventy percent, but the sudden change in the market disappointed our hopes, and having in mind your desire for speedy realization, and being uncertain of any immediate improvement, we parted with it."[9]

The final outcome had been more than satisfactory, with Kennedy netting $203,500, or about half the par value. Nevertheless, he had been uneasy: "This C. M. & St. P. speculation of the Bank has proved a very profitable one, but it might very easily have turned out otherwise." Kennedy had survived the panic of 1873, which had toppled even E. W. Clark & Co., Henry Clews & Co., Jay Cooke & Co., and Duncan, Sherman & Co. He was uncomfortable with unpredictable and uncontrollable situations—and with those ruthless entrepreneurs whom he perceived as thriving on them.[10]

▼   ▼   ▼

Certainly, Alexander Mitchell, the head of the Chicago, Milwaukee & St. Paul, was such a man. Kennedy, who traveled to Milwaukee several times to confer with Mitchell, basically mistrusted him. By promising a "favorable realization," Mitchell had tried to lure the liquidators into lowering their guard. But Kennedy warned Cameron in January 1879 that "we fear this [suggestion] must be taken with considerable allowance." To be sure, Kennedy could exercise substantial leverage, for he and his partner, John

Barnes, were known to be interested in the St. Paul, Minneapolis & Manitoba, which connected with Mitchell's Milwaukee line.[11]

In that essentially unregulated era, the Manitoba could exercise virtually total discretion in its territory, including allocating rights and privileges to other lines, and especially determining which connecting line it would use to forward freight. (Kennedy attributed his victory over Mitchell to his "intimate relations with and control of lines of Railway beyond St. Paul [the St. Paul, Minneapolis and Manitoba], upon which the C. M. & St. P. are largely dependent for Minnesota business.")[12]

Mitchell and Kennedy confronted each other in months of intense negotiations that finally were resolved in June 1879, when Mitchell bought the outstanding securities of the Western Union, and also of the Racine Warehouse and Dock, paying little for the stock, but much more for the bonds. Kennedy had triumphed; how did he do it?

Though Mitchell obviously held high cards, he was fundamentally vulnerable. This aggressive and capable railroad entrepreneur was creating a regional system, building or buying wherever an opportunity—such as the City of Glasgow Bank disaster—arose. Though his Milwaukee line did indeed own a controlling majority of the Western Union stock, developments elsewhere in the railroad wars suggested that this fifty-one percent might not suffice, that those hostile investors willing and financially able to mount a legal challenge might well manage to oust even an Alexander Mitchell. He would then risk having a rival invade the burgeoning Milwaukee territory, and might have to construct an alternative route. Only acquiring the remaining stock would give Mitchell firm, unassailable control.

There was another weakness in his armor: the Western Union bonds. On 1 February 1879, the Mitchell-dominated Chicago, Milwaukee & St. Paul defaulted on these bonds, refusing to pay interest. Not only would default depress the bonds' market value, the better for Mitchell to buy them cheaply, but it also would mean throwing down the gauntlet, testing the willingness and capacity of Kennedy—and the liquidators in Glasgow—to fight a long war. If victorious, they would gain much more money, but warring meant court appeals and legal costs, as well as the risk of defeat. If he intended to fight, Kennedy would appeal for a court-appointed receiver to defend the bondholders' interests after a foreclosure. If not, he doubtless would accept a quick compromise. In effect, Mitchell was trying to shake Kennedy and the liquidators loose; how would they react?[13]

Kennedy was sufficiently experienced to understand all too well what Mitchell was doing. Witness his lengthy report of 24 February to the liquidators, summarizing his negotiations with Mitchell, outlining the strengths and weaknesses of their case, and presenting the alternative strategies, either con-ciliatory or aggressive. Conciliation signified a quick sale and ready cash, though probably less than that obtainable from an aggressive stance, which might, however, require prolonged negotiations and court actions that would tie up both litigants indefinitely. Cameron replied from Glasgow for his col-leagues: "We are quite determined to prevent a wrecking liquidation and are prepared to follow the decided course you recommend." The liquidators, in effect, agreed with Kennedy's willingness to fight until victory.[14]

Kennedy opened another line of attack that spring by approaching a rival of Mitchell and the Chicago, Milwaukee & St. Paul, namely Albert Keep, the president of the Chicago & North Western Railway Company. Here was a potential buyer of the Bank's holdings in the Western Union. But Keep wanted complete control and was uninterested in buying the bonds. So Kennedy did not pursue Keep's bid. These discussions nevertheless put Mitchell on notice that he was not the only fish in the sea.[15]

Negotiations continued with him and with Julius Wadsworth, the Milwaukee's vice president. Kennedy asked ninety percent of par; Mitchell riposted with an offer in the seventy percent range. Kennedy already had reported to the liquidators, analyzing Mitchell's low bid tactics: "the idea evi-dently held by the C. M. & St. P. interest . . . that the liquidators *must sell*, and accept whatever they can get for the interest they represent." He urged them to fix a lowest acceptable bid. If Mitchell would not meet it, Kennedy pro-posed to take the offensive by bringing suit for the Western Union bondhold-ers, rather than submit to what he regarded as "sharp practice." So Kennedy instituted foreclosure proceedings in May, asking the courts to appoint a receiver. Kennedy's strategy was to litigate and negotiate simultaneously, using the courts to drive Mitchell toward an acceptable compromise.[16]

The Kennedy-Mitchell conferences in Milwaukee continued in March and April, with Kennedy astutely informing the liquidators that Mitchell's con-tention "that they would give us more for the stock and bonds than we could get anywhere else," was simply a tactic, nothing more. While on a European business trip, John Barnes, Kennedy's partner, traveled to Glasgow to broaden Kennedy's constant communications with the liquidators.[17]

In late May, Mitchell began to come around. Barnes received a proposal from John W. Cary and Sherburn S. Merrill, two ranking subordinates of Mitchell in the Milwaukee, to buy the seven percent Western Union bonds with five percent Milwaukee bonds. No cash was mentioned, but the five percent bonds certainly could be sold. This offer was somewhat better than those Mitchell had made previously, but Kennedy, perhaps encouraged thereby, chose to demand more. On his adversary's home ground,

Milwaukee, he proposed a rise to six percent interest, plus the payment of legal expenses and past interest; the Western Union stock would require a separate negotiation.[18]

By early June, Kennedy was able to cable the liquidators: "Have been in communication with the C. M. & St. P. Rd. daily last week. Our opinion is that C. M. & St. P. will make agreement issuing new six p. c. bonds. Guarantees payment of principal and interest, past due coupons will all be paid, Warehouse and Dock Coy.'s debt will also be arranged. Shall we settle on this basis? We recommend to your favorable consideration. We approve of such settlement. Reply by cable. No time is to be lost."[19]

What would be the price of the Western Union stock, and what would the new bonds bring? So the liquidators inquired. Kennedy replied, in an accurate prediction: "New bonds marketable ninety-three to ninety-eight, perhaps 100."[20] As rumors of the pending deal reached Wall Street, Western Union bonds rose from seventy-five to eighty-five.[21]

But what of the Western Union *stock*? Its price depended on profitability and dividends; for both, the line had a poor history and worse prospects. For the Milwaukee was in control, and could—as potential buyers understood—so direct its freight as to shape those profits and dividends. The liquidators, however, were honor-bound to squeeze every dollar they could out of the holdings of the City of Glasgow Bank. They balked over the dismissive treatment the stock was receiving, cabling Kennedy in early June, "Shall not assent to stock thrown in as a bonus. Must have substantial consideration." This strengthened his bargaining position with Mitchell. By mid-June, Kennedy managed to get $25,000 for the stock, though with great difficulty. The liquidators wanted still more, but Kennedy tersely cabled on 18 June: "Can do nothing more." They quickly replied: "You have our authority to close."[22]

There was a nagging postscript, however. The very day after giving the green light, Cameron sent a somewhat disingenuous cable, inquiring whether the $25,000 should have been £25,000; could there have been "a possible mistake" in the transmission? Kennedy replied curtly, "$25,000, not £25,000". Kennedy followed up on 20 June by cabling Glasgow "that our object throughout the negotiation has been to secure a settlement which would afford the largest possible realization to the Liquidators. This we are certain has been accomplished." He concluded: "The settlement proposed is one that you and we can both congratulate ourselves upon having effected."[23]

The settlement was signed on 25 June 1879.[24] Its terms were complex. In securing $25,000 for the stock, Kennedy agreed to help the Milwaukee exchange $574,000 of those Western Union bonds held by "outsiders," i.e., not by the City of Glasgow Bank, for a proportionate share of the $4 million in new six percent Milwaukee bonds. Kennedy and Barnes became watchdogs over the interests of the liquidators, who netted $350,000 to $400,000 more than the January offer whose acceptance Kennedy had recommended. Finally, these new bonds were listed on the New York Stock Exchange, to facilitate their sale by the liquidators.[25] The definitive appraisal was provided later by Alexander Mitchell himself: "I think the City of Glasgow Bank got a very good bargain," remarking—perhaps ruefully—that the liquidators were "very hard gentlemen to deal with."[26]

After the victory, Cameron wrote to Kennedy, trying to smooth away any tensions in their dealings: "Our hanging back was if possible to strengthen your hands in dealing with our antagonists, and when we saw that nothing more was to be made of it, we at once authorized you to conclude."[27]

Kennedy's rebuttal mixed politeness with irony: "We were very glad during our negotiations with the C. M. & St. P. Co. that we could rest upon the necessity of having to submit propositions to you before accepting, and that did no doubt strengthen us with our opponents; but it is, and will be, impossible for us to tell you how sharp, and sometimes dangerous for the success of the negotiations, was the correspondence and interviews with Mitchell and his coadjutors."[28]

▼   ▼   ▼

"I have no doubt," Kennedy had warned Cameron in late June 1879, that "you will be approached by parties trying to persuade you to sell out in such a way that *they* can make a considerable profit which will necessarily be so much lost to you." Kennedy might well have been referring to the attempt by—among others—William Menzies, the leader of the Scottish American Investment Company, to intervene in the sale of the $4 million in new six percent Milwaukee bonds.[29]

As we have shown, the men were longtime associates, having benefited substantially thereby. Now Menzies was attempting to gain by exploiting their relationship—and his indisputable position in representing the bond-holding "outstanders"—even as Kennedy held true to his obligations to the liquidators, and thus to the broader investment community. But Kennedy was experienced in reconciling apparent opposites without disrupting future business relationships, and he handled this problem deftly, yielding neither too much nor too little.

What did Menzies want? He may not have defined it precisely, even to himself. Obviously, it was to control some, perhaps *all,* of the bond sale, and, clearly, he wanted to avoid dealing on the open market like ordinary investors.

The question of how to sell the bonds was fluid, unresolved. Normally, a syndicate of several firms would be organized, offering the significant advantage of a substantial payment in advance. Should, however, the bonds simply be sold on the New York Stock Exchange? Kennedy recommended this and, reminding Cameron of their good business relations, offered "a lower rate of remuneration for this part of the work than . . . the customary charge"; Cameron was appreciative. But the piecemeal nature of a Stock Exchange sale made it very vulnerable to market fluctuations. Though there would be costs, a syndicate sale would be quicker and the net returns probably would be no higher, and possibly even lower.[30]

Menzies began intervening late in May, exploiting his long contacts with Kennedy and the Scottish financial community generally. One of the liquidators had spoken indiscreetly to Menzies, who treated this as a grant of authority to extract inside information from Kennedy. Without creating antagonism, Menzies soon tried to resolve the question of who had authority over what by appealing to the liquidators themselves. But they backed Kennedy, cabling him in June to "Act independently of Menzies."[31] And Cameron wrote privately to Kennedy: "We do not want you to feel uncertain of your position in conducting so important a piece of business. . . . I shall see that there is nothing done except through you." Kennedy nevertheless felt it necessary to inform Cameron that Menzies had intimated that the liquidators "are inclined to ask me [Menzies] to advise them."[32]

Menzies intensified the pressure, writing to Kennedy that "there is no wish on my part to interfere with you in any way, but I must look after the interests of this Coy. [Scottish American], and I shall trust, therefore, to your aiding us if you can do so." Kennedy objected, writing to Cameron "that we do not understand that our employment in this business is through our connection with his [Menzies'] Coy., or that we owe primarily any duty to his Coy. in connection with it." In visibly distancing himself from Menzies, Kennedy was consciously countering any suspicions that he harbored divided loyalties; after all, had he not been very closely associated with Scottish American for some years?[33]

All the while, both Kennedy in New York and Cameron in Glasgow were drawing the attention of various financiers to what promised to be a decidedly attractive bond issue.[34] Though Kennedy viewed these overtures as somewhat premature, for he and Cameron still were developing a prospectus for the bond sale and were discussing a likely price, the enthusiastic response of the financial community bolstered his hopes for a strong price, about par.[35]

The Menzies question continued to nag. Were the liquidators indeed as distant from him as they insisted? Any suspicions that Kennedy may have had were—presumably—laid to rest by a reassuring letter from Cameron in July: "Do not allow yourself to be controlled in this business in any way by Menzies, who has no warrant, and will not be encouraged without your knowledge." And Cameron was careful to send Kennedy copies of the letters with which Menzies bombarded him. So Kennedy was quickly informed when, in August 1879, Menzies told Cameron that he soon would travel to New York, and that he might purchase the six percent Milwaukee bonds. This proposal was not to be taken literally; it was really a not-so-subtle hint that Menzies might create difficulties unless he was included in any syndicate that might be formed. Cameron replied coolly, noncommittally, uninformatively.[36]

Kennedy was reassured by the failure of Menzies' thrusts. A letter to Cameron analyzed the situation: "Menzies' communications on the Western Union subject have now ceased. Our object in first bringing these under your notice was to protect ourselves from outside interference at a critical juncture in our negotiations with the C. M. & St. P. Co., and latterly, to guard you against his Company's evident desire to share profits which belong exclusively to yourselves. These needs being served, we need not further refer to the matter."[37]

Though Kennedy was privately disdainful, he remained publicly conciliatory, never vindictive. He understood full well that Menzies, as representative of both the "outstanders," and Scottish American, with its prestige and claims for preferential treatment, could not be excluded from a syndicate. As Kennedy wrote Cameron in early July: "We should expect that our friends at the SAI Co. should have such an interest as they desired." So Cameron caused no disturbance in August by suggesting that Kennedy give Menzies the information needed by a prospective buyer. By then, Kennedy had accepted Menzies' tactics as merely a passing nuisance. "Like yourself," he wrote Cameron, "we are surprised at the persistency which characterized Menzies' efforts to identify himself with 'Western Union' matters; but these annoyed us only when they threatened your interest, and can now, as you suggest, be allowed to pass unnoticed."

Menzies reached New York late in August 1879 and met with Kennedy. Past differences were readily forgiven, and all went well; as Kennedy informed Cameron: "Our conversations with him regarding past communications have resulted in mutual good understanding." And an agreement was reached to include Menzies in any syndicate selling the bonds. His aggressiveness and leadership of the outstanders, backed by the resources of Scottish American, apparently had succeeded.[38]

The key question for nearly three months had been: how best to sell the bonds? A syndicate? Or directly, on the New York Stock Exchange? Kennedy favored the latter, and Cameron agreed with him in late August, though both were upset by a minor market downturn that threatened to damage sales. And Cameron feared lest the liquidators, in waiting too long to begin selling, might expose themselves to a possible bear raid that would hurt prices. So Cameron informed Kennedy early in September that he was coming to New York. Kennedy fully agreed; his ominous references to "the altered state of our market . . . and other considerations" suggest that he wanted a decision—and soon.

After much discussion with various insiders, Cameron and Kennedy changed their views, choosing an underwriting syndicate that would guarantee the money, which was linked to public sales over several months. The uncertainties of an open sale may have seemed too great.

So they chose what seemed the safest route, and Cameron negotiated with John W. Ellis, an organizer of many railroad syndicates, who headed Winslow, Lanier & Co., a well-established New York investment banking house that was to lead the syndicate. It included: J. S. Kennedy & Co., M. K. Jesup & Co., the Scottish American Investment Company, the Clydesdale Bank of Glasgow (Cameron's bank), and Glyn, Mills, Currie & Co., the correspondent in London of Winslow, Lanier. Kennedy's enterprise had a twenty-two percent share, or some $757,000. The deal was formally concluded on 20 September 1879. Winslow, Lanier was to buy 3,081 Chicago, Milwaukee & St. Paul six percent bonds with a par value of $3,081,000, at ninety-eight percent, or $980 for each $1,000 bond. The syndicate in turn resold the bonds at slightly above 103 percent, which gave it just over four percent, or a very modest profit of about $125,000.[39]

So attractive an issue was expected to sell out very quickly. Cameron, his business completed, therefore departed for Scotland in mid-October, leaving the loose ends to Kennedy to tidy up. Not surprisingly, the latter already had given his business friends at the Bank of Montreal some of the business derived from transferring bond sales proceeds to the liquidators.

But Kennedy also faced a painful problem. As we have seen, the contributors, i.e., shareholders, of the City of Glasgow Bank were liable to depositors for the deposits. But some contributors, predictably, simply ignored the liquidators' demands that they fulfill this responsibility by meeting the bank's liabilities. Should the liquidators counterattack in court? Many wanted to, but Kennedy successfully advised against. The cost of collecting small sums from some dozens of scattered American and Canadian contributors far outweighed the benefit. He was equally realistic about the uncollectability of the trifling farm mortgages—worth $5,000 in all—and other minor assets ($6,000 in unsalable land, for example) that the Bank held in the Western

Union's territory. These minor problems Kennedy transferred to John Cary, the Milwaukee's general counsel, whose presence in southern Wisconsin offered some hope of collection, and whose bill for service to the liquidators Kennedy was settling.[40]

Meanwhile, the syndicate was surprisingly unsuccessful: out of a $2,976,000 issue, it had sold only $737,000 by December 1879. Certainly, the market was sluggish. But Alexander Mitchell's reputation for ruthless dealings made some investors leery of coming under his sway by investing in the Chicago, Milwaukee & St. Paul. Witness his treatment of the "outstanders," those minority investors for whom Kennedy had been designated as the agent in exchanging their Western Union bonds for those of the Milwaukee. They were angered by Mitchell's two-tier tactic—legal, but reprehensible—in paying them a lower price than he did the liquidators. And this created difficulties for Kennedy, which he expressed to Cameron in February 1880: "The action of the [Milwaukee] in refusing the outstanding 'Western Union' bondholders a settlement upon the terms allowed to you further intensified the discredit which its proceedings toward you had created," he reminded Cameron, "besides rendering your bonds, so long as any of the 'Western Union's' bonds remained outstanding, practically a *second* mortgage on the road."[41]

A fair settlement with the "outstanders" was essential if the new bonds were to sell, and only then would money begin flowing to the liquidators. So Kennedy and the formidable Alexander Mitchell once more began negotiating, finally reaching an agreement in February 1880, whose result was a proper offer for the "outstanders." This broke the log-jam, and sales soon rose to $1,121,000.[42]

Nevertheless, $1,855,000 remained unsold. Cameron kept prodding Kennedy: the liquidators were eager to get the cash needed to complete their work. In March, the syndicate tried to tap the Continental market by negotiating with a Frankfurt house to sell the remaining third of the bonds. An offer from a London banking firm also seemed promising. The syndicate closed down in April, but only after slightly shading the offering price. As before, Kennedy transferred the funds through George Stephen's Bank of Montreal. The final result of the syndicate came to an average 103 percent per bond flat: this represented little more than a modest success.[43]

How did Kennedy himself fare? The twenty-two percent of the bonds which J. S. Kennedy & Co. had in the syndicate, some $757,000, returned the meager profit of $25,000, which Kennedy—out of feeling for his hometown and some stockholders of the City of Glasgow Bank—simply gave to the liquidators.[44] And Cameron agreed that J. S. Kennedy & Co. should receive the reasonable fee of about $50,000 (£10,500) for its services. A minor query arose about this at the end, for Kennedy recalled in 1881 a talk with Cameron, and that, "as an old Glasgow man I did not want to charge an exorbitant fee, and that I had rather take a very small fee, or no fee at all, than not have the Liquidators satisfied. . . . All the work we had done up to that time we had made no charge for it, and that in view of the fact that I would turn in any profit I made out of the syndicate, that I thought about $50,000 would not be an exorbitant charge." Cameron replied that it "was a great deal of money," but "he could not say it was too high; and that he would talk it over on his return with his co-liquidators, and make me an offer," which proved to be for $50,000; Kennedy accepted.[45]

▼   ▼   ▼

In all the nerve-wracking complexities of the City of Glasgow Bank liquidation, Kennedy performed as an expert at the top of his form. He negotiated and litigated, coping masterfully, first with Alexander Mitchell, and then with William Menzies. And he profited quite modestly when some others might have exploited the difficulties of a defaulting bank thousands of miles away.

He did all this while simultaneously conducting a totally different campaign far away, in the upper Midwest, where the St. Paul, Minneapolis & Manitoba was being brought to life against heavy odds and with much risk. Kennedy's time, energy and wealth were deeply committed. His success in such complex ventures gives us some measure of his capacities.

NOTES

1. Liquidators of the City of Glasgow Bank against William Mackinnon [hereafter cited as Liquidators], 294; R. E. Tyson, "Scottish Investment in American Railways: The Case of the City of Glasgow Bank, 1856-1881," in *Studies in Scottish Business History*, edited by Peter L. Payne (New York: Augustus M. Kelley, 1967), 386-416, detailed the context; William Wallace, ed., *Trial of the City of Glasgow Bank Directors* (Glasgow: William Hodge & Company, 1905), reprinted the criminal trial record with an introduction; S. G. Checkland, *Scottish Banking A History, 1695-1973* (Glasgow: Collins, 1975), 469-481 focuses on the causes and effects as they relate to the history of Scottish banking and therefore fails to mention Kennedy.

   Liquidators of the City of Glasgow Bank against William Mackinnon (1881), Appendices B, C, and F, including both the American testimony and pertinent exhibits, constitutes the principal source cited. I should like to express my appreciation to the Glasgow, Scotland, office of Deloitte Haskins & Sells for furnishing a photocopy. Coverage by the *New York Times*, 3, 4, 5, 6, 19 October 1878 and on subsequent dates indicates an American awareness, concern, and knowledge as does that of the *Commercial & Financial Chronicle* 27 (12 October 1879), 369-71.

2. Liquidators, 1967.

3. Tyson, "Scottish Investment in American Railways," 406-8; John W. Cary, *The Organization of the Chicago, Milwaukee & St. Paul Railway Company* (1893, reprint; New York: Arno Press, 1981), 137-38.

4. J. S. Kennedy & Co. to J. Cameron, 30 April 1879, Liquidators, 2058; Liquidators, 2057.

5. J. S. Kennedy & Co. to J. Cameron, 6 May 1879, Liquidators, 2063-64; Liquidators, 2066.

6. J. S. Kennedy & Co. to J. Cameron, 7 May 1879, Liquidators, 2066; Mira Wilkins, *The History of Foreign Investment in the United States to 1914* (Cambridge: Harvard University Press, 1989), 136.

7. J. S. Kennedy & Co. to J. Cameron, 14 May 1879, Liquidators, 2071; Liquidators, 2086.

8. J. S. Kennedy & Co. to J. Cameron, 27 May 1879, Liquidators, 2090.

9. J. S. Kennedy & Co. to J. Cameron, 30 August 1879, Liquidators, 2185; Liquidators, 2190, 2192.

10. J. S. Kennedy & Co. to J. Cameron, 29 July 1879, Liquidators, 2160-61.

11. Liquidators, 344, 724, 726, 730; *Commercial & Financial Chronicle* 29 (13 December 1879): 631; J. S. Kennedy & Co. to J. Cameron, 15 January 1879, Liquidators, 1969.

12. J. S. Kennedy & Co. to J. Cameron, 10 June 1879, Liquidators, 2110.

13. Liquidators, 245, 1889, 1991, 1994, 1995; *New York Times*, 2 February 1879.

14. J. Cameron to J. S. Kennedy & Co., 25 March 1879, Liquidators, 2037; Liquidators, 2012-17.

15. Liquidators, 682, 2010, 2049.

16. J. S. Kennedy & Co. to Anderson, Jamieson, Haldane & Cameron, 24 February 1879, Liquidators, 2011; J. S. Kennedy & Co. to Anderson, Jamieson, Haldane & Cameron, 24 February 1879, Liquidators, 2008-9, 2017.

17. J. S. Kennedy & Co. to J. Cameron, 8 April 1879, Liquidators, 2046.

18. *New York Times*, 3 May 1879; J. S. Kennedy & Co. to Liquidators, Telegram, 27 May 1879, Liquidators, 2087; J. S. Kennedy & Co. to J. Cameron, 27 May 1879, Liquidators, 2088; Liquidators, 247, 280, 295, 314, 321, 346, 753.

19. J. S. Kennedy & Co. to Liquidators, Telegram, 2 June 1879, Liquidators, 2093.

20. J. S. Kennedy & Co. to Liquidators, Telegram, 3 June 1879, Liquidators, 2094.

21. Liquidators, 2096-97, 2102-03, 2114.

22. Liquidators to J. S. Kennedy & Co., Telegram, 6 June 1879, Liquidators, 2103; J. S. Kennedy & Co. to Liquidators, Telegram, 18 June 1879, Liquidators, 2122; Liquidators to J. S. Kennedy & Co., Telegram, 19 June 1879, Liquidators, 2123; Liquidators, 746, 752, 2118, 2121, 2122.

23. J. S. Kennedy & Co. to J. Cameron, 20 June 1879, Liquidators, 2125; Liquidators, 736, 2128, 2131.

24. J. S. Kennedy & Co. to Liquidators, 20 June 1879, Liquidators, 2124; Liquidators, 2123.

25. Liquidators, 247, 2131, 2133.

26. Ibid., 736, 2128, 2131.

27. J. Cameron to J. S. Kennedy & Co., 3 July 1879, Liquidators, 2143.

28. J. S. Kennedy & Co. to J. Cameron, 15 July 1879, Liquidators, 2149.

29. J. S. Kennedy & Co. to J. Cameron, 27 June 1879, Liquidators, 2131-32.

30. J. S. Kennedy & Co. to J. Cameron, 5 August 1879, Liquidators, 2166-67; Liquidators, 281.

31. Liquidators to J. S. Kennedy & Co., Telegram, 3 June 1879, Liquidators, 2094; Liquidators, 2079, 2079-80, 2082-83.

32. J. Cameron to J. S. Kennedy & Co., Private, 3 June 1879, Liquidators, 2095; Liquidators, 2107-8; J. S. Kennedy & Co. to J. Cameron, Private, 25 June 1879, Liquidators, 2129.

33. J. S. Kennedy & Co. to J. Cameron, 8 July 1879, Liquidators, 2145.

34. Liquidators, 2131-32, 2145.

35. Ibid., 2166, 2174-75.

36. J. Cameron to J. S. Kennedy & Co., 24 July 1879, Liquidators, 2158; J. Cameron to J. S. Kennedy & Co., 29 July 1879, Liquidators, 2159; Liquidators, 2183-84.

37. W. J. Menzies to J. Cameron, 4 August 1879, Liquidators, 2164; J. Cameron to W. J. Menzies, 5 August 1879, Liquidators, 2164; J. Cameron to J. S. Kennedy & Co., 5 August 1879, Liquidators, 2163; J. S. Kennedy & Co. to J. Cameron, 5 August 1879, Liquidators, 2165-66.

38. J. S. Kennedy & Co. to J. Cameron, 12 August 1879, Liquidators, 2174; Liquidators, 2172.

39. J. S. Kennedy & Co. to Liquidators, 12 September 1879, Liquidators, 2190.

40. Liquidators, 2217, 2234, 2239, 2264, 2265, 2267-69, 2270.

41. Ibid., 2184.

42. J. S. Kennedy & Co. to J. Cameron, 3 February 1880, Liquidators, 2230; Liquidators, 2220, 2229, 2232.

43. Liquidators, 2217, 2225, 2240, 2247, 2248, 2249, 2254, 2259, 2261.

44. Ibid., 258, 261, 2286-87.

45. Ibid., 329-30, 2201.

8   KENNEDY AND THE NEW YORK FINANCIAL WORLD

KENNEDY'S FIFTEEN YEARS OF prominence in New York banking from 1868 onward saw finance gradually evolve from a market based on personal relationships to one centering largely on transactions.

Personal and family contacts of course continued to mean a great deal. As we have seen, Kennedy often dealt with friends, relatives, friends of relatives, and relatives of those friends. But the number of players in the nation-wide game was increasing; family firms were evolving into managerial enterprises; and commercial banks and trust companies, with their ability to attract demand deposits and other forms of banking capital, were outstripping private banks.

All this favored larger and more impersonal financial intermediaries, with competition increasingly based on price rather than personal relationships. The number of *major* private banking houses in the United States was perhaps a dozen, certainly no more than twenty. From the lowliest clerks to the top men, their personnel totaled several hundred at most. Through their hands passed the lion's share of the financing of the railroads and other giant ventures that were propelling the American economy to new heights.

Kennedy's position in this great game was reflected in his expanding fortune. His net worth in 1878 was $500,000 (J. P. Morgan's then was $700,000), before surging upward to $1 million by 1880 and fully $2 million by 1882. By then, Kennedy was earning $200,000-$300,000 annually; and of course there was the increasing value of his investments in the St. Paul, Minneapolis & Manitoba; the Central Railroad of New Jersey; and lines in Texas and elsewhere.[1]

Many personal factors underlay this success: probity, good connections, the capacity for sheer hard work, and business acumen—especially a keen awareness of the need for liquidity, for having reserves of capital in hand to either defend against unforeseen onslaughts, or to snatch up fleeting opportunities. Kennedy also enjoyed his share of luck, of being born in the right place at the right time. But he also helped make his luck, first by settling in the United States shortly before the great railroad boom after the Civil War, and then by allying himself with such highly successful associates as Morris K. Jesup in the 1860s, George Bliss in the early 1870s, and James J. Hill in the late 1870s and thereafter. Never a lone wolf, Kennedy unerringly chose wise and scrupulous business associates. He was shrewd rather than lucky: luck alone cannot sustain so long and successful a career.

His Scottish background and contacts helped Kennedy flourish in the Anglo-American iron trade, which opened the door to his subsequent involvement with the Scottish American Investment Company, and the liquidation of the City of Glasgow Bank. Even his religious and marital affiliations were helpful, linking him first to the very prosperous Presbyterian community, and later to an old and well-established New York commercial family.

The railroad boom shaped Kennedy's elevation from commission merchant to private banker. His aim was to connect efficiently those with capital to those needing it, while always maintaining the reputation for honesty and reliability on which all else depended. In an era when the rules of high stakes business were sometimes painfully ambiguous, he fully understood the intimate linkage between business morality and personal success.

He also comprehended the need to balance diversification and concentration. The former offered safety, spreading investments sufficiently widely to insure against disaster. There was a cost, however: small investments could do little to stimulate growth—and income. Kennedy would take the risk of placing his eggs in a few baskets, which he personally could oversee as they matured, *if* a company had long-term potential; witness the Manitoba/Great Northern, for example. George Bliss and J. P. Morgan followed similar strategies; though never themselves operating railroad managers, they often were managing directors. And Kennedy himself was increasingly drawn into management, precisely to ensure the success of his investments: the two marched hand in hand.

In acquiring investments—which attracted him more than speculating or trading—in a fundamentally unregulated market, he drew on inside sources for information, relying far less on the rumor mill than on his own judgment. Market timing was less important than making astute choices.

All this he ran from his vest pocket, collecting intelligence, assessing personalities and contingencies, making decisions: like other private banking firms, J. S. Kennedy & Co. essentially was a one-man show, his junior partners having only fixed-term contracts. His initial partners, his relatives Henry Baker and John Barnes, had each invested a quarter of the capital, and had received a share of the profits, but exercised little power. As we have seen, they were forced out in 1877 and 1880, respectively. The firm was reconstituted in 1880, but with three partners clearly subordinate to Kennedy in age, authority and experience.

One was John Kennedy Tod, a nephew (his mother, Mary Tod, was Kennedy's sister), who was regarded as the heir apparent, Kennedy himself having no children.[2] Tod was then a mere twenty-eight (Kennedy was fifty), Glasgow-born, and previously employed in its important iron trade. He had visited the United States before settling permanently in 1879, when he entered J. S. Kennedy & Co., becoming a partner after Barnes left on 1 March 1880.[3]

Two other partners joined early in 1883. Like Tod, Oliver Hugh Northcote (who sometimes reversed his first and middle names) and Alexander Baring had been employed by the company for several years, and were among those entitled to exercise its power of attorney. But they *de facto* ranked below Tod in authority and status. Though young and without capital, both men had the aura of prominent and powerful families, precisely what Kennedy himself, an immigrant without inherited wealth or connections, lacked. Northcote, a son of the British political figure Sir Stafford Northcote, was also the younger brother of Henry Stafford Northcote, the son-in-law of Kennedy's long-time associate, George Stephen. With Barnes' departure, Northcote replaced him as Kennedy's man on the board of the Manitoba, but soon left, with Kennedy himself taking over.

Baring, who came from the famous Baring Brothers & Co., had entered the family business network, first as a clerk over three years in the late 1870s for its San Francisco agent, and then briefly as a clerk in New York. He moved to J. S. Kennedy & Co. in 1880, and was the only partner belonging to the New York Stock Exchange, joining it on 4 January 1883.[4]

As junior salaried partners without invested capital, Northcote and Baring received no profits from what then was the most important of Kennedy's ventures, the Manitoba syndicate. Matters were different with the Canadian Pacific syndicate, however: Tod received an eighth of the profits accruing to J. S. Kennedy & Co., while Northcote and Baring each got a sixteenth.

These men formed part of a staff of less than two dozen, including partners, clerks, bookkeepers and others. Their office had moved by the late 1870s from 41 Cedar Street to the newly-purchased 63 William Street. The financial advertisements of J. S. Kennedy & Co. demonstrated its transformation from a railroad commission merchant into a private international banker of high standing. Iron and steel companies no longer were mentioned, for it was in 1879 that the firm ceased serving as agents for the Cambria Iron Company and for Andrew Carnegie's Edgar Thomson Steel Company.

Private banking activities became central: serving as agents for banks, bankers and railroads; issuing commercial credit and letters of credit; collecting coupons, dividends and foreign and inland drafts; and offering investment securities on commission in all American, British and Dutch markets. The partnership was flexible enough to follow whatever opportunities arose, but it invested overwhelmingly in railroad securities: "I am familiar with [railroads]," Kennedy wrote, "and have been . . . more or less interested in . . . [their] management, . . . in the negotiation of their securities, and in ascertaining and advising upon their investment value."[5]

By the early 1880s, Kennedy's firm had significantly increased its general foreign and domestic banking business. Its bills sold quite well, and there were broad opportunities for capital placement through its European correspondents, which included firms of high standing. C. J. Hambro & Son, for example, was one of the largest merchant banks in London, while Kennedy's relationship to Melville, Evans & Co. of London provided yet another connection. H. Oyens & Sons of Amsterdam had already acquired an American reputation by representing the foreign shareholders of the Illinois Central. Hottinguer & Co. of Paris was a lesser member of the *Haute Banque*, the epitome of French high finance.

Kennedy also had such individual clients as James Robb, an important railroader and private banker in ante-bellum New Orleans, who later moved to Chicago. While developing railroad interests in adjacent states, he apparently met Kennedy, who then was in Chicago. The two corresponded frequently during the depression of 1873-77, as Robb joined so many railroad investors in watching unhappily while the market value of his once solid portfolio melted away. Kennedy had to inform him that his bonds had become unsalable, but did lend him a modest sum. Furthermore, Kennedy was unable to help Robb regain liquidity, by selling the art collection which once had ranked as the largest west of the Appalachians. Robb apparently had sufficient capital in the mid-1870s to continue accepting Kennedy's advice regarding an occasional purchase of various railroad securities, but the 1873 depression essentially forced him into retirement.[6]

What was the relative importance of Kennedy's various ventures? A definitive answer is impossible without account books and other documentation. But the Manitoba and the Canadian Pacific were far, far ahead of anything else in the early 1880s. J. S. Kennedy & Co. stood high on the investment pyramid, but not at its apex. There we find Drexel, Morgan & Co., Morton, Bliss & Co., and others which—unlike Kennedy & Co.—had dealt in government finance. These and such others of high stature as J. & W. Seligman & Co.; Winslow, Lanier & Co.; and Kuhn, Loeb & Co., managed major railroad financing, in which Kennedy & Co. participated only occasionally. Nevertheless, it was among the top dozen or so leaders, for Kennedy's career was marked by slow but incremental growth, with neither spectacular successes nor failures.

His social position was equally successful, in a quiet, unspectacular way. During the mid-1860s, he apparently lived at 42 West 21st Street, in the wealthy Madison Square district. He resided in New Jersey during 1870-72, and perhaps after. His last address was on the desirable south side of West 57th Street, first at #8, and then at #6, barely two blocks from the newly-completed Central Park.

This move signified Kennedy's rise, both financially and socially. He was surrounded by members of the elite Roosevelt family, which had moved uptown as their downtown neighborhood had gone commercial. So James Alfred Roosevelt owned #4, while his brother, the elder Theodore Roosevelt, built #6, a five-story town house, and one of three contiguous buildings designed by Russell Sturgis, a fashionable architect. Kennedy bought #6 in 1884 from the younger Theodore, the future president, and lived there in some opulence until his death in 1909. Kennedy had come a long, long way from the Scots mill town of his birth to the very edge of the old stock, seventeenth-century New York elite.[7]

But there was a price: mental exhaustion. Not ill-health in the organic sense, but certainly an exhaustion that Kennedy blamed for several psychosomatic illnesses and which he feared would cause still more. (In reality, he lived an active life to near eighty). In steering J. S. Kennedy & Co. for fifteen years through the reefs and shoals of Wall Street, Kennedy had carried very heavy responsibilities. Such was the nature of private banking, with some routine transactions, but others that were large, risky and demanding of constant personal attention. And this in an unregulated market, with memories of the panic of 1873 to demonstrate the danger of miscalculation. So exhaustion was not unknown, and Kennedy was not alone in retrenching in middle age, at age fifty-three. In any case, he was childless, and so rich that the further pursuit of wealth seemed almost gratuitous.[8]

In January 1883, he wrote Hill a long letter explaining that, despite imminent retirement from the banking world, he nevertheless would continue his involvement with both the Manitoba and the Canadian Pacific. A letter in October assured Hill that the forthcoming retirement would, in fact, leave Kennedy "free to give more time and thought to Manitoba matters," and this was indeed the case throughout the 1880s. Having become the vice president of the line in August 1882, Kennedy began transferring—in October—its business from J. S. Kennedy & Co. to his new railroad office.

So it was that Kennedy's life took a dramatic turn, as he liquidated J. S. Kennedy & Co. on 1 December 1883. No longer was he a private banker and railroad managing director. Instead, he was to become a railroad director and senior officer for the next five years, serving as the sole vice president and *de facto* money manager of the Manitoba. Kennedy had become officially what he always had been *de facto*: James Hill's emissary to the world of high finance. Other powerful financiers also had chosen to reposition themselves as they aged. Levi P. Morton and George Bliss, for example, had dissolved Morton, Bliss & Co. and formed the Morton Trust Co., while J. P. Morgan retained his nominal senior position in J. P. Morgan & Co. until his death. Not so for Kennedy, who more or less gave up his banking house to work for Jim Hill.

For J. S. Kennedy & Co. was succeeded by J. Kennedy Tod & Co., an entity new in law, though not necessarily in spirit. It was headed by Kennedy's thirty-one-year-old nephew, John Kennedy Tod, with Northcote and Baring continuing as junior partners. Kennedy's wealth of experience and the substantial start-up loan he provided more or less ensured his influence in the new firm—for a time. Its capital of $700,000 included this $300,000 loan, at six percent, to be repaid in three years, by 1 January 1887. There was some flexibility regarding repayment, which was made subordinate to any other debts the new company might incur, i.e., Kennedy was willing to take second place. The note was signed, however, not merely by Tod but by Baring and Northcote as well: their strong family resources offered Kennedy a further assurance of repayment.[9]

Inevitably, there was friction. Kennedy had age, wealth, prestige and experience. Tod and the others had little but youth and some family connections. Like many of the financial leaders of his day, Kennedy was accustomed to absolute power in his own domain. His partners were treated as subordinates, and it is hard to imagine him responding differently to Tod and the others. During the mid-1880s, however, Kennedy failed in opposing Tod's support of the Montana Central Railroad, an affiliate of the Manitoba, which then was driving westward into Montana. Kennedy contended that Tod's reputation might be hurt by an investment that smacked of speculation. Tod nevertheless asserted his independence, selling Manitoba stock—which was under attack in 1884—to British investors, and becoming involved during the 1890s in several railroad reorganizations. But it is not entirely surprising that Baring resigned in 1890 and Northcote in 1893, for the "Todizing" of the company had advanced in 1888, when William Stewart Tod, yet another Kennedy nephew, had been admitted to partnership.

Also in the late 1880s, Robert Elliott Tod, still another nephew, began representing Kennedy's interests in the Chicago area. He was a director and an officer in companies promoting the Indiana twin cities of East Chicago and Indiana Harbor, as well as the canal connecting Lake Michigan with the Calumet River. In 1898, Robert Tod followed the pattern of Kennedy nephews by becoming a partner in J. Kennedy Tod & Co.; he left in 1911, acting thereafter as an executor and trustee of Kennedy's estate. Just two years later, the company was dissolved.[10]

In all this, Kennedy was serving as a *pater familias*, bolstering his Scots relatives (his firm, for example, even bought stationery from one of them), and especially his Glasgow nephews, the sons of his sister Mary Tod. They in turn were following his lead in leaving the old country for greater opportunities in the new. And all went well with John, Robert and William Tod.

But it did not with their younger brothers, James and Andrew Tod. They had arrived in the early 1880s, and Kennedy had dispatched them to St. Paul, where his many connections might give them a leg up in small-scale lumbering and flour milling. The nephews nevertheless began losing money at once, and kept it up. James was honest and willing, but his costly speculations in the grain futures market demonstrated his incompetence; Kennedy paid the losses and kept James on as a remittance man. Andrew, however, gradually emerged as either a knave, a fool, or both.[11]

Kennedy's influential friends in St. Paul—particularly James Hill and, for a time, Richard Angus—were drawn into these troubles. For Kennedy implored them to assist, influence and intervene both verbally and financially with the nephews, who would neither listen to reason nor keep their worried uncle in far-off New York informed regarding their careers. Andrew in particular was tapping Kennedy occasionally for small business loans.[12]

Kennedy found it difficult to complain. He had failed to understand the changes then affecting lumbering and flour milling: both were becoming larger, more concentrated and more heavily capitalized. Weyerhaeuser in lumber, and Washburn Crosby and Pillsbury in flour milling, had emerged to dominate their industries. The scope for small enterprises was diminishing; Andrew's entrepreneurial failures were not entirely his fault.[13]

But his irresponsible, and ultimately criminal, behavior was another matter. He apparently left St. Paul for New York in 1884. Kennedy sent him back, with admonitions to do better. To no avail; the Mille Lacs Lumber Co. was now heavily in debt, and Andrew was replaced as its president. Kennedy complained often to Hill—who by now was deeply involved, and who rightly saw Andrew as simply a ne'er-do-well—about Andrew's incompetence, while admitting that he could do little about it. The two older men finally hired an attorney to examine the books of Andrew's flour mill; Kennedy then advanced a $12,000-$15,000 loan to cover Andrew's obligations, not the first loss that simply had to be absorbed.[14]

The truth was that Andrew embezzled nearly $150,000 from Kennedy by 1885, falsified the books, and ultimately disappeared without a trace. Many years later, in 1899, Kennedy admitted to Hill that, "when I look back . . . to see the amount of money I advanced to Andrew G. Tod, I am very surprised at it . . . I was so busily engaged that I did not keep the run of the large amount of money he was getting." Not surprisingly, Andrew later was cut out of Kennedy's will, though it is surprising that so shrewd and experienced a financier should have been exploited so easily by a young scoundrel who happened to be one of the family; apparently, that excused everything.[15] Having no children of his own, Kennedy perhaps was overly indulgent with these two nephews.[16]

By the mid-1880s, Kennedy stood as a very well connected retired banker, involved with James Hill in the St. Paul, Minneapolis & Manitoba railroad, and also in other interests that did not entail sustained operating responsibilities. In the New York banking world, one was the Central Trust Company. Another was Bank of the Manhattan Company, a century-old commercial bank of great significance in the city, and thus throughout the country. Kennedy was a director from January 1881 until his death in 1909, and his relatives, the Bakers, maintained the connection thereafter.

There was friction during 1882-83 with the current bank management; Kennedy stood among those directors who felt that it could do better. Bank presidents in that era were little more than high-priced hired hands. The directors held real power and enjoyed wide prestige. Kennedy pressed for prudence, for the bank to maintain an average weekly reserve of not less than 25 percent of its liabilities. And, in April 1883, he moved that the board receive a full accounting of all non-performing assets. Both actions increased the power of the directors. Kennedy gained an ally in December 1883, when John Sloane joined the board of directors, the first of Kennedy's friends, relatives, or business associates to do so. Kennedy led a drive to ease out the bank's president, but not at the price of a $5,000 severance payment. Kennedy pressed for a much lower offer, and the other directors agreed.

All this set the stage for Kennedy to become president *pro tem* of the bank during December 1883-February 1884. In these three months, he coped with the difficulties created by a director who had divulged confidential information. Kennedy also instituted some innovations, for which the board of directors voted him $1,000 in appreciation. To help the new president through the change of leadership and also the depression of 1884, Kennedy served as vice president until his resignation in 1888 for health reasons.

Nevertheless, he played a critical role in helping the bank during the international financial crisis of 1890. Baring Brothers & Co., the most prestigious British private banking house, which was deeply involved in the American economy, suddenly fell into major difficulties. The waves reached far and wide in the New York financial community, whose Clearing House Association had assumed the role of lender of last resort. Bank of the Manhattan Company wanted to borrow Clearing House Loan Certificates, which existed for such emergencies, but needed collateral. In a fast-breaking situation where time was desperately short, Kennedy took the risk of putting up $500,000 in personal securities—for which he probably received a modest return. Quite understandably, the other directors expressed "their appreciation of Kennedy's generous kindness."

Ill-health led the bank president to resign in May 1893, leaving Stephen Baker as the highest ranking officer. Baker was not only Kennedy's nephew and the son of his former partner, Henry Baker, but had been Kennedy's private secretary and confidential agent in the mid-1880s. The Baker family had a long-standing association with the bank, though Baker himself lacked banking experience. So Kennedy returned as president *pro tem* from August through December of 1893, and helped to navigate the bank through the financial distress of the time, before stepping aside for Baker to become president.[17]

The fall of 1907 brought New York a dangerous replay of the 1893 crisis. Now it was the trust companies, unregulated and at times reckless in their competition for business with the commercial banks and each other, that sparked the explosion. In offering high interest to attract deposits, these companies had to make high-risk investments. So the first rumors of trouble brought a run on the financial intermediaries, as depositors raced for their money. The Clearing House Association functioned as it had in 1890, trying to stem the panic.

Again Kennedy stepped in for Bank of the Manhattan Company, as did two other directors. But the panic went deeper, the sums required were much greater, and he far outstripped these men in advancing fully $1.8 million as the collateral that enabled the Bank to obtain Clearing House Loan Certificates. For this he got $1.9 million in bills receivable, which probably assured a reasonable return. Nonetheless, Kennedy had rescued the Bank in a dire moment, and the board of directors publicly expressed its gratitude.[18]

It was during this panic that Kennedy played some role in assisting the Central Trust Company of New York, of which he was a trustee from 1882 until his death in 1909. This old-line, conservative enterprise, the fourth largest in the city, nevertheless was threatened by the general tumult: without their own self-help association, each trust company stood entirely alone. So

Kennedy offered his resources—though it is unclear whether they were accepted—to a rescue committee comprising the trust company presidents.[19]

Kennedy's relationship to the Central Trust paralleled that with Bank of the Manhattan Company. Both represented less a source of immediate profit (at his death in 1909, he owned a mere 150 out of 8,357 Central Trust shares, though each had risen from $100 when bought in 1875 to about $2,175 in 1900), than a potential connection to investment capital—and capitalists. The Central Trust had been founded in 1875, and Frederick P. Olcott, who became its president in 1884, commanded it during the great expansion of New York trust companies then underway. These companies profited from their unregulated status and their freedom to maintain lower reserves, the better to encroach on the banks' traditional turf, blurring the line between the two entities by lending to railroads and other large and growing enterprises. As the trust companies outstripped the banks in growth, so these companies also began acquiring the role of railroad trustees from the corporate lawyers and private bankers who had for long held these positions.

Kennedy found as fellow Central Trust trustees such major New York financial luminaries as J. Pierpont Morgan; Oliver Harriman, a prosperous merchant; Percy R. Pyne, the president of the National City Bank; Samuel Thorne, a Manitoba director during the mid-1880s; and Charles Lanier, head of the private banking firm of Winslow, Lanier & Co.

The Central Trust did well, gaining eminence in railroad mortgages during 1880-1900, and maintaining its dividends even during the 1884 and 1893 financial crises. In 1887, it accepted Kennedy's proposals for a profit-sharing plan for both officers and employees. Benefiting from Kennedy's contacts and experience, it joined the Farmers' Loan and Trust Company (a National City Bank affiliate) in becoming heavily involved in railroad reorganizations and trusteeships.[20]

Kennedy provided a personal connection between his crucial interest, the St. Paul, Minneapolis & Manitoba, and both Bank of the Manhattan Company and the Central Trust. The latter not only acted as the trustee for the Manitoba during the 1880s, but created related trusteeship connections as well: in 1884, by accepting a bond issue of the Minneapolis Union Railroad Company, a Manitoba affiliate; in 1887, with first mortgage bonds from the Montana Division of the Manitoba; and in 1889, with Great Northern first mortgage bonds. The Kennedy-Central Trust Company connection was extended to some of his other railroad holdings; profits accrued on all sides.

This is not to impose precise patterns on the catch-as-catch-can world of railroad investing, but simply to note how interests could interlock and interact. In 1890, the Central Trust helped reorganize the Houston & Texas

Central Railroad Company, in which Kennedy had been involved for twenty years. In 1905, the Central Trust served as the trustee of the first mortgage bonds of the Mason City & Fort Dodge Railroad, an Iowa line that had been closely held by Hill, Kennedy and others. Finally, in 1907, the Central Trust accepted the registrarship of the Great Northern stock subscription certificates.

Kennedy's role as a director or trustee was by no means limited to Bank of the Manhattan Company and the Central Trust Company. His web of connections and relations grew with the similar positions he held after 1887 with the Morgan-dominated National Bank of Commerce; after 1895 with the Title Guarantee and Trust Company; and after 1896 with the United States Trust Company. Only death in 1909 ended his activities: in 1898, for example, he helped secure a loan to Hill by the United States Trust Company.[21]

In all this, Kennedy was extending his life-long career as the quintessential intermediary, linking those needing financial services with those ready to furnish them. Everyone profited by this reduction of transaction costs. As a seminal figure in the American banking world, whether as commission merchant, private banker, or director and trustee of powerful financial institutions, Kennedy helped accelerate the growth of the economy.

NOTES

1. R. G. Dun & Co. Collection, 2 June, 10 November 1881, 7 March 1882, 7 January, 30 April, 21 June 1883, New York City, 348:900, A107, A163; J. S. Kennedy to J. J. Hill, 30 April 1883, 11 February 1887, Hill Papers.

2. R. G. Dun & Co. Collection, 1, 6 January 1883, New York City, v. 348, p. 900, sub-p. A163; Alexander Baring, *My Recollections, 1848-1931* (Santa Barbara, Calif.: Schauer Printing Studio, 1933), 12, 77-78, 82-83, 90, 192; Peter Eisenstadt, New York Stock Exchange, to SE, 24 April 1987.

3. J. S. Kennedy & Co. to J. J. Hill, 28 February 1880, R. B. Angus to J. S. Kennedy, 4 March 1880, Hill Papers, James Jerome Hill Reference Library, St. Paul, Minnesota; R. G. Dun & Co. Collection, 1, 22 March, 18 May, 12 November 1880, New York City, v. 348, p. 900, sub-p. A107.

4. R. G. Dun & Co. Collection, 12 November 1880, 7 March 1882, New York City, v. 348, p. 900, sub-p. A107; J. S. Kennedy & Co. to J. J. Hill, 28 February 1880, Hill Papers; *Commercial & Financial Chronicle* 30 (15 May 1880): 519; J. S. Kennedy to R. B. Angus, Private, 24 July 1880, James J. Hill Correspondence, President's Office, Great Northern; Merrill Denison, *Canada's First Bank A History of the Bank of Montreal* (Toronto: McClelland & Stewart, 1967), 2: 204; Heather Gilbert, *The Life of Lord Mount Stephen* (Aberdeen: Aberdeen University

Press, 1976, 1977), 1: 71, 2: 18, 42; "Announcement," January 1883, James J. Hill Correspondence, President's Office, Great Northern.

5. R. G. Dun & Co. Collection, New York City, v. 348, p. 900, 10 May 1878, sub-p. A53; 22 July, 3 May, 29 May, 6 November 1879, sub-p. A107; J. S. Kennedy to R. B. Angus, 21 January 1880, James J. Hill Correspondence, President's Office, Great Northern; Vincent P. Carosso, *The Morgans: Private International Bankers, 1854-1913* (Cambridge: Harvard University Press, 1987), 682; Poor's *Manual of Railroads of the United States*, advertisement, 1878, 22; 1879, 26; Kennedy deposition in Sahlgaard v Kennedy, 1881, Farley v Hill, Transcript of the Record, 2: 1743; John S. Barnes, "My Egotistigraphy," 1910, Typescript, New-York Historical Society, 326.

6. R. G. Dun & Co. Collection, 20 November 1880, 7 March, 1 June 1882, New York City, v. 348, p. 900, sub-pp. A107, A163; *Commercial & Financial Chronicle*, 36 (April and June 1883): advertisements; Poor's *Manual of Railroads*, 1881, 24; 1882, 35; 1883, 30; Dorothy R. Adler, *British Investments in American Railways, 1834-1898* (Charlottesville: University Press of Virginia, 1970), 145-46; Stanley Chapman, *The Rise of Merchant Banking* (London: George Allen & Unwin, 1984), 53; C L N Oyens & Van Eeghen to SE, 2 November 1989; J. S. Kennedy to James Robb, 1873-77, James Robb Collection, Historic New Orleans Collection, New Orleans, Louisiana.

7. John Milnes Baker, *The Baker Family and Edgar Family of Rahway, N.J. and New York City* (Middletown, N.Y.: Trumbull Publishing, 1972), 67, 345; "Russell Sturgis," *Dictionary of American Biography*, 18: 181-82; "Russell Sturgis's Architecture," *Architectural Record* 25 (June 1909): 410; David McCullough, *Mornings on Horseback* (New York: Simon and Schuster, 1981), 127, 135-36, 140, 225, 231, 283, 286; Edmund Morris, *The Rise of Theodore Roosevelt* (New York: Coward, McCann & Geoghegan, 1979), 74-75; Karin M. E. Alexis to SE, 20 July 1989; Karin May Elizabeth Alexis, "Russell Strugis: Critic and Architect," (Ph.D. diss., University of Virginia, 1986), 98-105; Karin M. E. Alexis, "Russell Sturgis: A Search for the Modern Aesthetic—Going Beyond Ruskin," *Athanor* 3 (1992): 31-40; Robert Sink to SE, 26 March 1990.

8. J. S. Kennedy to J. J. Hill, 16 January 1883, Hill Papers.

9. J. S. Kennedy to J. J. Hill, 30 October 1883, G. Stephen to J. J. Hill, 7 June 1883, J. S. Kennedy & Co. to Correspondents, 1 December 1883, J. J. Hill to J. S. Kennedy, 7 November 1883, J. S. Kennedy & Co. to J. J. Hill, 30 November 1883, Hill Papers; R. G. Dun & Co. Collection, 1, 20 December 1883, New York City, v. 348, p. 900, sub-p. A163; Note signed by J. Kennedy Tod, H. O. Northcote, and Alexander Baring, 1 December 1883, Baring Archives.

10. J. Kennedy Tod to J. J. Hill, 1 February 1886, Hill Papers; Baring, *My Recollections*, 85; E. G. Campbell, *The Reorganization of the American Railroad*

System, 1893-1900 (New York: Columbia University Press 1938), 93-94, 183-84, 213-14, 230; Maury Klein, *The Great Richmond Terminal* (Charlottesville: University of Virginia Press, 1970), 254; *Who Was Who in America*, 1: 1243; J. S. Kennedy to J. J. Hill, Private, 29 May 1884, Hill Papers; [James C. Burton, ed.], *Arthur Young and the Business He Founded* (New York: Privately Printed, 1948), 10; "Robert Elliott Tod," *National Cyclopedia of American Biography*, 33: 497; *Cyclopedia of American Biography*, 9: 435-36; Powell A. Moore, *The Calumet Region: Indiana's Last Frontier* (n. p.: Indiana Historical Bureau, 1959), 221-22, 224, 226, 229, 236, 239.

11. R. B. Angus to J. S. Kennedy, 7 February 1880; J. S. Kennedy to R. B. Angus, Private, 6 March 1880; R. B. Angus to J. S. Kennedy, Private, 22 April 1880; J. S. Kennedy to G. Stephen, 10 May 1880; R. B. Angus to J. J. Hill, 11 January 1881, Hill Papers.

12. J. S. Kennedy to J. J. Hill, 15 February, 13 June 1882, James J. Hill Correspondence, President's Office, Great Northern; J. S. Kennedy to J. J. Hill, 9 November 1882, Hill Papers.

13. J. J. Hill to J. S. Kennedy, 5 January 1883; J. S. Kennedy to J. J. Hill, Private, 9 January 1883, Hill Papers.

14. J. S. Kennedy to J. J. Hill, 18, 23 February, 5, 10 April, 28 May, 6 June 1884; J. S. Kennedy to J. J. Hill, Confidential, 1 March 1884; J. J. Hill to J. S. Kennedy, 6 April, 31 May 1884, Hill Papers.

15. J. J. Hill to J. S. Kennedy, 19 January 1885; J. S. Kennedy to M. C. Healton, 25 October 1895; Andrew Gray Tod to W. C. Toomey, 18 November 1898; J. S. Kennedy to J. J. Hill, 29 December 1899, Hill Papers; Mille Lacs Lumber Company Balance Sheet, 28 February 1911, Hill Papers; Norma J. Hervey to SE, 21 January 1991.

16. J. J. Hill to J. S. Kennedy, 10, 12 January 1885; J. S. Kennedy to J. J. Hill, 16 January 1885, Hill Papers.

17. Bank of the Manhattan Company directors, Minutes, Board of Directors, vol. 10, inside cover, 10 January 1881, 28 December 1882, 19 April, 6, 11 December 1883, 15, 21, 25, 28 February 1884, 6 February 1886, 6 June 1887, 26 March, 9 April 1888, 5 December 1889, 17 November, 2 December 1890, 8 January, 9 November 1891, 11 May, 7 August, 2 October, 14 December 1893; MSS "History of the Manhattan Co.," 52-53, Chase Manhattan Bank Archives, New York, April 1930; Dolores Greenberg, *Financiers and Railroads, 1869-1889: A Study of Morton, Bliss & Company* (Newark: University of Delaware Press, 1980), 92-93; R. G. Dun & Co. Collection, 1 November 1886, New York City, v. 348, p. 900, sub-p. A162; J. W. Sterling to J. J. Hill, 27 February 1884; J. S. Kennedy to J. J. Hill, Private, 24 April 1885, J. J. Hill to J. S. Kennedy, Personal, 12 May 1885; J. S. Kennedy to J. J. Hill, 8 January 1891; J. S. Kennedy to J. J. Hill, Telegram, 10 July

1885_ Hill Papers; Vincent P. Carosso and Richard Sylla, "U.S. Banks in International Finance," in Rondo Cameron and V. I. Bovykin, eds., *International Banking 1870-1914* (New York: Oxford University Press, 1991), 48-71.

18. Minutes, 28 October 1901, 16 January 1908, 1 November 1909, Bank of the Manhattan Company.

19. Central Trust Company, board of directors minutes, 19 December 1882, 4 March 1884; executive committee minutes, 23 December 1884, 4 April 1887, 6 November 1889; board of trustees minutes, 15 April, 21 May, 19 August 1890, 4 April 1905, 8 January 1907; J. J. Hill to J. S. Kennedy, 22 July 1887, Hill Papers.

20. Edward Ten Broeck Perine, *The Story of the Trust Companies* (New York: G. P. Putnam's Sons, 1916), 150, 152; H. Peers Brewer, "The Emergence of the Trust Company in New York City: 1870-1900," (Ph.D. diss. New York University Graduate School of Business Administration, 1974), 100; MSS History of the Central Trust Company, early 1930s, 14, 19, Manufacturers Hanover Bank Archives, New York; *New York Times*, 9 August 1896, 20: 1, 11 January 1900, 4: 4, 7 October 1903, 16: 1; Harold van B. Cleveland and Thomas F. Huertas, *Citibank, 1812-1970* (Cambridge: Harvard University Press, 1985), 41, 358n. 43; Carosso, *The Morgans*, 621; [United States Trust Company], *Promise Fulfilled A Story of the Growth of a Good Idea, 1853-1953* (New York: United States Trust Company of New York, 1953), 53; J. S. Kennedy to J. J. Hill, 2 December 1898, Hill Papers.

21. J. J. Hill to J. Kennedy Tod, 21 July 1884; J. S. Kennedy to J. J. Hill, 8 November 1884, Hill Papers.

9 KENNEDY, HILL AND THE MANITOBA, 1880-1885: OBSTACLES SURMOUNTED; PROSPERITY ATTAINED

THE GREAT WORK OF KENNEDY'S life undoubtedly was his involvement as banker and fiscal agent with the fledgling St. Paul, Minneapolis & Manitoba. Not only did this evolve into one of the great lines that opened up a vast span of previously unsettled territory, but it also propelled to the fore one of the memorable empire builders of American railroading: James J. Hill.

Railroad construction was shaped by terrain—and controlled by weather, particularly during the five to six month building season of the snow-swept plains near the Canadian border. The decisions regarding what route to follow, with all that it signified for gradients, roadbeds, curves and straightaways, would shape a line's future—and its profitability—for decades to follow. Poor decisions would saddle it with a debt load and operating costs that could mean default or eventual annexation by more powerful rivals. Superior decisions could mean success, power and profits. The stakes were gigantic, the leaders intensely competitive, and the consequences vital for everyone from financiers in New York, London and Amsterdam, to scattered settlers far out on a prairie empty but for the great Iron Horse and its obedient boxcars.[1]

The cost of a mile of track ranged from $10,000 to $50,000. And the 1880s saw more of it built than in any decade before or after. Building on such a scale meant massive spending, hence intense competition for funding. Once the Manitoba was formed in May 1879, it became Kennedy's task to provide the financing needed to outstrip other lines in the great march across the northern plains. Of these there were many: the Northern Pacific; the Chicago & North Western; the Chicago, Milwaukee & St. Paul; and the Chicago, Rock Island & Pacific. And new competitors would likely emerge, given the opportunity. So it was fortunate indeed that Kennedy was able to state (to Hill in 1882) that "I will always be able to get control of at least one million [dollars] any time I want it."[2]

In that simpler era, Kennedy & Co. performed a variety of tasks that few private banks now would commingle for the same enterprise. His house issued bonds for the Manitoba, acted as its transfer agent, reported on its mortgages, bonds, stocks, etc., and invested for the personal accounts of its owners and managers—especially that of Hill himself. This multiplicity of tasks, plus the broad range of duties he performed as a financier, afforded Kennedy (and other private bankers) a profitable flexibility that, however, was later to be criticized as inconsistent with his fiduciary duties to either the Manitoba or its financial intermediaries and investors. In promoting the Manitoba's credit while serving two, if not more, masters, Kennedy was hardly a disinterested or impartial adviser. All sides nevertheless were satisfied: neither the Manitoba nor its investors ever had good cause to believe that Kennedy had betrayed his trust.[3]

The relationship between Kennedy and Hill was inherently complex. Hill was inordinately ambitious, hard-driving and hard-working, but as yet was untested in building so big an enterprise. Though well known in St. Paul, he was not in the New York financial circles where key decisions were made. Hill eventually won renown as a master of entrepreneurial management, not only saving a nickel here and a dollar there, but far outstripping other leaders in making critical building and operating decisions. But that too lay in the future.

With very limited personal resources, Hill nevertheless got in on the ground floor of the new Canadian Pacific. He also was striving to maintain his position in the Manitoba, a line with which he identified personally and in which, as general manager (he became president in August 1882), he stood above his fellows in both devising and implementing strategy. Like many such front-line commanders, he tended to underestimate the problems his associates faced in the rear.

A major one lay in conflicts over borrowing strategy. Building of course entailed borrowing. But should it be short-term, which was cheaper, though it required frequent refinancing? Why borrow more than needed, or for longer than necessary? Or should it be long-term, which cost more but, not requiring refinancing, was more stable and less vulnerable to market fluctuations and crises?

Hill, a risk-taker, favored short-term—and generally prevailed. Kennedy, who bore the direct responsibility, and who had experienced crises when credit vanished overnight, favored long-term. Kennedy wanted Hill to correlate financing with construction, where advance warning was absolutely essential. Hill argued back that he needed the freedom to react immediately to sudden competitive building.

Though Kennedy's pleas generally were ignored, the two men got along surprisingly well, learning to trust each other. Perhaps it was the thousand miles separating them. Perhaps it was the mutual admiration of two supremely competent and creative entrepreneurs. Perhaps it was the immense satisfaction of pioneering, building into the unknown, opening the wilderness to plow and profit. And undoubtedly it was the firm backing that Kennedy offered the man from St. Paul in the arcane world of high finance, advice that profited Hill no less than it did the Manitoba.

Their association even managed to survive Kennedy's irritation over slip-shod record-keeping by the Associates. This dispute surfaced in the mid-1880s. In January 1886, years after he might have ended the trusteeships he held over various St. Paul & Pacific mortgages, Kennedy still lacked the legal authority, i.e., a court order, to do so. This blocked him from paying the Associates the $25,000 which had accrued to him as the trustee.

After so many years of delay, Kennedy grew exasperated—as his correspondence demonstrates. Much of his career had been spent cleaning up financial wreckage: witness his work on the City of Glasgow Bank. Through no fault of his own, he now found himself saddled with a minor disruption, and he reacted typically, with references to poor health and uncertain mortality. Though only fifty-six, Kennedy nevertheless complained to Hill that he could not risk having the matter unsettled upon his death (which actually lay twenty-three years away). And Kennedy threatened to dispatch a good lawyer to St. Paul to settle the matter conclusively, unless, of course, the competent George Young, Hill's lawyer, chose to do so. Not surprisingly, Young did exactly that—and quickly, soon informing Kennedy that the accounts were ready for closing.[4]

This minor annoyance did not disturb a relationship between Hill and Kennedy that solidified in the early 1880s, as Hill bought into the Canadian Pacific, while also retaining his Manitoba holdings. All this, with very little money; Kennedy made up the difference. In December 1879, he wrote to Hill, "we learn that you desire to subscribe to the Syndicate for the purchase of [the] $2,000,000 . . . 2nd Mortgage 6% bonds to the extent of $125,000. We shall place this amount to your debit and carry it until 1 March at the rate of 5%." Typically, Hill was borrowing short and investing long, no doubt counting on future income. No less typically, Kennedy was carrying him against that day, for varying reasons. Keeping the stock in the family not only maintained good relations with Hill, but also kept outsiders out, a constant threat in an era when railroads often changed hands unexpectedly and their owners collapsed into bickering.[5]

So it was again in February 1882, when J. S. Kennedy & Co. advanced $100,000 to help Hill with a Canadian Pacific buy, following up in October by offering to finance it outright. Kennedy received *carte blanche* in applying

Hill's Manitoba securities as collateral for the good of that line, a mark of unusual confidence between men whose association was relatively new.[6]

Kennedy backed Hill even more forcefully—and ingeniously—in 1883. Kennedy borrowed from J. S. Kennedy & Co. in Hill's name, informing him that "you can readily understand that it does not do for me or my firm to appear as large borrowers in the market." As always, Kennedy was alert to the danger of a bear attack that would almost surely be inspired by rumors that he was borrowing, hence was vulnerable. So Kennedy revealed that he was not informing his partners that he and Hill were buying Manitoba stock through their joint account. No ulterior motive was present. Secretiveness simply was Kennedy's style, saying as little as possible to anyone about market operations in a very thin market. Hill himself was no stranger to the dangers inherent in a bear-filled market: in selling Manitoba bonds that May to raise the cash needed to buy the bonds of a Manitoba proprietary company, he asked Kennedy for secrecy.[7]

Kennedy took the lead during September in yet another convoluted transaction with Hill, who—as so often—had come up short after plunging too deeply in buying both Manitoba and Canadian Pacific securities. Kennedy found a solution. Hill remitted to Kennedy, as the Manitoba vice president, the surplus earnings, which the railroad then lent to J. S. Kennedy & Co. Kennedy followed by loaning the necessary amount to Hill, enabling him to pay for his Canadian Pacific buy, while pledging his securities as collateral. Kennedy also was buying Canadian Pacific, and he paralleled Hill in borrowing to do so, rather than selling Manitoba. Though Kennedy, with his greater wealth and easy access to the New York credit market was in a more liquid position than Hill, both were willing to stretch rather than lose the immense possibilities represented by the construction of both lines.[8]

In mid-1884, Hill again appealed to Kennedy for financial aid. He had borrowed $250,000 from Bank of the Manhattan Company, no doubt with Kennedy's assistance, and no doubt to preserve and even expand his railroad holdings. Now there was a financial crisis, and Hill needed an extension on the loan—which Kennedy, as a director, helped him obtain. But Kennedy's constant warnings that Hill was skating on very thin financial ice had come true: the latter found himself in a disturbed market, and following the bank's other prime customers in paying a full 6 percent interest.[9]

But nothing could stop Hill's zest for more—and more. Should he, Hill asked Kennedy in January 1885, sell Manitoba stock? No, Kennedy replied; it would weaken the quotations and look bad. And don't sell Manitoba consolidated bonds either, Kennedy advised. These he expected to rise, for investors were impressed by a line whose revenue was increasing, whose operating costs were low (thanks largely to Hill's excellent leadership), and which therefore was paying interest from earnings even during a financial crisis. Kennedy assured Hill that he himself would finance any of Hill's borrowings. To be sure, J. S. Kennedy & Co. had been dissolved in December 1883, but Kennedy's connections remained as good as ever. As a trustee of New York's Central Trust Company, for example, he interceded in April 1885 with its president, Frederick P. Olcott, to get Hill a short-term loan of $200,000.[10]

Kennedy also coped with Hill's occasional talk about retrenching his overstretched finances. "I will be sorry," Kennedy wrote to Hill in April 1885, "if you have to sell any of your stock in the face of what may possibly soon happen [i.e., financial danger], still I can appreciate your feeling and desire 'to owe no man anything'." Ironically, Hill then was reaching firmer ground—though he apparently did not yet realize it. The Manitoba was prospering, and with it, his reputation and financial contacts, particularly in 1884, when John Jay Knox, a close friend and former Minnesotan, became president of New York's powerful National Bank of the Republic. As the Comptroller of the Currency during 1872-84, Knox had gained close contacts with the national financial community; all this benefited Hill, and lessened his dependence on Kennedy.[11]

The financial relationship that Kennedy built with Hill after 1879 was one aspect of the larger connection with the Associates as a whole and with the Manitoba they controlled. Drawing on his experience during the 1860s with the Chicago & Alton, Kennedy now served as the Manitoba's fiscal agent, handling both banking and purchasing, and receiving a fixed fee, plus substantial commissions. Obviously, there was a potential for conflict of interest in a situation where the agent might represent both buyer and supplier.

So trust could not be assumed but had to be earned, as Kennedy put it in a long letter to Stephen in July 1880: "I hate anything . . . that is not open and above board and thoroughly understood by all concerned." Kennedy was anxious lest the other associates not fully understand the benefits his work conferred, and he pointed to both the successful sale—in very difficult circumstances—of Manitoba bonds in 1879, and to his further success in saving money when buying locomotives from Baldwin; the commission it paid he voluntarily credited to the Manitoba. Was all this understood and appreciated by men who—excepting Stephen—were not knowledgeable about finance? Kennedy had his doubts: "Hill seems to think," he mentioned to Stephen, "he can make all his purchases better than we can and I am very certain that as a rule he cannot." Furthermore, "I had supposed by the purchase of rails, etc. we originally made and which were commended by none other than Hill, that we had shown some capacity but he now seems to have forgotten it."

There was, finally, the question of Kennedy's remuneration, some of which went to expenses. His remarks to Stephen show much flexibility: "You can determine how to deal with the question and fix the compensation at $5,000, $10,000, $15,000 or any other amount you see fit and as I said before whatever you do will be entirely satisfactory to me"; the Associates chose $15,000. Was Kennedy's insistence on his disinterestedness entirely sincere? Undoubtedly he preferred more to less, but his real strategy ignored short-term gains in hope of gaining the Associates' confidence, the better to strengthen his position with a Manitoba line for whose future he had great expectations. And he judged rightly.[12]

So Kennedy began devoting himself to the Manitoba's day-to-day operations, within months becoming more important than Stephen, who was tied to Montreal, where the Canadian Pacific's birth pangs were generating intense patriotic fervor as the 1880s wore on. This left the way open for Kennedy, with his vast experience and access to the latest New York financial news, to analyze, advise and recommend. So he urged both Stephen and Hill to borrow immediately, before interest rates rose still further, thus conserving cash in paying for a shipment of rails.[13]

Kennedy's leadership was central in December 1879 to a substantial—$2,000,000—Manitoba second mortgage bond syndicate. He soon informed Smith that the firsts had begun finding buyers, but that the seconds were lagging. Kennedy & Co. took some $200,000 worth. So did both Stephen and Smith, while the over-stretched Hill could not join in until April 1880, when he took a relatively puny $125,000. D. Willis James and Samuel Thorne, of Kennedy's New York business world, helped greatly by each purchasing $150,000. The fear of any railroad entrepreneur—that the buying public simply would not respond at a satisfactory price—was being averted, thanks largely to Kennedy's connections.[14]

But the problem was not truly resolved, nor could it be, so long as so much capital was required for construction whose return was both uncertain and so far off. Kennedy and his fellow financiers were selling dreams of future wealth, and the wise investor knew very well the fine line between dreams and nightmares. That skepticism meant that fully twenty-five percent—$500,000—of the second mortgage issue remained unsold in August 1880. What should be done, Richard Angus, the vice president, inquired of Kennedy? Should the bonds be further discounted, in hope of attracting investors, or should they be used as collateral for borrowing?

Kennedy offered to buy the bonds at once (probably for resale) for cash, but this old campaigner was careful to make the facts of life absolutely clear to his associates, scattered as they were among Montreal, St. Paul, and New

York. They must stand united, *not* bringing out any new bonds—which would depress the market—until he had disposed of the already-existing bonds, plus others held to support the market. "I note what you say," he told Angus, "about money matters and I will take care of all your [i.e., Manitoba] wants. I do not want you to borrow any money except through my firm." Like all private bankers, Kennedy tried to grasp the reins tightly, fearing clients who might borrow excessively by turning to multiple sources.

So he bought $203,000 of the seconds, taking over the balance in September. He informed Angus in December 1880 that Kennedy's firm had formed a syndicate with two other firms to reach out to investors when the market turned favorable. Angus and Stephen, though certainly appreciative, were also a little concerned: was the Manitoba becoming overly dependent on J. S. Kennedy & Co.?[15]

Perhaps it was, but Angus nevertheless had turned to Kennedy that September for another $200,000, which the Manitoba needed on 1 October to pay interest. Kennedy delivered the goods: $250,000 for 60 days. A year later, however, the Manitoba did indeed—momentarily—turn away from him, resorting to Stephen's Bank of Montreal for $400,000. The untried Manitoba, as yet lacking the creditworthiness needed for extensive borrowing, used a promissory note personally endorsed by Angus, Hill, and Stephen.

The economic recovery was helping the Manitoba do well financially, but it sensed political trouble ahead. And with good reason: the Granger movement was gathering momentum among the prairie wheat farmers, who were struggling with long-term declining prices, as production increased in Argentina, Australia, Russia and of course the United States itself. The farmers, with their traditional vision of competition as involving many buyers and sellers, were oblivious to the inherently oligopolistic nature of railroads. The rates charged by competing railroads between any two points had to be identical, even though both costs and profits varied. But the farmers could see only their own difficulties, not the nuances of fixed costs, entrepreneurial skills, decisions regarding routes, and the like. They found it easy to blame the railroads for what seemed unconscionably high rates and profits.

The lines responded with what later was termed "creative accounting," in which everything possible—even the purchase of durables—was charged to operating expenses. As Kennedy cautioned Hill in January 1880, it was essential to boost operating expenses as high as possible and thereby artificially deflate earnings. Hence the ambivalence with which Kennedy later responded to Hill's record in keeping operating expenses well below those of comparable lines: low expenses meant high profits and a likely public outcry. Far better to veil Hill's accomplishments by keeping costs hidden.[16]

The two leaders feared a counterattack from the Minnesota state government, of which Kennedy was—privately—contemptuous. He was later to write, "I have always found in dealing with legislatures that you cannot reason with them, the majority comprising them are men who are ignorant, stupid, and full of prejudice, and who do not desire to know the truth and the more you try to enlighten them, the more stubborn and unreasonable they become." No doubt there was some truth to the adage that no man's property is safe while the legislature is in session. Nevertheless, here was mirror imaging with a vengeance, with no compromise—or even dialogue—possible between opponents armored in self-righteousness and mutual contempt. And here too was a precursor of later federal intervention—and regulation.[17]

The Manitoba's success became visible to all when it began paying dividends late in 1882. With it came realignment at the top. George Stephen, for long eager to involve himself with the Canadian Pacific, nevertheless had remained with the Manitoba, where his prestige proved invaluable. Now he felt free to step aside as president in favor of Hill, whose ability by now was fully appreciated in the inner circle. Kennedy also moved up, becoming a member of the board of directors in August, and the vice president soon thereafter. He was stepping into Stephen's former role, as chief financial adviser, money raiser, and ambassador in New York to the international financial community. Kennedy's ascendancy offered continued assurances of sound management in an era when this was by no means certain.

Kennedy quickly made his presence felt. "As the company now has its own office here [New York]," he suggested to Hill in September, "I would be obliged by your telegraphing and writing about earnings and all other matters to me as vice president . . . I hope to be ready to take over the Company's business from my firm [J. S. Kennedy & Co.] on 1 Oct. at latest." Though Kennedy's salary was $10,000, $5,000 below that of fiscal agent, other factors made the new position well worth it. For one, a maturing rail line performed its own services, and no longer needed a fiscal agent. By this time, Kennedy may have anticipated closing J. S. Kennedy & Co., and therefore sought a position which was attractive but not overly-burdensome.[18]

But this change also brought up a minor but irksome piece of unresolved Manitoba business. Immediately after its creation in May 1879, the line had issued thirty-year first and second mortgage bonds, with well-respected financial figures—including Kennedy—as trustees to protect the bondholders. The trustee also served as a recording clerk and a receiving and paying teller, small but necessary tasks for which he received a modest fee.

Here lay yet another potential conflict of interest about which Kennedy, always sensitive about his image, was very conscious. As fiscal agent, he was required to pay the fee which, as trustee, he himself was to set. Would anyone believe that he had abused his position? he asked Angus in mid-1881, when they were discussing his fee, a trifling $826.00 for that fiscal year. In 1882, Kennedy recommended to Hill that there be an independent audit to underscore the legitimacy of his fee for trustee services, which totaled a mere $7,000. As always, reputation mattered.[19]

The Manitoba's board of directors originally had included only Canadians and Minnesotans. Kennedy's arrival marked the beginning of a "New Yorkization" process that gradually—and quite amicably—saw Canadian influence diminish, as the financiers of Montreal plunged into the great Canadian Pacific project. Kennedy brought to the board as active directors two long-time business friends: in late 1882, D. Willis James, a partner in Phelps, Dodge & Co. and, in 1884, Samuel Thorne, the president of the Pennsylvania Coal Co. Both had owned substantial amounts of Manitoba securities virtually from its birth, knew other potential investors, and, with coal, iron and steel interests that would attract any railroad, could bring invaluable inside advice, contacts and information to the Manitoba.[20]

Kennedy never had everything his own way, however. Hill was, and remained, the Manitoba's dominant personality, particularly regarding the short-term financing to whose uncertainty Kennedy had long objected. Their differences continued, even as the Manitoba changed direction in 1881-82. Having connected isolated bits-and-pieces of existing track to create a link to Winnipeg, the line shifted westward, into the Dakota Extension and the Great Plains they signified. Before, the line had borrowed short-term, building trackage whose length and solidity were then certified by an independent third party. With these assurances in hand, bonds could be issued, albeit piecemeal, just as the track itself was being built piecemeal, a slow process from which Kennedy sought escape. "Another year," he admonished Hill in December 1881, "we must manage things differently."[21]

If financing was one complex issue, dividends were another. None were paid in 1879-81. Modest profits were indeed accruing, but most of the stock in this new company was held by its principals, who felt no need to satisfy a mass of stockholders, preferring instead to plow cash back into the growing Manitoba. But net income soared in 1882, and the pressure for a quarterly dividend no longer could be overlooked. The only question was: how much? Kennedy's view was "I would not make it more than 2% and I do not see how we can make it less," he told Hill in October, "let me know your views." Hill agreed; two percent it was.

The economy, however, was beginning to decline, and this was intensified in May 1884 by a bank panic; recovery came in 1885. Kennedy reacted in

June 1884 by suggesting that the quarterly dividend be reduced to 1.5 percent; Hill agreed and it was done that fall. In retaining much of its cash, the line would please conservative investors, oriented toward regular and consistent interest and dividend payments.[22]

So was Kennedy, concerned since late 1882 lest too much of his capital was going into the Manitoba. The figures were disquieting. He had advanced about $800,000 to the Manitoba, and still another $150,000 to the Canadian Pacific. And he was anticipating Manitoba obligations of another $800,000. No doubt he could finance this need, but at what cost to his liquidity? The man who had informed Hill early in 1882 that he himself "could always get control of one million any time I want it," was confessing in November about wanting to "get into a little better shape financially . . . with all my other business and the money required for it I am really bothered."

The liquidity needed to exploit fleeting opportunities, to bolster his prestige, and to maneuver with other financiers, seemed to be evaporating. And how might all this affect the other commitments of J. S. Kennedy & Co.?[23] There was a dire warning in the fate of Jay Cooke & Co., which had collapsed in 1873 because it had lacked effective control over the runaway spending of the Northern Pacific management. "I find," Kennedy complained to Hill that November, "that I am without any authority to sell or hypothecate the [Dakota Extension] bonds and though this may be a matter of form I wish to have a resolution properly passed to protect me for my advances to the Company and for other purposes."[24]

There were further anxieties that November. The Manitoba needed more construction money, and Kennedy was expected to provide it—at once. There was nothing new in this, but there was in his solution, which used his acquaintanceship with several trustees of the Equitable Trust Company in New London, Connecticut, to help the Manitoba obtain $500,000 *immediately*, in return for bonds which the Equitable presumably would resell to other institutions. The money was lent to Kennedy, who gave "my *individual* note for the amount with collateral." Clearly, Kennedy's personal credit was stronger than that of the Manitoba. No less clearly, he was getting in very deep.

Frustrations were mounting with Hill, whose eagerness to squeeze the maximum of construction mileage out of every dollar could lead to trouble. So it had late in 1882 with the Union Depot Company in St. Paul, a Manitoba proprietary which twice had been remiss in paying interest to its bondholders. Kennedy twice had intervened to prevent default, guaranteeing payment of what were, after all, relatively small sums. But he resented being put in this position: unhappy bondholders would weaken the Manitoba's reputation.

Ultimately, Hill was responsible, but he had paid little attention. "I must have money," Kennedy demanded with irritation, "for I cannot stand the strain any longer." Yet stand it he did for another half dozen years.[25]

He complained further to Hill in January 1883: "I hope you will . . . continue to make me remittances as . . . I am still largely in advance to the Company" [i.e., the Manitoba]. Hill acknowledged Kennedy's anxiety in May: "I note . . . the purchase by you of the $574,000 [of the new consolidated bonds] in the hands of the Company. I fully appreciate the valuable services your house rendered this Company the past winter, and desire as far as I can to give you an equivalent for it." Hill continued in a similar vein: "We will go on and pay what we can from earnings after paying construction estimates etc. I would like to draw on account of bonds sold." Hill was informing Kennedy that, while the Manitoba had some financing in hand, he took it for granted that J. S. Kennedy & Co. would make up the predictable shortage.[26]

As of August 1883, the Manitoba owed J. S. Kennedy & Co. fully $600,000 on an open account, i.e., an unsecured debt. Kennedy made it very clear that he needed some payment, writing to Hill in October that, "I have been left to finance the Company as best I could, making advances without any security whatever to the amount of nearly $1 million and yet whenever the Company had any money I loaned it out and got them all the interest I could on it." A debt of $600,000 had ballooned enormously in a mere three months; of course Kennedy was anxious.[27]

Despite his constant complaints, Kennedy did not hold back financially when the Manitoba seemed threatened. This held true even after the dissolution of J. S. Kennedy & Co. in December 1883. Even during the 1884 crisis, Kennedy urged rapid construction to forestall building by two rivals, the Northern Pacific, and the Chicago, Milwaukee & St. Paul. "I am willing," he informed Hill that spring, "to lend the Company $500,000 on its obligations to return them bond for bond after the new road is completed."[28]

And Kennedy went farther still that April, offering to bring potential investors from the East during his visits to St. Paul. "I am doing all I can to get a few gentlemen of the right stamp to come out with me," he advised Hill, "but as it draws near the time they all seem to have some excuse or another for not doing what they all express a very strong desire to do. All I can say is that if I do not bring 6 or 8 good men with me or as many of that number as I possibly can, it will not be my fault."[29]

Given the financial crisis, Kennedy had to walk a fine line, seeking capital for the Manitoba's expansion, yet doing so very discreetly: to be perceived as needy was to invite an attack by the bears, for whom crisis spelled opportunity. So Kennedy warned Hill that May, "You can readily understand that in the present condition of financial matters here I do not wish to appear as a borrower if I can help it, or if I must, I want to make it for as small an amount and as short a time as possible." It was important to look both liquid and solvent, avoiding uncertain ventures. Accordingly, Kennedy advised Hill later that month, "We [Kennedy, James and Thorne] find that it would be unwise to attempt to force the making up of a syndicate now to take the $650,000 we are about to issue. . . . Thorne and [Oliver] Harriman will each take $25,000 . . . and I think I can place $100,000 more . . . privately." Kennedy was too wise in the ways of the market to risk going public with ventures whose possible failure might damage his credibility. And he now realized that he had underestimated the severity of the financial panic, which left overloaded bankers unwilling to buy more securities. In his campaign to bolster the Manitoba's image, Kennedy urged Hill to not only—somehow— accumulate cash reserves, but to discreetly advertise this fact: "Were it known in the Street that we had a few hundred thousand in hand which we were lending, it would help us immensely."[30]

Though Kennedy did not go so far as to cancel his customary extended (two or even three month) summer vacation in Western Europe, he took strong legal and financial precautions to enable his associates at the Manitoba and the Central Trust Company to act against unforeseen events. But cash flow problems remained. Kennedy wrote Hill early in July to ask for money to cope with an unexpected shortage, an unusually large number of bonds being presented for redemption. The sum involved—$134,000—was merely the latest demand on Kennedy's finances. Kennedy tried to prod Hill: "I need not urge you to hasten all such remittances as rapidly as you can, for I had made no preparations to make any advances on this account."[31]

Kennedy's anxieties turned out to be misplaced. In writing to Hill after returning from Europe in late September 1884, he still was very cautious regarding the financial situation. But a bountiful wheat harvest in the Great Plains soon filled the coffers of the Manitoba with much-needed revenue. The Kennedy-Hill correspondence suddenly became buoyant and optimistic, free from the fear of a cash crunch with which the men had lived for so long. Hill remitted $50,000 to Kennedy in November, a mere first installment of the hefty $800,000 he anticipated sending by late December; Kennedy of course was delighted. He observed to Hill before Christmas that, "If you can continue to send on remittances I can carry a loan I have made . . . until the dividend is payable. . . ." And on 31 December, he offered a cheerful summa- tion to Hill: "We finish the year with not only enough money on hand to pay all our interest due 1 January but a good cash balance besides. We were never in such good financial condition before, and I cannot tell you what a relief it is to me, from the anxious days and sleepless nights I have had in times gone by and which I hope and believe, for all our sakes, will never return."[32]

Kennedy continued to sustain the Manitoba's building program during 1885. This often necessitated short-term borrowing that, being repaid quickly, found no place on the balance sheet. The Manitoba, a "wheat line" that gained its greatest revenue during the harvest, was subject to seasonal fluctuations which complicated its financing. Kennedy remained as steadfast as ever, finding time during a fishing vacation to correspond with Hill regarding a $150,000 loan.[33]

▼   ▼   ▼

By the mid-1880s, the Manitoba was solidly established as a major railroad in the Great Plains. Hill had shown stunning abilities as a builder and operator, and Kennedy as a resourceful and courageous financier. His role, which was indispensable in the early days of hand-to-mouth financing, was gradually altering as the Manitoba gained prestige and prominence in the financial world. Its operating income more than doubled, rising from $1.5 million in 1880 to $3.8 million in 1889. Operating mileage almost quintupled, from 656 in 1880 to 3,030 by 1889. Bonded debt quadrupled, from $16 million in 1880, to $61 million in 1889; the line's credit rating also improved. The stockholders were amply rewarded, particularly once dividends began to flow in 1882. When organized in 1879, the Manitoba's stock had only nominal value; in 1881, when Kittson sold his stock to other insiders, the price had risen to $60 a share; within five years, Manitoba stock sold at par—$100, and above.

Kennedy had metamorphosed his career—and himself. For years he had intervened as a financier for many a railroad in various stages of growth and decline, profit and loss. He had achieved remarkable personal wealth, but no intimate or sustained connection with a particular line. His Manitoba relationship was strikingly different. Here he joined others—especially Jim Hill—in an uncertain pioneering venture into the great unknown. And they were hugely successful.

NOTES

1. J. S. Kennedy to J. J. Hill, 17, 30 April 1884, Hill Papers.

2. J. S. Kennedy to J. J. Hill, 3 October, 4 November 1882, Hill Papers.

3. J. S. Kennedy to J. J. Hill, 9 July 1884, Hill Papers.

4. J. J. Hill to J. S. Kennedy & Co., 6 October 1879; G. Stephen to J. S. Kennedy & Co., Telegram, 8 May 1880; R. B. Angus to J. Kennedy Tod, 28 July 1880, Hill

Papers. J. S. Kennedy & Co. to R. B. Angus, 5 August 1880, James J. Hill Correspondence, President's Office, Great Northern. J. S. Kennedy & Co. to R. B. Angus, 16 August 1880; J. J. Hill to J. S. Kennedy, 4 January, 12 February 1882, 12 July 1885, 23 January 1886; J. J. Hill to J. S. Kennedy & Co., 29 July 1882; J. S. Kennedy to J. J. Hill, 21 July 1882, 7 October 1883; J. S. Kennedy to J. J. Hill, Private, 16 January 1885; J. S. Kennedy to J. J. Hill, 19 January 1886, Hill Papers.

5. J. S. Kennedy to J. J. Hill, 17 December 1879; R. B. Angus to J. S. Kennedy, Private, 20 January 1880, Hill Papers.

6. J. S. Kennedy & Co. to J. J. Hill, 26 November, 17 December 1879, 25 March 1881, 2, 9 February, 13 , 15 March 1882, Hill Papers; J. S. Kennedy & Co. to R. B. Angus, 25 October 1880, James J. Hill Correspondence, President's Office, Great Northern; J. J. Hill to "My Dear Mr. Kennedy," 5 March 1881; J. J. Hill to J. S. Kennedy & Co., 21 April, 24 December 1881, 16, 29 March, 17, 31 July, 2 August 1882; J. J. Hill to J. S. Kennedy, 18 February 1882; J. S. Kennedy to J. J. Hill, 16, 20 March, 10 August, 2 September, 3 October 1882, Hill Papers.

7. J. S. Kennedy to J. J. Hill, Confidential, 5 February 1883; J. S. Kennedy to J. J. Hill, 4 May, 14 August 1883, Hill Papers.

8. J. S. Kennedy to J. J. Hill, Private, 18 September 1883; J. S. Kennedy to J. J. Hill, 22 September 1883, Hill Papers.

9. J. S. Kennedy to J. J. Hill, 5 June 1884, Hill Papers.

10. J. S. Kennedy to J. J. Hill, 13, 18 January 1885, Hill Papers.

11. J. S. Kennedy to J. J. Hill, Private, 24 April 1885; J. S. Kennedy to J. J. Hill, 1 May 1885, Hill Papers.

12. J. S. Kennedy to G. Stephen, 29 July 1880, James J. Hill Correspondence, President's Office, Great Northern; R. B. Angus to J. S. Kennedy & Co., 28 August 1880, Hill Papers.

13. J. S. Kennedy to R. B. Angus, 20 August 1880; J. S. Kennedy & Co. to J. J. Hill, 2 December 1880, James J. Hill Correspondence, President's Office, Great Northern; J. S. Kennedy to J. J. Hill, 5 September 1882, Hill Papers.

14. J. S. Kennedy to J. J. Hill, 10 September 1879; J. S. Kennedy & Co. to G. Stephen, 21 November, 15 December 1879, 20 April 1880, James J. Hill Correspondence, President's Office, Great Northern.

15. R. B. Angus to J. S. Kennedy, 5 August 1880; J. S. Kennedy to R. B. Angus, 9, 13, 20 August 1880, R. B. Angus to J. S. Kennedy & Co., 16 August 1880, J. S. Kennedy & Co. to R. B. Angus, 18 September, 23 December 1880, James J. Hill Correspondence, President's Office, Great Northern.

16. J. S. Kennedy & Co. to J. J. Hill, 16 January 1880, James J. Hill Correspondence, President's Office, Great Northern; J. S. Kennedy to J. J. Hill, Private, 9 January 1884; J. J. Hill to J. S. Kennedy, 12 January 1884, Hill Papers.

17. J. S. Kennedy to J. J. Hill, 16 January 1883; J. S. Kennedy, St. Augustine, Fl., to J. J. Hill, 13 February 1885, Hill Papers.

18. Kennedy testimony, Farley v Hill, Transcript of the Record, 2, 3K, 1607; J. S. Kennedy to J. J. Hill, 8 August, 7, 30 September 1882, Hill Papers.

19. Kennedy deposition in Sahlgaard v Kennedy, Farley v Hill, Transcript of the Record, 2: 1759; J. S. Kennedy to J. J. Hill, 5 September 1882; R. B. Angus to J. S. Kennedy & Co., 27 November 1880; J. S. Kennedy to R. B. Angus, 4 August 1881, James J. Hill Correspondence, President's Office, Great Northern; R. B. Angus to J. S. Kennedy, 8 August 1881, Hill Papers.

20. D. W. James to J. J. Hill, 9 February 1885; J. S. Kennedy to J. J. Hill, Telegram, 30 April 1884; J. J. Hill to J. S. Kennedy, 6 May 1884, Hill Papers.

21. R. B. Angus to J. S. Kennedy & Co., 13 September 1880, 13 September 1881; J. S. Kennedy & Co. to R. B. Angus, 18, 25 September 1880, James J. Hill Correspondence, President's Office, Great Northern; J. S. Kennedy to J. J. Hill, 21 December 1881, Hill Papers.

22. J. S. Kennedy to J. J. Hill, 3 October 1882, 3 June 1884; J. J. Hill to J. S. Kennedy, 5 October 1882, Hill Papers.

23. J. S. Kennedy to J. J. Hill, 9 November 1882, Hill Papers.

24. J. S. Kennedy to J. J. Hill, 24 November 1882, Hill Papers.

25. J. S. Kennedy to J. J. Hill, 4, 9, 21 November 1882; J. J. Hill to J. S. Kennedy, 18 February 1882, Hill Papers.

26. J. S. Kennedy to J. J. Hill, 9 January 1883; J. S. Kennedy to J. J. Hill, Personal, 16 January 1883; J. J. Hill to J. S. Kennedy, 5 May 1883, Hill Papers.

27. J. J. Hill to J. S. Kennedy, 10 May 1883; J. S. Kennedy to J. J. Hill, St. Moritz, Switzerland, 23 August 1883; J. Kennedy Tod to J. J. Hill, 29 August 1883; J. S. Kennedy to J. J. Hill, 30 October 1883, Hill Papers.

28. J. S. Kennedy to J. J. Hill, 17, 30 April 1884, Hill Papers.

29. J. S. Kennedy to J. J. Hill, 30 April 1884, Hill Papers.

30. J. S. Kennedy to J. J. Hill, Private, 29 May, 3, 7, June 1884, Hill Papers.

31. J. S. Kennedy to J. J. Hill, 9 July 1884, Hill Papers.

32. J. S. Kennedy to J. J. Hill, 25 September, 24 November, 23, 31 December 1884; J. J. Hill to J. S. Kennedy, 22 September, 1, 5 October, 10 November 1884, Hill Papers.

33. J. S. Kennedy to J. J. Hill, 1 July 1885, Hill Papers.

10 LOCOMOTIVES AND RAILS

KENNEDY RAISED MONEY for the Manitoba, and helped spend it as well, particularly on those biggest of big-ticket items for a growing railroad: locomotives and rails.

As the 1880s wore on and the management of the line grew more complex and articulated, so its routine purchasing became internalized, with salaried managers buying technical products directly from manufacturers; the days of the commission merchant—such as Kennedy had been—were vanishing fast. But there still was a place in purchasing for so experienced and, above all, so well-connected and influential a man, in those twin specialties—locomotives and rails—which helped determine a line's operating earnings, and indeed its very survival.[1]

Until about 1880, relatively small and inexpensive locomotives were easily produced. But the 1870s inaugurated the Bessemer era, that of conversion from iron to steel rails. In 1880, steel comprised thirty percent of track mileage; the figure soared to eighty percent by 1890. This translated into more powerful and efficient locomotives that could pull longer trains with heavier loads at higher speeds. With a dozen or so large-scale locomotive builders specializing and meeting more stringent standards, technological advancement was rapid: pulling power actually doubled during 1870-1910.[2]

Here was progress, and the railroaders fostered it. But it meant higher capital costs and the need for more systematic decision-making. Steel rails, for example, were a complex product, with more and greater variables—curved or straight? light or heavy? freeze resistant or not?—which required delicate negotiations and decisions in an exclusively made-to-order market that might confuse the ordinary purchasing agent, but which Kennedy handled adroitly.

The British advantage in the cost and quality of rails, so apparent as American rail imports doubled during the booming late 1860s, had ended as American competitors lunged ahead in the 1880s. British firms did, however, continue to provide specialized rails for bridges and also mountain curves, where American rails had become notorious for cracking and breaking.

129

Steel had emerged in the 1870s as a major industry. Prior to 1883, while Kennedy was most active as a commission merchant, even pig iron production more than doubled, while that of steel simply skyrocketed. By 1900, the capitalization of its relatively few, vertically integrated firms had increased six times and their output over eleven times, while their labor force (including that of iron) had quadrupled.

Rail production was central to this upward trajectory. The combination of technological innovation and economies of scale sharply slashed the price of both iron and steel rails. But making rails was a delicate, tricky task, requiring not only masses of capital but also—in the absence of a true science of metallurgy—the skills and intuition of a small pool of highly experienced craftsmen. Rail making could not, therefore, easily satisfy sudden upsurges of railroad construction, and this brought on decades of problems. One was speculation in rails, with market prices fluctuating substantially, certainly month to month, and even week to week.[3]

All this greatly affected the Manitoba. As a wheat line, subject to the frigid temperatures of the Great Plains, and running long, heavily-laden trains at the highest practical speed during the brief and demanding harvest season, it required heavy and frost-resistant rails. And it needed these delivered during the short summer construction season, precisely when competition was stiffest.

The commission merchant mediated these transactions, collecting privileged information, watching the market's ups and downs, trying to get the best price for his client. With few parties involved, there was a virtually one-to-one relationship between customer and merchant, whose payment was 1 percent from the manufacturer.

The locomotive industry also had its complexities. Locomotives were not a stock item. Virtually all were custom-built. Their price moved upward from about $12,000 in the 1870s to $20,000 or so as they grew in power. Their *unit* price, however, was not fixed but was highly negotiable, hence responsive to buyers with strong bargaining positions. Reliability was vital: time lost in repairing a disabled locomotive was time lost forever. And their increasing sophistication was a mixed blessing for buyers: an expensive purchase last year could be undercut by major innovations in next year's model.

Delivery was another factor to consider. A moderate saving was possible if the delivery was timed *precisely* to the harvest itself, when locomotives were most needed. But building began only after orders were received, and the more prestigious builders felt free to decide which line to satisfy first: the buyer had little say. Yet it would be disastrous if freight sat idle—or, even worse, if a competitor grabbed it—for want of a locomotive. So no line wanted to be dependent on any one builder. Yet significant economies of scale could be achieved if a line placed its entire order with a single builder. And steady customers could expect preferential treatment, especially regarding date of delivery.[4]

Should the economy contract, however, the shoe would be on the other foot, as Kennedy pointed out to Hill in mid-1882. "The locomotive builders are . . . applying to me for orders which would indicate that they are getting short of work, and prices in this case . . . will undoubtedly be lower before very long."[5] So the industry's structure, coupled with the boom and bust cycle so typical of capital goods industries, meant delays, waiting lists, premiums for accelerated deliveries, and a general climate of uncertainty and fluctuation.

Building was dominated by the Baldwin Locomotive Company of Philadelphia, which built several hundred locomotives annually, and which was the first and—by the late 1870s—the largest such firm in the country. The Rogers Locomotive Works of Paterson, New Jersey, was its principal competitor. Baldwin set the pattern, while Rogers—its family leadership in disarray, and its once-prestigious operations disturbed by a major fire in 1879—scrambled to keep up; the other builders trailed behind.

Kennedy was in his element as the central figure in the Manitoba's locomotive purchases during 1879-December 1883, when he left this role upon liquidating J. S. Kennedy & Co. Few men were as much at ease with the complexities and uncertainties inherent in the technological change that he had witnessed from childhood onward. He had decades of negotiating experience, now easily applied to three vital questions: quality, delivery and price. He had gained insights into the Rogers company in the 1850s and 1860s, while partnered with Morris Ketchum Jesup, who, together with Morris Ketchum, were its principal financiers. Kennedy's connections as a commission merchant helped him uncover who had paid what for locomotives. He had easy access to the financing on which transactions depended. And he had the associates required either to organize a complex deal, or to defend the Manitoba against a counterthrust.

By 1879, Kennedy and Hill were sharing doubts about the situation at Rogers. Hill was urging Kennedy to find out why the new Rogers' locomotive cost substantially more than a similar Baldwin.[6] Hill compared Baldwin and Rogers locomotives that August, favoring the former for its greater reliability. But Baldwin's price was higher than Hill wanted to pay, and Kennedy's angling for a discount proved fruitless.[7]

The issues were clear. Kennedy and Hill wanted both discounts and delivery in advance of the late summer-autumn boom in traffic. And they were prepared to maneuver, bargain, or even threaten to have their way.

In March 1880, with the harvest just six months away, Kennedy informed Hill that a partial shipment had arrived, and that he was trying to keep Baldwin on schedule, hastening "the completion of the remaining locomotives as much as possible."[8] Kennedy cautioned the next month that the Manitoba should place its orders immediately; in August, he again warned Angus, the Manitoba's vice president, that: "[the] locomotive market is tight. If you anticipate needing more locomotives by next spring, order now."[9]

In April, Angus authorized Kennedy to ascertain Baldwin's price for ten more locomotives. Kennedy was to buy—*if* Baldwin could deliver by 1 September.[10] But Angus was apprehensive about delivery: should the Manitoba hedge by finding another supplier, the Pittsburgh Locomotive Works, for example? Kennedy demurred, arguing for quality: "The builders [Baldwin] produce excellent work," he reminded Angus, "and we think your interests would be well served if placed in their hands." This time it was Angus who balked, and Kennedy was forced to cancel the Baldwin order; the Manitoba, he informed the Philadelphia company, had switched to another builder.[11]

In March 1881, Kennedy closed an order for twenty-five locomotives from Baldwin. Though he undoubtedly received a reasonable discount for so substantial an order, he did admit to Hill: "The price is high and the delivery way ahead, but it seems to be the very best that can be done at present both as regards price and delivery." In December, Kennedy began urging Baldwin to hurry the delivery, but to no avail. The following March, he performed his classic role as an intermediary between buyer and seller, with J. S. Kennedy & Co. guaranteeing prompt payment on the order. As an old-line, established, mercantile company, its credit stood higher than that of the new, untried Manitoba.

But April came, and Baldwin still had not delivered. Hill wanted to deduct $500 for each locomotive arriving late, but Kennedy disagreed, informing Hill that "we think there might be some difficulty in making good your claim against Baldwin for loss sustained through delay." For Kennedy it was a question not merely of law, but of prudence: as so often, he opposed actions that yielded a paltry return, while risking damaging good relations with a major player.[12]

While Baldwin's quality was consistently high, Rogers' locomotives could be problematic. In December 1879, for example, Hill bolstered his arguments by actually shipping broken parts to Kennedy, who was dealing with Rogers. He later informed Hill that Rogers had pledged to make good, but also inquired whether their representatives had inspected the defective locomotives. Still, Hill and Kennedy both wanted to maintain the Rogers connection, if only because Baldwin deliveries were unreliable.[13]

The Rogers company also cared about the Manitoba conection. Kennedy informed Hill in August 1880 that one of the Rogers family personally urged "that his company should be allowed to supply you with a few locomotives when next you are in the market . . . [and] he is extremely anxious to be allowed a chance of proving to you that [his] engines will in every respect meet your wants as well as those of Baldwin." Rogers even was prepared to undersell Baldwin. Kennedy backed the Rogers proposal, mentioning his long and favorable experience with the Rogers product, and suggesting that Hill split the order between Rogers and Baldwin.[14]

To Kennedy, whose priority clearly was delivery on time, and who was anxious about becoming overly dependent on Baldwin, the deficiencies in Rogers' product were aberrations, to be taken in stride. With personal contacts all-important, he opposed approaching an unknown builder who might—or might not—provide timely deliveries.

Hill, an operations man above all else, and without previous railroad experience, saw things differently. The Rogers' deficiencies meant inoperable locomotives, unhaulable freight and distraught customers. Kennedy, with his long relationship to Rogers, was willing to be generous; Hill was not. So he sent Kennedy a bill of complaints in September 1880, regarding the decline in Rogers' quality. Kennedy nevertheless won one round in the argument when Angus ordered him to buy ten Rogers locomotives. Kennedy assured Hill regarding their quality; Rogers offered to build two to demonstrate their high quality.[15]

By the autumn of 1880, however, Hill had become completely disenchanted with Rogers' locomotives. But he himself was still untried as an operations chief, and so avoided a showdown over what was, after all, a relatively minor issue. Hill was willing to drop a claim for damages against Rogers, but would buy no more from them, pointing out that the builder had not offered restitution for the losses the Manitoba had suffered due to breakdowns in Rogers' locomotives.[16]

Hill once again shipped defective parts to Kennedy, who replied in January 1881, "I have duly forwarded the pieces of defective shell plates to Rogers for his inspection. There can be no question that this material is of the most defective quality, and I am glad that you have supplied me with this additional proof that the complaints I made on your behalf were founded." Rogers and the Manitoba now reached a financial settlement.[17]

Nevertheless, the Manitoba continued to do business with Rogers, with Kennedy favoring this action, until he, having dissolved J. S. Kennedy & Co. in late 1883, put railroad purchasing aside.[18]

▼   ▼   ▼

As with locomotives, so it was with rails: Kennedy—and J. S. Kennedy & Co.—served as an indispensable middleman between buyer and seller from 1868 onward. Having begun by representing two British firms—Bowling Iron Co. and the West Cumberland Hematite Iron Co.—in the early 1870s, he moved toward American firms thereafter. Particularly in the 1880s, he bought steel rails from the Lackawanna Iron & Coal Co. (later the Lackawanna Steel Co.), a well-known and prestigious firm in Scranton, Pennsylvania. Kennedy was connected with this firm through old business relationships with William E. Dodge and D. Willis James, both of Phelps, Dodge & Co., the New York metals mercantile house.[19]

There also was a connection with Andrew Carnegie, a fellow Scotsman, who had organized the renowned Edgar Thomson Steel Co. Ltd. in Pittsburgh during the late 1870s, as a component of the Carnegie empire. J. S. Kennedy & Co. acted as the agent for the Thomson Co. during 1877-79, creating a link that was to prove very valuable when Kennedy led the way after 1878 in buying rails for the St. Paul & Pacific and for its successor, the St. Paul, Minneapolis & Manitoba.[20]

Kennedy also was connected to the eminent Cambria Iron Company, which had opened during 1852 in Johnstown, Pennsylvania, as an integrated firm with a rolling mill. By 1875, it stood as the very largest American iron and steel company, a technological pioneer in producing rails, sheet steel and all the outpourings of the Bessemer era. As a commission merchant, Kennedy had been a selling agent for Cambria iron and steel rails during 1874-79, before Cambria developed its own marketing personnel as part of its vertical integration.[21] J. S. Kennedy & Co. was used in March 1877 by Farley of the St. Paul & Pacific to buy steel rails from Cambria, and even was asked by Farley in May to pay the bill: the line would repay Kennedy as soon as possible. Farley later informed him that "I am well satisfied about the quality of Cambria rails . . . and think the price very reasonable."[22]

As so often, Kennedy was representing both buyer and seller, in a somewhat ambiguous relationship that nevertheless satisfied those involved. He brokered a much more complex and potentially risky transaction in mid-1878, when he persuaded the Cambria to accept surprisingly thin credit—debentures whose issuance required, first, judicial authorization, and then buyers—when selling rails to the St. Paul & Pacific, to which Kennedy had already lent some of the cash it required. The Cambria, also needing ready cash, then sold a quarter of the debentures it received to Kennedy himself. In effect, Kennedy was serving as a catalyst of economic growth by helping both buyer and seller finance a deal in which he believed. He calculated well; had he not done so, there would have been disaster all round.

But the Cambria itself fell short. The order may have been placed too late. Or the economic resurgence of 1878 may have brought more orders than it could fill. Whatever the reason, not all the rails were delivered, and the St. Paul & Pacific lost critical time in August, when it had to suspend construction. Hill was angry, but he and the others realized that they could not do better elsewhere: Kennedy's connection to the Cambria was an invaluable asset. So George Stephen informed Hill, "Kennedy has thoroughly impressed them [i.e., the Cambria] with the great importance of timely delivery, and they know they cannot get their debentures until the road is finished."[23]

By 1880 or so, high-quality competition to the Cambria had appeared in the Chicago area, an iron manufacturing center for some thirty years. The North Chicago Rolling Mill Company was in the vanguard. Kennedy acquired an indirect connection here through his young nephew, Robert Elliott Tod, who represented Kennedy's interests while serving an apprenticeship in the 1880s with Joseph Thatcher Torrence, a prominent Chicago-area iron manufacturer and organizer of local transportation systems. Until Tod left in 1898 to join J. Kennedy Tod & Co. in New York, he was very well placed to provide his Uncle John with the inside information essential to wise decisions.[24]

These primarily revolved around buying steel rails: when? in what quantities? at what price? with what financing? and from whom? In January 1880, Kennedy had discussed prices with Richard Angus of the Manitoba. Rails then stood at about $80 per ton, and Kennedy was correct in forecasting a rise, possibly in anticipation of general prosperity. Of course this would cost the Manitoba—and Kennedy supported Angus' decision to buy at the North Chicago Rolling Mill—but a rise might also help by discouraging construction by weaker rivals.

Prices, however, were dropping by May, when Kennedy offered Angus some advice. "The market here [New York] is very demoralized, and several speculative parcels have recently come into the market. We believe that we could today buy iron rails at $46 or $47 per ton, and steel rails at $65 per ton, and *probably even less*. . . . Should you want any, therefore, we recommend before purchasing to let us, at least, try what we can do at this end, as we think we can really save you money." This drop of nearly twenty percent, from $80 to $65, suggests just how important it was to heed the advice of a Kennedy, shrewd in judgment, sagacious in negotiation, and well-supplied with an insider's market information (though his direct connection to Cambria had ended in 1879, he nevertheless learned the price it was charging other lines), if a line were to avoid incurring a crushing load of debt.[25]

A year later, in April 1881, Kennedy cautioned Hill against then buying steel rails: "might buy cheaper for later delivery." And he followed in February 1882 with suggestions to Hill regarding how to pay for the surprisingly early arrival of an order of steel rails from the North Chicago Rolling Mill and from the Joliet Co., another Chicago-area manufacturer. The Manitoba had enough cash to pay partially, and Kennedy offered his notes for the remainder if necessary, but asked: "Why cannot you get them to take your notes three or four months in payment with interest added and in that way help us to finance until we can make other arrangements?"[26]

By July, the 1882 railroad construction season was well under way. Although he doubted that Hill needed more steel rails, Kennedy nonetheless reported a softening—to $45 a ton—in the Eastern market. And he passed on a rumor that Collis P. Huntington of the Central Pacific had recently bought 10,000 tons at that price for fall delivery. "We are waiting," Kennedy notified Hill in August, "to hear . . . about steel rails. We think we can make a better trade with the Cambria Iron Company than can be made anywhere else and we would like to give them the order."[27]

In October, rumor had it that Carnegie had sold 11,000 tons at $46 per ton, a record low price. Kennedy then offered Cambria $44 a ton, but doubted if this would be accepted. "The market is going down," he forecast in November, "so that there is no need to be in a hurry buying."[28]

▼　　　▼　　　▼

Kennedy's involvement in locomotive and rail transactions fell into two realms: 1) as an agent during the 1870s for several leading manufacturers, first British and then American; and 2) as a buyer first for the St. Paul and Pacific, and then for the new Manitoba railroad. Kennedy was dedicated to economic growth in general, and to that of the Manitoba line in particular. His skill lay in making the economic mechanism mesh more efficiently by greasing its wheels through advice, finance, negotiation, personal intervention, and all the expedients that a nimble and imaginative mind could offer.

There was, however, a painful irony in all this: Kennedy's very success in spurring big business forward helped render the commission merchant obsolete. For, as time passed and the railroads and their iron and steel counterparts grew larger and more capable, they had less need for Kennedy and his fellows. That he could take timely action to disengage from a declining occupation, the better to join a thriving railroad that was eventually to reach the far Pacific, suggests how well he understood the changing world around him.

Notes

1. Glenn Porter and Harold Livesay, *Merchants and Manufacturers* (Baltimore: Johns Hopkins University Press, 1971), 104-5.

2. John H. White, *A Short History of American Locomotive Builders in the Steam Era* (Washington, D.C.: Bass, 1982), 9, 11, 13; Harold C. Livesay, "Marketing Patterns in the Antebellum American Iron Industry," *Business History Review* 45 (Autumn 1971): 269-70, 291, 295; Harold C. Livesay and Glenn Porter, "The Financial Role of Merchants in the Development of U.S. Manufacturing, 1815-1860," *Explorations in Economic History* 9 (Fall 1971): 64, 79; Harold C. Livesay, *Andrew Carnegie and the Rise of Big Business* (Boston: Little Brown, 1975), 32, 84; Peter Temin, *Iron and Steel in Nineteenth-Century America* (Cambridge: MIT Press, 1964), 266-67, 270-71, 282; Muriel Emmie Hidy, *George Peabody: Merchant and Financier, 1829-1854* (New York: Arno Press, 1978), 328, 331, 333-34, 336, 338, 345; Ann M. Scanlon, "The Building of the New York Central: A Study in the Development of the International Iron Trade," in Joseph R. Frese and Jacob Judd, eds., *An Emerging Independent American Economy, 1815-1875* (Tarrytown, N.Y.: Sleepy Hollow Press, 1980), 99, 102, 104, 117; Harry H. Pierce, "Foreign Investment in American Enterprise," in David T. Gilchrist and W. David Lewis, eds., *Economic Change in the Civil War Era* (Greenville, Del.: Eleutherian Mills-Hagley Foundation, 1965), 45; Vincent P. Carosso, *The Morgans: Private International Bankers, 1854-1913* (Cambridge: Harvard University Press, 1987), 51, 95, 113-15, 159-60, 688n. 72; *Historical Statistics of the United States*, 1976, 208-9, 732; *Commercial & Financial Chronicle* 10 (26 March 1870): 416; 13 (25 November 1871): 720; 14 (5 April 1872): 472; 17 (27 September 1873): 440; William K. Hutchinson, "Import Substitution, Structural Change, and Regional Economic Growth in the United States: The Northeast, 1870-1910," *Journal of Economic History* 45 (June 1985): 325; Jeremy Atack and Jan K. Bueckner, "Steel Rails and American Railroads, 1867-1880," *Explorations in Economic History* 20 (July 1983): 261.

3. J. S. Kennedy to R.B. Angus, 8 March, 24 May 1880, James J. Hill Correspondence, President's Office, Great Northern.

4. John H. White, Jr., *American Locomotives An Engineering History, 1830-1880* (Baltimore: Johns Hopkins University Press, 1968), 21; White, *A Short History of American Locomotive Builders*, 13, 15, 27, 87; L.R. Trumbull, *A History of Industrial Paterson* (Paterson, N.J.: Carleton M. Herrick, 1882), 123; Porter and Livesay, *Merchants and Manufacturers*, 85, 102-6.

5. J. S. Kennedy to J. J. Hill, 20 July 1882, Hill Papers; J. S. Kennedy to R.B. Angus, 20 August 1880, James J. Hill Correspondence, President's Office, Great Northern.

6. J. J. Hill to J. S. Kennedy, 14 April 1879, Hill Papers.

7. J. J. Hill to J. S. Kennedy, 20 August, 25 December 1879, Hill Papers; J. S. Kennedy & Co. to J. J. Hill, 27 August, 26 December 1879, James J. Hill Correspondence, President's Office, Great Northern.

8. J. S. Kennedy & Co. to J. J. Hill, 4 March 1880, James J. Hill Correspondence, President's Office, Great Northern.

9. J. S. Kennedy & Co. to R.B. Angus, 10, 13, 15, 19 April, 26 August 1880, James J. Hill Correspondence, President's Office, Great Northern.

10. R.B. Angus to J. S. Kennedy & Co., 10 April 1880; J. S. Kennedy & Co. to R.B. Angus, 16 April 1880, Hill Papers.

11. R.B. Angus to J. S. Kennedy & Co., 16 April 1880, Hill Papers; R.B. Angus to J. S. Kennedy & Co., Telegram, 17 April 1880, Hill Papers; J. S. Kennedy & Co. to R.B. Angus, 10, 13, 15, 19 April 1880, James J. Hill Correspondence, President's Office, Great Northern.

12. J. S. Kennedy to J. J. Hill., 18 March 1881; J. S. Kennedy & Co. to J. J. Hill, 12 May 1882, James J. Hill Correspondence, President's Office, Great Northern; J. S. Kennedy to J. J. Hill, 27 December 1881, 6 February 1882; J. J. Hill to J. S. Kennedy & Co., 27 April, 8 May 1882, Hill Papers.

13. J. J. Hill to J. S. Kennedy & Co., 22 December 1879, Hill Papers; J. S. Kennedy to R.B. Angus, 8 March 1880, James J. Hill Correspondence, President's Office, Great Northern.

14. J. S. Kennedy & Co. to J. J. Hill, 28 August 1880, James J. Hill Correspondence, President's Office, Great Northern.

15. J. J. Hill to J. S. Kennedy, 1 September 1880, Hill Papers; J. S. Kennedy & Co. to J. J. Hill, 9 September 1880, James J. Hill Correspondence, President's Office, Great Northern.

16. J. S. Kennedy & Co. to J. J. Hill, 25 October 1880, James J. Hill Correspondence, President's Office, Great Northern; J. J. Hill to J. S. Kennedy & Co., 29 October 1880, Hill Papers.

17. J. S. Kennedy & Co. to J. J. Hill, 22 January 1881, James J. Hill Correspondence, President's Office, Great Northern.

18. J. S. Kennedy to J. J. Hill, Private, 18 September 1883, Hill Papers.

19. "George W. Scranton," *Dictionary of American Biography*, 16: 513-14; Wayland Fuller Dunaway, *A History of Pennsylvania* (New York: Prentice-Hall, 1925), 654, 656; Daniel Hodas, *The Business Career of Moses Taylor* (New York: New York University Press, 1976), 86, 89, 102-16, 148-50, 226-29, 260-64; Victor S. Clark, *History of Manufactures in the United States, 1860-1914* (Washington D. C.: Carnegie Institution, 1928) 232; "Daniel Willis James," *Dictionary of American Biography*, 9: 573-574; Robert Glass Cleland, *A History of Phelps Dodge 1834-1950* (New York: Alfred A. Knopf, 1952), 17, 30, 36-37, 42-43, 67-68, 274; James

M. Swank, *History of the Manufacture of Iron* (Philadelphia: American Iron and Steel Association, 1892), 412; Redlich, *History of American Business Leaders*, 140; Scanlon, "The Building of the New York Central," 117; Burton W. Folsom, Jr., *Urban Capitalists: Entrepreneurs and City Growth in Pennsylvania's Lackawanna and Lehigh Regions, 1800-1920* (Baltimore: Johns Hopkins University Press, 1981), 29; *Iron Age* 30 (10 August 1882): 24; Richard Peters Jr., *Two Centuries of Iron Smelting in Pennsylvania* (Philadelphia: Pulaski Iron Company, 1921) 39.

20. Livesay, *Andrew Carnegie*, 81, 97, 103, 123, 132; Wall, *Andrew Carnegie*, 307, 309, 324, 359-60, 365, 471; Robert V. Bruce, *The Launching of American Science, 1846-1876* (New York: Alfred A. Knopf, 1987), 341; Louis M. Hacker, *The World of Andrew Carnegie, 1865-1901* (Philadelphia: J. P. Lippincott Company, 1968), 387-88; Jonathan Hughes, *The Vital Few* (New York: Oxford University Press, 1965), 229; Porter and Livesay, *Merchants and Manufacturers*, 136, 140n. 28, 141, 144-45, 148; Swank, *History of the Manufacture of Iron*, 411; *Commercial & Financial Chronicle* 25 (22 December 1877): 648; 26 (23 February 1878): 200; 26 (8 June 1878): 584; 27 (13 July 1878): 52; 28 (4 January 1879): 26.

21. Porter and Livesay, *Merchants and Manufacturers*, 58, 60, 65, 73; Livesay, "Marketing Patterns in the Antebellum American Iron Industry," 291-92, 294; Livesay and Porter, "The Financial Role of Merchants in the Development of U.S. Manufacturing," 69; John W. Oliver, *History of American Technology* (New York: Ronald Press, 1956), 319; Dunaway, *A History of Pennsylvania*, 665-66; William T. Hogan, *Economic History of the Iron and Steel Industry* (Lexington, Mass.: Lexington Books, D.C. Heath and Company, 1971), 1: 55-56, 94-95; James M. Swank, *History of the Manufacture of Iron in All Ages* (Philadelphia: American Iron and Steel Association, 1892), 411; Fritz Redlich, *History of American Business Leaders: Iron and Steel*, vol. 1 (Ann Arbor, Mich.: Edwards Brothers, 1940), 98; *Commercial & Financial Chronicle*, 19 (26 December 1874): vii; 20 (29 May 1875): xxxii; 21 (24 July 1875): 96; 23 (30 September 1876): 338; 26 (23 February 1878): 200; 26 (8 June 1878): 584; 27 (13 July 1878): 52; 28 (4 January 1879): 26; *Iron Age* 16 (25 November 1875): 5; 24 (11 December 1879): 5, 11; 20 (5 July 1877): 5; 21 (28 March 1878): 5; 22 (4 July 1878): 5; 23 (27 March 1879): 5; Peters, *Two Centuries of Iron Smelting*, 53; Judge Joseph Masters, "Brief History of the Early Iron and Steel Industry of the Wood, Morell & Co., and the Cambria Iron Co. at Johnstown, Pa.," Official Souvenir Program, 11th Department Encampment, United Spanish War Veterans, Johnstown, Pa., 7, 8, 9 June 1915, 9-21; [Bethlehem Steel Corp.], "History of the Bethlehem Steel Corp.," Charles M. Schwab Memorial Library, Bethlehem, Pennsylvania, unpub. ms., circa 1950, 1-3; [Bethlehem Steel Company], "History of the Evolution of the Cambria Plant Bethlehem Steel Company 1852-1935," unpub. ms., 1935, 1, 3-4, 6; "Robert W. Hunt," *Dictionary of American Biography*, 9: 932; Richard A.

Burkert, "Iron and Steelmaking in the Conemaugh Valley," in Karl Berger, ed., *Johnstown—The Story of a Unique Valley* (Johnstown: Johnstown Flood Museum, 1985), 265-66.

22. J. P. Farley to J. S. Kennedy & Co., 23 March, 31 May, June [undated but probably mid-June] 1877; J. S. Kennedy & Co. to J. P. Farley, 8 July 1878, Farley v Hill, Transcript of the Record, 2: 1718, 1495.

23. J. S. Kennedy & Co. to J. P. Farley, 18 June, 8 July 1878, Farley v Hill, Transcript of the Record, 2: 995, 1495; J. S. Kennedy to J. P. Farley, Private, 10 July 1878, Farley v. Hill, Transcript of the Record, 2: 1001; J. J. Hill to J. S. Kennedy, 21 August 1878, J. J. Hill to J. S. Kennedy & Co., 28 August 1878, Hill Papers.

24. Hogan, *Economic History of the Iron and Steel Industry*, 1: 235, 239-42; Kenneth Warren, *The American Steel Industry, 1850-1970* (Oxford: Clarendon Press, 1973), 62-63; Clark, *History of Manufactures*, 67, 235-37, 581; Edward C. Kirkland, *Industry Comes of Age Business, Labor, and Public Policy, 1860-1897* (New York: Holt, Rinehart and Winston, 1961), 208, 218; Joseph Frazier Wall, *Andrew Carnegie* (New York: Oxford University Press, 1970), 1067n. 38; American Iron and Steel Association Bulletin 30 (7 February 1896):26; 12 (24 July 1878):170; 16 (11 January 1882): 13; Frederick Merk, *Economic History of Wisconsin During the Civil War Decade* (Madison: State Historical Society of Wisconsin, 1916), 142, 147n. 5; Herbert N. Casson, *The Romance of Steel* (New York: A.S. Barnes & Company, 1907), 18; Livesay, *Andrew Carnegie*, 166, 182; Bernhard C. Korn, "Eber Brock Ward," (diss., Marquette University, 1942), 114, 165, 167, 171; Swank, *History of the Manufacture of Iron*, 318, 411; Redlich, *History of American Business Leaders*, 107-8, 110, 119, 123, 137, 157; *Iron Age*, 16 (25 November 1875): 23; 24 (11 December 1879): 29; "Joseph Thatcher Torrence,"*Dictionary of American Biography*, 18:594; "Robert E. Tod," *Cyclopedia of American Biography*, 9: 435-436; "Joseph Thatcher Torrence," *National Cyclopedia of American Biography*, 2: 523; "Robert Elliott Tod," *National Cyclopedia of American Biography*, 33: 497; William D. Edson, *Railroad Names* (Potomac: Maryland: Privately printed, 1984).

25. J. S. Kennedy & Co. to J. J. Hill, 23 April 1881, J. S. Kennedy to R.B. Angus, 19 April 1880, James J. Hill Correspondence, President's Office, Great Northern.

26. J. J. Hill to J. S. Kennedy & Co., 2 February 1882; J. S. Kennedy to J. J. Hill, 6 February 1882, Hill Papers.

27. J. S. Kennedy to J. J. Hill, 20 July 1882, Hill Papers.

28. J. S. Kennedy to J. J. Hill, 30 October, 9 November 1882, Hill Papers.

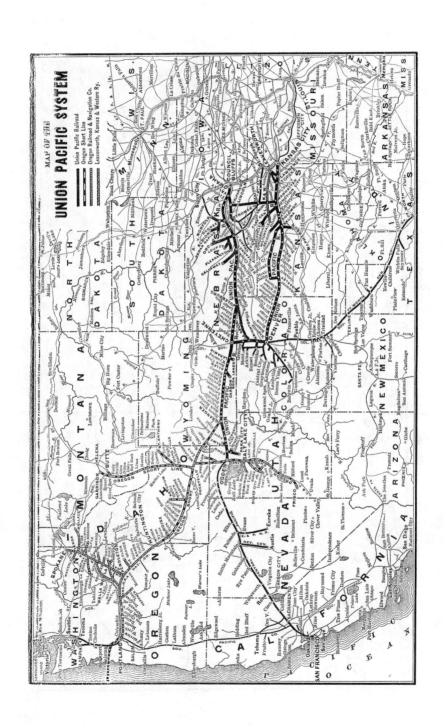

MAP OF THE

UNION PACIFIC SYSTEM

Union Pacific Railroad
Oregon Short Line
Oregon Railroad & Navigation Co.
Leavenworth, Kansas & Western Ry.

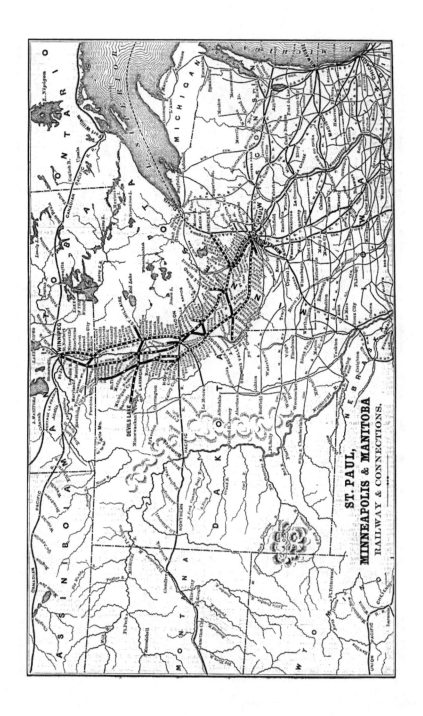

ST. PAUL,
MINNEAPOLIS & MANITOBA
RAILWAY & CONNECTIONS.

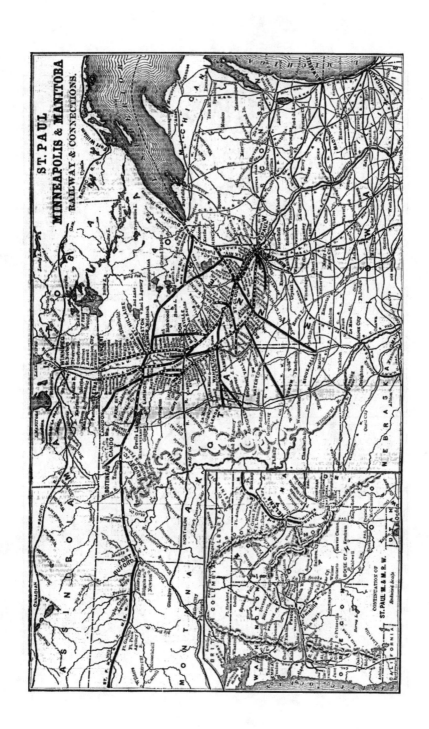

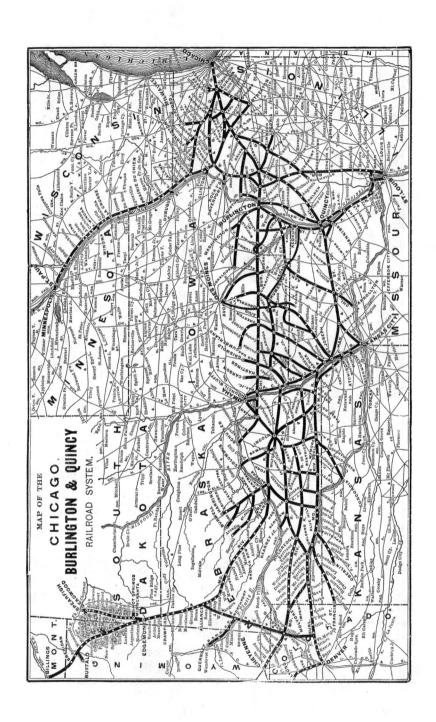

MAP OF THE
CHICAGO,
BURLINGTON & QUINCY
RAILROAD SYSTEM.

11 ENTER THE BOSTONIANS

THE GREAT IRONY FACED by Hill, Kennedy and the others leading the Manitoba in the early 1880s was that increasing success brought greater volatility in the price of Manitoba securities and serious complexities in financing. A solution was eventually found in 1885, by bringing in new, truly committed investors—the Bostonians who controlled the Chicago, Burlington & Quincy line—but only after four years of mutual assessment, decision-making, bargaining and negotiation.

The situation had developed as follows. The Manitoba was very much a growth stock, successful in financing (thanks to Kennedy), and equally so in construction and operations (thanks to Hill). And there was noticeable proof in the dividends it began paying late in 1882.

The stock's high price, relative to earnings, attracted enthusiastic speculators. The bulls bought and sold to drive prices up, using legitimate news and not-so-legitimate rumors to trap unwary buyers. The bears thrived on bad news, and worked to force prices down by generating panic among unknowing investors. The Manitoba did, to be sure, enjoy some protection through the centralization of its holdings in the hands of Kennedy and the former George Stephen Associates: of its 200,000 shares, no more than 70,000 were traded. Should the floating supply increase unexpectedly, however, the line might face unpredictable price fluctuations.

The threat derived from subtle, yet decisive, divergences at the peak of the Manitoba pyramid. As we have seen, George Stephen and Donald Smith were combining their involvement in the Manitoba with leadership of the Canadian Pacific project. Here was an idea whose political and nationalistic time had come; virtually every Canadian public figure stood behind it. It required mobilizing every dollar that a capital-short Canada could yield. And so Stephen and Smith had to sell small blocks of 1,000 or so from their Manitoba holdings (probably about 25,000 shares each), shifting the proceeds into the Canadian Pacific venture.

Such sales of course depressed the price of Manitoba stock, and this troubled Hill and Kennedy—though there was little they could do about it, aside from discussing the issue with Smith and Stephen. The two Americans understood that their Canadian associates had little choice but to support the Canadian Pacific. The question was how to avoid the chaos inherent in unpredictable sales to unknown—and very possibly ill-intentioned—buyers. For the market was extremely "thin," i.e., sales of relatively small amounts result in highly volatile prices.

As the leader in financing the Manitoba, Kennedy faced a corollary problem: how to use such "unreliable" stocks in securing loans? Certainly the bankers were impressed by the Manitoba's long-term prospects. But it was risky for them to accept as collateral a stock so unpredictable and wide-ranging in price as to create difficulty should a loan happen to go bad. Witness Hill's statement to Kennedy in September 1882 that he was unhappy about the increase in Manitoba stock to 165 because large blocks were being sold; he preferred steadier, consistent prices at around 150-55.[1]

The predictable occurred. On 10 October, Kennedy sold 1,100 shares of Stephen's stock. These—and other—sales pushed Manitoba stock down, with Kennedy suggesting to Hill in late October that the fluctuations would continue so long as it was uncertain at what intervals and in what amounts the Canadians would try to market some of their holdings. And this Stephen and Smith, driven by the inherently unforeseeable requirements of the Canadian Pacific's construction crews, did not themselves know. As Kennedy later wrote, the large Canadian holdings—which might be sold at any moment—hung over the Manitoba like the sword of Damocles. In effect, events were in the saddle, and men could only ride.[2]

Inevitably, news of these sales reached the press, and Kennedy complained that, despite his best efforts, this had a bearish effect on Manitoba stock. He proposed listing it on the London Stock Exchange: the broader the market, the less the Manitoba stock would become the plaything of speculators.[3]

Kennedy and Hill were working closely together, buying and selling on joint account to try to stabilize the Manitoba stock price and thus retain control. In January 1883, for example, Kennedy decided to cease buying unless the price declined two or three points. Hill readily deferred to his judgment: "In regard to the purchase of stock, I can hardly advise you, but . . . I am satisfied to do as you think best, being on the ground and able to judge from day to day."[4]

Without informing Hill, however, Kennedy had kept this trading secret from his junior partners in J. S. Kennedy & Co. Such secrecy was hardly unknown in a business world where partners whose relationship was essentially unequal often went their own way, and doubtless Kennedy, as the senior, could rationalize it in terms of the overriding need for security. But his secret trading might well injure any partner who also was trading in Manitoba.

So Kennedy was embarrassed when Hill inadvertently spilled the beans in a letter that had been sent to the firm, not to Kennedy personally. The letter also referred to Kennedy's use of $71,462 of Hill's money in settling a transaction, Kennedy himself having been short of personal funds at that time. Kennedy explained matters to Hill in February 1883:

> My firm here referred your letter to them of [the] 1st to me. I am sorry you wrote them on the subject as I did not want any one here to know that you and I had been buying Manitoba stock and now I have had to admit and explain to them all about it so far as the 500 shares referred to in the letter are concerned . . . I had not the money at the moment to pay my half so I drew the whole amount [$71,462] from my firm and had it charged to your account. On the 18 January having plenty of money then on hand I paid up my half of the cost . . . My firm knew nothing about the transaction except that so much money was at one time drawn from and at another time so much paid in your account.[5]

Kennedy's intense penchant for secrecy had caught him in a web of his own making.

Throughout 1883, Kennedy and Hill continued to try to stabilize Manitoba stock, buying or selling as circumstances required. In May, Hill asked Kennedy to sell all of Hill's stock over 30,000 shares, leaving him with $3,000,000 at par. The price was left to Kennedy's judgment; Hill later wrote Kennedy that "you are on the ground and know what you can do."[6]

After a price decline of several months, the latest of a long series of bear attacks came in July 1883; Kennedy and his associates responded very aggressively. Initially, Kennedy alone supported the market. But he lacked the resources to withstand the bears, and so joined in a pool of 40,000 shares that Stephen formed to fight back by buying Manitoba shares; Kennedy and Hill each contributed one-fifth.

The onslaught continued, nevertheless, and with it, the sharp fluctuations in Manitoba stock prices that bedevilled Kennedy personally, not least during his customary European vacation that summer. "I had intended remaining here for a little while longer," he wrote to Hill in late August from St. Moritz, "but the advices I have had about the bear raids in New York on the Manitoba and the Canadian Pacific stocks and the unsettled aspect of affairs generally have made me feel uneasy so that I cannot derive any pleasure or comfort from a longer stay over here and will therefore leave . . . I hope the bears will get caught and get such a twisting that they will not have the courage to attack the stock again."[7]

The pool was the only instrument readily at hand with which to counter-attack speculators. Though a small pool of like-minded men would doubtless hang together, they might well lack sufficient resources. A larger pool would indeed have the resources, yet probably would lack the cohesion and sense of common purpose required for a united front. In pools to defend the Manitoba and the Canadian Pacific, Kennedy trusted Hill completely, Stephen and Smith slightly less, and other financiers—who might be tempted by immediate profit—still less. For example, Kennedy abruptly withdrew from a Manitoba pool in October 1883, informing Hill that Thomas Pearsall, an investor and broker for George S. Scott & Co., which was managing the pool, actually had lent stock to the bears; Kennedy felt betrayed. In another case involving a pool member, Kennedy was outraged to discover that a good friend of Stephen and Smith had actually sold 1,400 shares of Manitoba, while buying 2,700 shares of Canadian Pacific.

"I am sure you will feel just as I do," Kennedy privately protested to Hill, "that it is folly . . . [for] you and I to be in a pool to protect Manitoba stock if some of our friends are going either directly or indirectly to advise or allow their friends to sell out the one in order to buy the other, and that we had better even at some sacrifice and inconvenience close the pool."[8] Kennedy was partially mollified when the rules were slightly changed and the pool was revived.

But he essentially distrusted pooling, wanted to end this particular example, and informed Hill that Stephen would accept their decision. The pool simply wasn't successful; it benefited the brokers, who drew commissions, but not the participants; and Kennedy felt no need for brokers to make decisions that he could make for himself. In a word, pooling made him "miserable."[9] "The whole thing," he wrote later, "is an outrage. I was never in such a thing and I certainly never will be again; it has made my life miserable for I feel that I am being humbugged and cheated and I cannot and will not endure it."[10]

The Manitoba pool was in fact dissolved in mid-November 1883; Kennedy was pleased. But this dissolution encouraged the bears, whose raids soon drove the stock down to its par of $100. This in turn spurred purchases by the solid, permanent investors whom Kennedy and Hill wanted. The constant leakage of Canadian shares nevertheless remained very worrisome, and, in March 1884, the price of Manitoba stock slid—unaccountably—to $90. Kennedy soon discovered that Duncan McIntyre, who had brought the

Canadian Central into the Canadian Pacific, had sold 2,500 of Smith's holdings—and that Kennedy and Hill could do nothing whatever about it.[11]

The bear raids continued during the stock market panic of May 1884,
though Kennedy did receive limited help from sales by J. Kennedy Tod & Co.
to English and Scots investors.[12]

In October, Kennedy reported to Hill that the bears, having pushed
Manitoba stock below eighty, were bragging that it would soon fall to seventy
or even sixty. Kennedy, though ordinarily quite cool in difficult situations,
was furious at men whom he saw, not as normal, hard-bargaining businessmen, but as wreckers and destroyers. "I feel like doing something to try and
stop such people from making money out of their neighbors by such methods, and if the earnings are likely to turn out better than they did in the cor-
responding month last year . . . to go on and buy stock enough to give the
bears a twist."[13]

The Manitoba had faced a complex situation for at least four years. It was
young and booming, eager to use every dollar to expand, yet without the
solid wealth needed to both continue constructing and also solidify its position. Kennedy did indeed have wealth, and Hill was putting all his limited
funds into the line, whereas Stephen and Smith were taking money *out*,
rather than putting it *in*. How, then, to solve the problem? Kennedy and Hill
conceived of a solution: find an ally, reliable, reasonable and rich. As we shall
see, this brought them to the Chicago, Burlington & Quincy, an outpost of
Boston rectitude and sagacity in the Midwestern plains.

The Burlington, a large, exceptionally well-managed line with dispersed
ownership, was operating more than 3,000 miles of track in the early 1880s,
extending from Chicago south to St. Louis and west to Denver. It compared
favorably to the Pennsylvania as the best managed railroad in the country.
Social class, family relationships, and shared backgrounds in the "Athens of
America" contrasted sharply with the managerial elite of most railroads. The
Burlington was dominated by John Murray Forbes and his cousin, Charles
Elliott Perkins, who led a like-minded group of wealthy and prominent
Bostonians. Their traditions were those of international trade, especially the
China trade, in which the enormous distances and the virtual impossibility of
enforcing moral strictures made integrity and mutual trust absolutely essen-
tial. The Bostonians therefore were far less interested in quick profits than in
solid long-term relationships that could bring consistent yields.

But, like all railroads in that free-wheeling era, the Burlington had to be
prepared to fight for survival against other lines. One strategy involved
alliances with neighbors, if only to ensure preferential treatment for freight
(in those unregulated days) when it entered the neighbor's turf. Such

alliances could be consolidated through purchasing sufficient stock to place a friendly representative on the board of directors.

The Bostonians also had to contend with another survival issue: of the several lines battling in the intensely competitive market of the trans-Mississippi West, which would triumph and which would go under? An alliance with the Manitoba might give the Burlington an edge in its expansion to the Twin Cities—and perhaps beyond.

More general considerations also favored an alliance. Experience had taught railroaders that it was unwise to reach too far, that it was very difficult to either finance or manage sprawling enterprises; far better to organize them into divisions, more responsive and accessible to meticulous leadership. All these calculations, both general and strategic, underlay the inspection trips which Perkins conducted in 1883 over both the Manitoba and the Northern Pacific; not surprisingly, he informed Forbes that he favored the Manitoba. Henry D. Minot, a Forbes grandson, studied both railroads in 1884. So momentous a potential transaction was being conducted very cautiously.

High-level discussions began in April 1885, when Forbes and Perkins arrived in St. Paul to further study the Manitoba and start testing the waters with Hill. He informed Kennedy that he had told Forbes that, "while we had a good money making property and were not seeking a customer, I thought any arrangement that would strengthen our system and be of real benefit to us would be fairly considered."[14]

Buyer and seller gradually edged closer over the next several months. The Burlington was interested in expanding from Chicago to the Twin Cities. So it sought terminal rights at the Manitoba's facilities in St. Paul, as well as the use of Manitoba trackage from there across the Mississippi into Minneapolis. Above all, the Burlington, eager to guarantee traffic for its northern expansion, wanted the Manitoba to direct a specified amount of its freight via that line to Chicago. There also was the question of the number of shares that Hill, Kennedy, Stephen and Smith would sell to the Forbes consortium; the two Canadians were, as we have seen, eager to gain cash for the ever-expanding needs of the Canadian Pacific. Finally, the Bostonians wanted Minot to join the Manitoba board of directors and also become a vice president. Minot, living in St. Paul, would function as an ambassador, representing the Bostonians, and passing them the latest information from the Manitoba headquarters.[15]

Word began circulating by summer that Hill was willing to offer $5 million in Manitoba stock to the Burlington men. Nevertheless, uncertainties remained regarding what they would do and when: Forbes had at least a dozen prospective investors—many of them relatives—to nudge into line.

Kennedy was miffed by the continued uncertainty. He wrote Hill on 1 July to announce that there was definite information from brokers that the Bostonians were buying. Yet neither he nor Hill had received a direct offer as yet.[16]

An alliance also had its appeal to Kennedy. To join with the powerful Burlington offered a way to defend the Manitoba against incursions by the Chicago, Milwaukee & St. Paul, and also by the Chicago, Rock Island & Pacific. Both he perceived as "bent on revenge," as they contested territory in the Manitoba's backyard, in Iowa and southern Minnesota.[17]

So Kennedy wrote to Hill in July that "it is therefore all the more important that we make the alliance that now presents itself, and that we make it as soon as we can . . . and then I think our jealous neighbors and especially the Rock Island and the Milwaukee and St. Paul will be very careful about what they do for they must know the inevitable consequences should they provoke conflict."[18]

Kennedy himself was not personally disturbed by the need to offer some of his 25,000 Manitoba shares to the Bostonians; the capital he gained would enable him to follow his preference of diversifying his holdings. Moreover, the minority block the Bostonians would obtain sufficed for influence, but not control. That remained securely in the hands of Hill, Kennedy, Stephen and Smith.

So Kennedy traveled to Boston that summer of 1885 to close the deal, wiring Hill that a Forbes emissary had predicted that all would go well, though Forbes needed time to settle various legal technicalities.[19] Kennedy met with Albert E. Touzalin of the Burlington, and Henry Lee Higginson of Lee, Higginson & Co., the Boston private banking firm. He reported to Hill "that he [Touzalin] and two others of his associates had . . . [conferred] with Forbes who had returned to town with them, and . . . that Forbes would not close until they had ascertained through one of their counsel that the mortgages of the St. Paul & Pacific had all been properly foreclosed and . . . that 'little Minot' [Henry D. Minot] had suggested this as a matter that should be looked into . . . and when Forbes took a position there was no use trying to move him from it."[20]

Too many players were involved among the Bostonians for a quick decision, however, and this in turn meant a leakage of information regarding what would, after all, be a major boon to the Manitoba. Inevitably, its price rose, as buyers were attracted. Stephen and Smith had promised to sell to the Bostonians at par; they could hardly be expected to do so as the price rose above it. What to do? Hill and Kennedy were forced to intervene to try to bring the price down by selling, though this would cost them when they eventually bought the stock back. Conceding all this, Touzalin was apologetic. Kennedy impressed on the Bostonians that he and the other associates would indeed sell their Manitoba stock to them well below par, but only if it were held for investment. This moral guarantee was, in fact, a corollary to the ultimate agreement.[21]

That was signed on 3 August 1885. It involved Kennedy on one side, and Touzalin, Higginson, and Charles A. Whittier, a Higginson partner, on the other. Railroad securities were marketable at seven to ten times their earnings. The $5,000,000 the Bostonians now paid certainly was in that range, though close to its upper end. The purchase occurred in two stages. First, Kennedy contracted to sell—at below the market price—12,500 shares owned by Stephen and Smith. Then, in mid-September, Kennedy sold 7,500 shares from the joint account held by him and Hill: 4,750 shares from Kennedy's total, and 2,750 from Hill.[22]

This two-stage formula reflected caution and prudence: would the Bostonians honor their moral commitment to hold, rather than sell, the Manitoba stock? By consulting the stock transfer books at his disposal, Kennedy learned that they had indeed been true to their word, and stage two therefore could proceed.[23]

▼   ▼   ▼

Kennedy suggested to Hill in October that they sell some Manitoba stock, as a recently-formed pool apparently had raised the price. With the Manitoba now firmly controlled by him and Hill, Kennedy felt free to follow his natural bent toward diversification, fearing the risks of excessive investment in any one company.[24]

The speculators nevertheless remained interested in the growing and profitable Manitoba, despite its increased solidity. Furthermore, although the Canadian Pacific had been completed, there was always the possibility that Stephen and Smith, preferring to hold less Manitoba and more Canadian Pacific, might be tempted into selling by an attractive offer. Speculative success required participation—or at least toleration—by either Kennedy or Hill.

Witness the action in February 1886 of Thomas Pearsall, who offered either to buy or option Kennedy's entire holding of some 20,000 shares. Kennedy refused, capably analyzing the situation for Hill:

Pearsall, in addition to the parties he is working with here, is working with our friends in Montreal [Stephen and Smith] and that they are ready for any scheme that will run the stock up. They want to capture either you or me. . . . If either of us were to sell out entirely, that means resigning our positions as director and officer of the Road and then we would be chargeable with bad faith by those who have taken an interest in the property on the faith of our connection with it.

Kennedy's position was quite clear: "I will be delighted," he concluded, "to see the day when the speculative element is completely eliminated from the stock."[25]

Pearsall was not dissuaded, however. In October, he proposed yet another bull pool to Kennedy. The strategy was simple enough. Kennedy, Hill, Stephen and Smith were all to hold their stock off the market, thus driving the price up until they—and certainly the two Canadians—could rake in big profits by selling. Kennedy was noncommittal, but dismissed this scheme, writing to Hill:

> I am not going to tie up my stock in order that a ring of speculators may safely . . . go to work to "jeremy diddle" the market, get prices up fictitiously, and then dump out their stock on the innocent public at a good profit, and I am sure you are not going to aid or abet any such scheme. . . . They simply want us to hold the cow while they milk it, and I think we have both had enough of that sort of thing already. Very possibly Stephen and Smith are to be in the pool and get their share of the "swag" for tying up their stock. You and I cannot afford to be . . . mixed up with such schemes. I think we have both established a reputation for fair and honest dealing and as officers of the Company the stockholders look—and have a right to look—to us to protect their interests in every respect and how then could we either by express consent or by silence give aid to such a scheme as Pearsall proposes? Were we to do so and should it become known, as sooner or later it probably would, you would find that the credit of the company would soon stand very different from what it now does.[26]

Though Hill agreed, Stephen and Smith—who no longer were Manitoba directors or officers—may well have joined in Pearsall's scheme, which was carried out. The rumor mill was used to encourage heavy sales to unsophisticated outsiders. Much to Kennedy's satisfaction, the pool ended by mid-October 1885.[27]

The Manitoba-Burlington alliance took tangible form when the Chicago, Burlington & Northern opened for traffic in mid-1886. The Northern did indeed rent the Manitoba's terminals in the Twin Cities, as well as the track connecting them. Kennedy opposed granting the same privilege to other lines, anticipating that the Manitoba itself would eventually need the facilities.[28]

By the decade's end, the Manitoba had emerged unscathed from the speculators' attacks. Stephen and Smith had ceased to be vital stockholders. In any case, the Canadian Pacific had been completed, and they no longer felt pressured to constantly sell their Manitoba stock. The Bostonians were too conservative to be tempted by the speculators. Finally, the Manitoba's net operating income stabilized during 1883-89, even as it financed its construction by selling bonds, rather than capital stock. So the speculators turned to more attractive targets.

The new relationship with the Bostonians had broad significance. It brought together two groups who were eventually to coalesce into one, when the Manitoba/Great Northern bought the Burlington in 1901. And it brought to the Manitoba's headquarters in St. Paul a new vice president, Henry D. Minot, "young Minot,"—he was twenty-six, and Forbes' grandson—as both the watchdog of Bostonian interests and tangible proof to the financial world that the Manitoba now had direct access to the Boston investment community. Kennedy soon wrote to Hill that "it is certainly to your interest and mine to have a good block of our stock amongst such Boston investors as Minot appears to be associated with." What mattered about Minot was who, not what, he knew.[29]

There was, nevertheless, a certain inherent tension between Minot's loyalty to his associates in Boston, and his new position as the *de facto* second vice president at the Manitoba headquarters in St. Paul and as a member of the executive committee: tact and sensitivity were required on all sides. Minot, however, was very eager to make a name for himself. The Manitoba, and especially the closeness to Hill it afforded, was to be his opportunity.

The key to that opportunity, apparently, was financing. Hill ran the line, and Minot fully accepted that reality. But Kennedy, at age fifty-five, and far off in New York, may have seemed vulnerable to this highly ambitious young man, with his Lee, Higginson connection to the Boston capital market. Minot even suggested to Hill in November 1885 that Kennedy might, perhaps, sell much of his Manitoba stock and then resign from the board of directors. That would, of course, leave the way wide open for Minot himself.

It was not long before Kennedy grew aware of these ambitions. Though he had dealt with Hill for many years, theirs was a long-distance relationship, primarily by letter. Minot, however, now stood at Hill's right hand. And Kennedy was disturbed by various pinpricks from Minot. The latter, for example, asked for a personal share of the Manitoba stock sold to the Bostonians. Kennedy believed that Minot's cut should come from those sold to Lee, Higginson & Co., but he and Hill ultimately decided to each provide 1,000 Manitoba shares for Minot to buy—at par.[30]

Minot went farther in the autumn of 1885 by urging Kennedy to place 5,000 shares with him, at well below market price, to be sold to conservative Boston investors. Kennedy wanted immediate payment, but Minot refused, and Kennedy brusquely ended the deal.[31] This skirmish opened a war of attrition, as Kennedy, accustomed to deference and perhaps worrying that Minot wanted, eventually, to shunt him aside, found himself bombarded by self-aggrandizing letters from Minot that bore unsolicited advice and suggestions. Minot, for example, suggested that, "as a matter of propriety and prudence," he himself take over Kennedy's task as the agent in transferring stock. At one level, Minot's proposal was perfectly reasonable; at another, it was grossly insensitive.[32]

Minot also differed from Kennedy in wanting to bring Lee, Higginson in on a small-scale transaction by which Hill, Kennedy, D. Willis James, Samuel Thorne and others bought—in a private venture, unconnected with the Manitoba—the Mason City & Fort Dodge Railroad in Iowa. Kennedy dismissed as absurd Minot's contention that using the Boston house as the lead banker would help deceive the railroad world regarding the true backers of the line. Kennedy also was disturbed by what he regarded as excessive personal profits for Minot and Lee, Higginson. This Minot of course denied, insisting that he could succeed honestly and had no reason "to seek any illegitimate success," but Kennedy was not satisfied, and voiced his accusations to others—including Hill—in the Manitoba circle.[33]

Thorne intervened as peacemaker, trying to heal a rift that not only might damage relations with the Boston investors, but even between Hill—who found Minot useful—and the New York side of the Manitoba: Kennedy, James and Thorne himself.[34] But Kennedy continued finding fault with Minot, weighing in on 25 February 1886, with a twenty-three page, handwritten letter to Hill cataloguing Minot's various indiscretions and outright errors and misjudgments. The financing of the Mason City & Fort Dodge project remained the principal issue, with Kennedy demonstrating that those supplying the capital would receive little, while Minot and especially Lee, Higginson—whose efforts would be marginal—would do very well.[35]

The battle shifted to a new front the following month, that of minutes, records and information generally. First, Minot and Kennedy battled over placing Manitoba information in the minutes of the board of directors. Western railroads invariably had been more secretive than were their older, more established Eastern brethren, and the Manitoba was no exception. Kennedy wanted as little as possible on the record: why give anything away to Stephen and Smith—and the Canadian Pacific? Minot, however, sought to emulate the Burlington, which was impressing the financial community by publishing selected corporate records; shouldn't the Manitoba do the same? Although Hill agreed, and a three-volume draft had been prepared, Kennedy—predictably—was opposed, even hinting to Hill that Minot had ulterior motives: "For whose benefit have they [the documents] been prepared?"[36]

Other incidents followed, with Minot and Kennedy essentially playing to Hill as they themselves exchanged criticisms over passing information between the offices in St. Paul and New York. There was, for example, the question of timely reporting by Minot to Kennedy on the Manitoba's construction plans in Montana. Kennedy insisted that he had not been informed; Minot disagreed—and eventually was proven right. Thereafter, Minot chose to provide Hill with carbon copies of all correspondence to Kennedy.

After a patronizing letter from Minot in October 1886, Kennedy appealed—angrily—to Hill: "I desire . . . to treat Minot courteously and show all the respect that is due him, but when he undertakes to write to, and of, his superiors as he has done . . . I think it but proper that your attention should be called to it, for it is not the first time he has done it, and that he should be informed by you just what subjects he is at liberty to write about or discuss with me."[37]

Kennedy may have been particularly touchy because he and Hill had recently been selling St. Paul & Duluth stock. They had kept Minot in the dark, and he had played into their hands by recommending its purchase to various Bostonians. As a further criticism of Minot, Kennedy pounced on the recent success by the Rock Island line in buying the Des Moines & Fort Dodge Railroad, which he and Hill themselves had wanted. Minot had failed in conducting the negotiations, as Kennedy chose to remind Hill.[38]

By late 1886-early 1887, Minot's future was becoming clouded. He had considered resigning the previous summer, doubting that he was accomplishing much for himself, for the Manitoba, or for the Boston investors. Kennedy, who had a history of demolishing younger rivals, insisted confidentially to Hill in January 1887 that Minot must go—and at once. Hill, who respected and needed Minot's administrative skills and appreciated the links he provided to Boston capital, was not so sure: could they wait until June? Kennedy disagreed and demanded immediate action.[39]

The real question of course was the reaction of the Bostonians to Minot's departure. Would they back him strongly, moderately, or not at all? For Hill, this was a vital issue; for James, who was tilting against Minot, it was significant but not decisive; and for Kennedy, who wanted Minot out no matter what, it had become entirely irrelevant.

Kennedy played his trump card that summer: a threat to resign. "I supposed Minot's case had been settled in view of his treatment of me. I will leave the Company if Minot is re-elected to the board." This threat, or promise, was successful. Minot resigned that summer as vice president and as a director. But Hill immediately found a place for him as president of the Eastern Railway of Minnesota, a Manitoba subsidiary. And Hill showed how important Minot was for him in 1889, when Hill reconstituted the Manitoba board—from which Kennedy, James and Thorne had resigned—with both Minot and his brother, William, Jr., as members. (Minot died in a railroad accident the following year.)[40]

The Mason City & Fort Dodge Railroad, a critical battle in the Minot-Kennedy altercation, continued to be troublesome for those involved in its finances. Barely a hundred miles long, it had some appeal to Hill, first as a coal carrier between the Iowa coal fields and the Manitoba line, and then, by the mid-1880s, simply as an unconnected feeder line to the Manitoba. And Hill brought in Kennedy and a very few others; this was to be a closely-held enterprise, not the open and more public venture that Minot had envisaged.

The purchase agreement in early 1886 called for Hill, Kennedy and Henry W. Cannon (a friend of Hill) to subscribe to a bond issue needed to expand and improve the line. It was hoped that Kennedy's name might help sales abroad. The line essentially became a joint venture between Kennedy and Hill, with each owning about forty percent of the stock, while the remainder was split between five associates.[41]

But the line quickly proved disappointing. Its cost was high, the Iowa coal fields it was supposed to tap were themselves problematic, and its location on the extreme southern edge of the Manitoba's territory undercut its role as a possible feeder line. Many years later, Kennedy was to write, "we have never received a return of a single dollar, either in interest on the bonds or dividends on the stock. . . ." But even at the time, Kennedy recognized these problems: by November 1886, he was urging Hill to find a buyer.[42]

Fully fifteen years passed before this happened, in part because Hill remained unwilling or unable to grapple with the issue. In April 1887, the Illinois Central expanded in Iowa. Kennedy hoped that it might be interested in the Mason City, and volunteered to open negotiations. He found yet another prospect in the Chicago, Milwaukee & St. Paul, but Hill replied with a contrary suggestion that they expand the Mason City by building to Omaha. Nothing came of this, nor of Kennedy's more realistic suggestions; as trial balloons, they all floated away.

Ten years passed before one came to earth. In July 1898, Kennedy discovered that A. B. Stickney, the leader of the expanding Chicago Great Western, was considering building a line between Mason City and Omaha. Had an opportunity arrived to dispose of the Mason City, whose purchase would cost

Stickney less than building a new line? The Chicago, Milwaukee & St. Paul was another potential buyer. Hill, at first mildly interested in selling, then said no.

Kennedy, always eager to liquidate unprofitable investments, was not dissuaded for long. "James, Thorne, and myself," he wrote Hill, "feel it is necessary that something be done to protect our interests in the Mason City road which has been so disappointing from the very first, and if we do not make some arrangements now that we have an opportunity, we may practically lose our entire investment." But nothing substantial happened for a full year; Kennedy was extremely disappointed by Hill's rejection of his suggestions.[43]

Kennedy nevertheless kept trying. In April 1899, he informed Hill that rumor had it that the Chicago, Milwaukee & St. Paul was seriously considering building to Duluth. Would the Milwaukee consider buying the Mason City's existing line at a price comparable to that of building its own new line? Kennedy grumbled, "I may say for myself and also for James and Thorne, that we are most desirous to get out of the investment at any sacrifice. . . ." Again the result was nil, until 1901, when Hill—at last!—sold the Mason City & Fort Dodge and the related Webster County Coal Company to the Chicago Great Western for $1.5 million.[44]

▼　　　▼　　　▼

The infusion of reliable, non-speculative capital which the Bostonians brought to the Manitoba stabilized its financial situation—and shielded it against speculators—thus freeing it for the great drive into Montana that followed in the late 1880s. But there was a price. The entrance of newcomers brought difficulties to what previously had been an exceptionally cohesive cadre of leaders, men who had shared years of work, worry and mutual support under very trying circumstances. Kennedy, in what was hardly his finest hour, responded by forcing Hill to choose between Minot and himself. Predictably, Hill chose Kennedy, thus restoring the relationship that Minot had threatened.

NOTES

1. J. J. Hill to J. S. Kennedy, 15 September 1882; J. S. Kennedy to J. J. Hill, 30 October 1882, James J. Hill Papers, James Jerome Hill Reference Library, St. Paul, Minnesota.
2. J. S. Kennedy to J. J. Hill, 15, 17 November, 29 December 1883, 9 January 1884, Hill Papers.

3. J. S. Kennedy to J. J. Hill, 1, 9, 24 November 1882, Hill Papers.

4. J. J. Hill to J. S. Kennedy, 10 January 1883; J. S. Kennedy to J. J. Hill, Personal, 16 January 1883, Hill Papers.

5. J. S. Kennedy to J. J. Hill, 5 February 1883, Hill Papers.

6. J. J. Hill to J. S. Kennedy, 4 May, 14 August 1883, Hill Papers.

7. J. S. Kennedy to J. J. Hill, St. Moritz, Switzerland, 23 August 1883; J. W. Sterling to J. J. Hill, 26 July 1883, Hill Papers.

8. J. S. Kennedy to J. J. Hill, Private, 10 October 1883, Hill Papers.

9. J. S. Kennedy to J. J. Hill, 10 November 1883, Hill Papers.

10. J. S. Kennedy to J. J. Hill, 12 November 1883, Hill Papers.

11. J. S. Kennedy to J. J. Hill, 1 March 1884, Hill Papers; "Duncan McIntyre," *Dictionary of Canadian Biography*, 12: 635-37.

12. J. S. Kennedy to J. J. Hill, 12 May 1884, J. S. Kennedy to J. J. Hill, Private, 29 May 1884, Hill Papers.

13. J. S. Kennedy to J. J. Hill, 11 October 1884, Hill Papers.

14. J. J. Hill to J. S. Kennedy, 21 April 1885, Hill Papers.

15. J. J. Hill to J. S. Kennedy, 29 April, 1 May 1885; J. J. Hill to H. D. Minot, 8, 12 June 1885; J. J. Hill to J. S. Kennedy, Personal, 8 June 1885; H. D. Minot to J. J. Hill, 22 June 1885, Hill Papers.

16. J. S. Kennedy to J. J. Hill, Ristigouche, Canada, 1 July 1885; J. J. Hill to J. S. Kennedy, 20 June 1885, Hill Papers.

17. J. J. Hill to J. S. Kennedy, 8 June, 13 July 1885; J. S. Kennedy to J. J. Hill, 3 July 1885, Hill Papers.

18. J. S. Kennedy to J. J. Hill, Rye Beach, N.H., 18 July 1885, Hill Papers.

19. J. S. Kennedy to J. J. Hill, Boston, 21, 22 July 1885, Hill Papers.

20. J. S. Kennedy to J. J. Hill, Boston, Telegram, 22 July 1885; J. S. Kennedy to J. J. Hill, Rye Beach, N.H. 23 July 1885, Hill Papers.

21. J. S. Kennedy to J. J. Hill, Rye Beach, N.H., 23 July 1885, Hill Papers.

22. J. S. Kennedy to J. J. Hill, Rye Beach, N.H., 1 August 1885, J. S. Kennedy to J. J. Hill, Private, 25 August 1885; J. S. Kennedy to J. J. Hill, 26 August 1885, Hill Papers.

23. J. S. Kennedy to J. J. Hill, 18 September 1885, Hill Papers.

24. J. S. Kennedy to J. J. Hill, Confidential, 12 October 1885; J. S. Kennedy to J. J. Hill, 14, 20 October 1885, Hill Papers.

25. J. S. Kennedy to J. J. Hill, Confidential, 1 February 1886, Hill Papers.

26. J. S. Kennedy to J. J. Hill, 5, 9, October 1886, Hill Papers.

27. J. J. Hill to J. S. Kennedy, Telegram, 11 October 1886; J. J. Hill to J. S. Kennedy, 11 October 1886, Hill Papers.

28. J. S. Kennedy to J. J. Hill, 15 October 1886; J. S. Kennedy to J. J. Hill, Private, 16 October 1886, Hill Papers.

29. J. S. Kennedy to J. J. Hill, 3 September 1885, Hill Papers.

30. J. S. Kennedy to J. J. Hill, Private, 25 August 1885, Hill Papers.

31. J. J. Hill to J. S. Kennedy, 23 September 1885; H. D. Minot to J. J. Hill, 5 November, 5 December 1885, Hill Papers.

32. H. D. Minot to J. S. Kennedy, 22 January 1886, Hill Papers.

33. H. D. Minot to J. Kennedy Tod, 23 January 1886; H. D. Minot to J. S. Kennedy, 12, 17 February 1886; J. S. Kennedy to J. J. Hill, Private, 16 February 1886; H. D. Minot to J. S. Kennedy, Personal, 19 February 1886; J. S. Kennedy to J. J. Hill, 20 February 1886, Hill Papers.

34. H. D. Minot to J. S. Kennedy, Telegram, 23 February 1886; S. Thorne to J. J. Hill, 24 February 1886, Hill Papers.

35. J. S. Kennedy to J. J. Hill, 25 February 1886, Hill Papers.

36. J. S. Kennedy to J. J. Hill, 21 May 1886, Hill Papers.

37. J. S. Kennedy to J. J. Hill, Private, 4 October 1886; J. S. Kennedy to J. J. Hill, 16 April 1886, Hill Papers.

38. J. S. Kennedy to J. J. Hill, 12 November 1886, Hill Papers.

39. J. S. Kennedy to J. J. Hill, Confidential, 20 January 1887; J. S. Kennedy to J. J. Hill, 11 February 1887, Hill Papers.

40. D. W. James to J. J. Hill, 17 July 1887; J. J. Hill to J. S. Kennedy, 22, 26 July 1887; J. S. Kennedy to J. J. Hill, 22 July 1887, H. D. Minot to J. J. Hill, 12 August 1887, Hill Papers; *New York Times*, 15 November 1890, 1: 5; *Boston Transcript*, 15 November 1890, 9: 4.

41. Richard S. Prosser, *Rails to the North Star* (Minneapolis: Dillon Press, 1966), 140; H. Roger Grant, *The Corn Belt Route: A History of the Chicago Great Western Railroad Company* (De Kalb: Northern Illinois University Press, 1984), 56, 60; Memorandum of agreement in regard to purchase of securities of the Mason City & Fort Dodge Railroad Company, 5 January 1886; J. S. Kennedy to J. J. Hill, 4, 5, 17 February 1886, Hill Papers.

42. J. S. Kennedy to J. J. Hill, 22 November 1886, 13 April 1899, Hill Papers.

43. Grant, *Corn Belt Route*, 58; J. S. Kennedy to J. J. Hill, 17 January 1890, 8 January 1891, 27 July 1898, 13 April 1899, 31 December 1900, Hill Papers.

44. J. S. Kennedy to J. J. Hill, 13 April 1899, Hill Papers; Grant, *Corn Belt Route*, 62; E. T. Nichols to W. C. Toomey, 16 March 1901; J. J. Hill to directors of the Mason City & Fort Dodge, 16 March 1901; W. C. Toomey to E. T. Nichols, 16 March 1901, Hill Papers.

12 MONTANA OR BUST

THE 1880S SAW THE St. Paul, Minneapolis & Manitoba become a leader among American railroads. Although more mileage was built by American railroads during this decade than in any other, the Manitoba expanded even faster. It had served the Red River wheat country with just over 500 miles of track in 1879, connecting the Twin Cities and Winnipeg. Coupled with an infusion of millions in additional capital, its mileage rose to about 1,200 by 1883, placing it among those twenty-one lines that stood over 1,000 miles.

The Manitoba was just entering its take-off stage, having become profitable, paid interest consistently on its bonds, and initiated dividend payments. It built a mere 100 miles in the panic year of 1884. This dropped to fifty in the following year of depression, and then shot upward to nearly 400 in 1886 and over 700 in 1887, before falling to a still-impressive 400 in 1888. This grand total of over 2,850 miles nearly equaled the distance across the entire continent, with the Pacific Coast still beyond the horizon.

▼   ▼   ▼

The Manitoba was, in fact, becoming an essentially east-west line—with implicit regional ambitions on a grand scale—in part because the advent of the Canadian Pacific in the mid-1880s had more or less pre-empted its advance north from the Twin Cities. Montana, where copper had been discovered near Butte in 1866 and later at Helena, now became the primary objective; both cities were reached in 1886. Transportation costs for copper, a classic high bulk-low value commodity, plummeted, while settlers flocked in, making Montana a state in 1889.

New objectives required new organizational forms, and the Manitoba spun off three separate companies: the Montana Central Railroad, which linked Butte, Helena and Great Falls; the Great Falls Water Power & Townsite Company, which exploited topography to generate water power; and the Red

157

Mountain Consolidated Mining Company, which provided the Manitoba with its own source of copper, ensuring a modicum of freight should the existing mines stay with the Northern Pacific.

For Hill, Kennedy and the others had to be cautious. They were entering battle with the Northern Pacific, which had reached the potential riches of the Montana copper country before them, in 1883, but whose ill-placed lines boded ill for its future. It had, in fact, fallen into receivership in 1873. Though Hill and Kennedy were little concerned about taking on this vulnerable adversary, they nevertheless had to cover their flanks.

For the Montana Central was an expensive project. It penetrated difficult terrain, in which heavily-loaded freights labored over steep gradients and sharp curves. Long and severe winters hampered construction. A sparse and scattered population meant difficulties in recruiting *ad hoc* laborers to bolster the existing construction gangs.

Unlike the Manitoba, which had opened up new land for immediate settlement as it surged rapidly across the Dakota Territory, the Montana Central extension was built in several stages. First came a stretch linking Butte, Helena and Great Falls, connecting them at Billings to the Northern Pacific's route in southern Montana. Subsequently, the Manitoba's main line linked up with this segment, having entered the state through the Milk River Valley well to the north, a route superior in location and certainly in cost to that of the Northern Pacific.

This creativity in selection surfaced again when Major A. B. Rogers (ret.), Hill's field engineer, surveyed a new Helena-Butte route that was shorter and enjoyed more favorable grades than its predecessor. Even the opposition offered grudging approval, as Thomas Oakes, a Northern Pacific vice president, told Hill "that with the absence of river crossings and low grades, the extension of the Manitoba road into Montana would ruin the Northern Pacific."

Potential investors saw in the Montana Central a massive enterprise, to be constructed extremely rapidly over great distances. Not until the far-distant Butte-Helena copper mines were reached could there be substantial income. To fall even twenty miles short in a 600 or 700 mile burst would therefore mean to invest huge sums while gaining virtually no revenue until the line was completed the following year. And that delay would give the Northern Pacific more time to further tighten its monopoly on traffic. Such a huge construction surge entailed, above all, massive, well-timed purchases of rails; a shortage could be disastrous. So the hasty financing improvisations by which Kennedy and his associates had always managed to find a million or two for Hill's last-minute needs, no longer would suffice. Large-scale, systematic financing was needed, and that meant finding major capitalists.[1]

The mobilization of capital began in March 1886, after long discussions between Hill and Kennedy, when Hill formally invited Kennedy's participation. They drew, not only on such established Manitoba investors as J. Kennedy Tod, D. Willis James and Samuel Thorne, but on such newcomers as John Murray Forbes, Charles Elliott Perkins and still others.[2]

Kennedy wanted to strike decisively to head off the Northern Pacific, which recognized the threat emanating from the Manitoba's sudden assault. This news no doubt was gratifying, but Kennedy then was facing the re-emergence of the old, time-worn differences with Hill regarding their respective styles of financing. Neither man was solely concerned with personal wealth *per se*: both had plenty. The stakes were more complex, subtle and personal than that.[3]

The question for Kennedy was: how best to cope with risk? Not only was it a matter of finances, but of psychology, emotions, in a word: *anxiety*, the anxiety that underlay the bouts of sickness to which he often referred, or the long summer vacations which he thought necessary. So his general *strategy* for coping with the unpredictable risks of the capital market was to simplify, regularize, and safeguard the borrowing process, eliminating as much uncertainty as possible by a long-term strategy. His specific *tactic* was to choose a moment when the market was favorable, and then reach out to the public by floating a very large bond issue with the most prestigious consortium of banks that could possibly be assembled. In this late spring of 1886, Kennedy wanted to sell consolidated bonds, which would replace two or more outstanding issues by merging indebtedness in one issue, itself secured by a consolidated mortgage.

Hill also paid a psychological price: severe migraines. Nevertheless, this empire builder, always eager for more and grander accomplishments—and wide recognition—saw matters differently. He tended to underestimate construction costs, assuming that less money need be raised than, in fact, often turned out to be the case. This was a corollary of his commitment to cutting costs, i.e., increasing profits, as the great goal that justified virtually any risk. In pushing the Manitoba across the plains, Hill would have been delighted to have the last dollar, the last rail and the last spike all arrive simultaneously at the last possible moment at the last site—with *nothing* whatever left over. This was cost-cutting with a vengeance. It was also a pursuit of perfection that put enormous strain on those of his associates who wanted calmer, less anxious days. And it is no coincidence that Kennedy, James and Thorne all resigned (amicably, to be sure) as directors of the Manitoba by the late 1880s, even though Hill—needing their advice no less than their moral support— very much wanted them to stay.

It followed that Hill's general preference in raising capital was not long but short-term, and less rather than more. His goal of course was saving money. Should things go wrong, however, he relied on Kennedy and the other New York directors to extricate the Manitoba—often at the last possible moment—from its troubles. So Kennedy, knowing Hill full well, prodded him in June 1886 to make a decision. The money market was highly favorable at the moment, though Kennedy feared lest railroad expansion, and heavy borrowing generally, might clog the market with unsold bonds. Hill estimated that the Manitoba needed about $3,000,000 for current construction, of which a million would come from retained earnings.[4]

Kennedy recommended a contrary, ultra-conservative course, with the Manitoba using its surplus, not to press westward into thinly-settled prairies, but to straighten curves, reduce grades, otherwise improve facilities, and take other actions that would lower long-term operating costs. Kennedy also proposed changes in various Manitoba departments, urging Hill to follow the example of the Pennsylvania, the self-styled "standard railroad of the world," and also of the highly regarded New York Central.[5]

Hill, nevertheless, was in the driver's seat; growth therefore remained dominant. Kennedy, James and Thorne, the inner circle of financiers, did their best to raise the money needed, with James suggesting that the Manitoba try to do so with four percent bonds in London, where the prestigious Baring Brothers & Co.—which had financed so much American railroad borrowing—seemed willing to talk. This idea, however, died aborning.[6]

Meanwhile, a far more fruitful relationship was blossoming between Kennedy and Jacob Schiff of the no less prestigious Kuhn, Loeb & Co. Their meeting represented a breakthrough by Kennedy—and the Manitoba—to the very highest level of international finance. Discretion was the watchword (Kennedy met twice with Schiff before identifying him to Hill), with much deference granted Schiff by Kennedy, who fully understood the benefits this association would likely bring the Manitoba in its later dealings.[7]

"I had a long interview," Kennedy privately wrote Hill in late September, "with James and a prominent banker [Schiff] here whose firm deals largely in railroad bonds both in this and the London market . . . James and I were impressed by what he said and we have made up our minds that even if we have to take a comparatively low price to start with we should make the rate of interest 4%." This cryptic reference to a "comparatively low price" went to the heart of the matter. Kuhn, Loeb would form a syndicate to finance the Manitoba expansion. The syndicate of course would offer bonds, but what rate of return would attract the buying public? Should it be 4 or $4^1/_2$ percent?[8]

Kennedy and the other Manitoba men wanted four percent. Obviously, this would lessen the Manitoba's long-term interest payments, the burden that had crushed so many railroads. But there was another, less tangible, more subtle factor. They wanted the Manitoba to enter the select circle of top lines paying only 4 percent. Schiff disagreed: $4^1/2$ percent it must be, or the price would have to be too low to yield sufficient cash for construction.

Kennedy and James agreed—though reluctantly—while meeting Schiff in early October. They recognized the force of his argument. Good relations with Kuhn, Loeb were vital, moreover, if only to finance a possible drive from Montana to Puget Sound. Hill, in fact, recently had sent Major Rogers to reconnoitre and map a likely route (Kennedy treated the resulting report with great secrecy). As Kennedy put it to Hill, "People all seem to be waking up to the idea that sooner or later we will become a transcontinental line." If the current deal went well, Kennedy speculated that Schiff might be more accommodating about a 4 percent rate in the future.[9]

Even as the negotiations proceeded, there was the nagging question of what to do about the Boston investors clustered loosely around Lee, Higginson & Co. The Burlington line they already controlled; for the Manitoba they had high hopes. They may well have construed their investment in it only the year before as constituting a moral claim to its future security business, and thus a lever to advance themselves in the American financial hierarchy.

Now Kennedy was by-passing them and their banking house, which he felt was incapable of raising large sums. "The most I can do for Lee, Higginson & Co. when our negotiation [with Kuhn, Loeb] is completed," he maintained to Hill, "is to ask the parties to offer them an interest in the syndicate. They are not the kind of people we can negotiate with, neither have they the connections in Europe that are necessary to enable us to accomplish our purposes. Of course you understand that as well as I do." Lee, Higginson did not, in fact, protest or complain about the transaction with Kuhn, Loeb. Not only were the Bostonians participating (as subordinates, to be sure) in the syndicate then being formed, but they may also have realized that they simply lacked the capacity to manage it. That was up to Kuhn, Loeb, which demonstrated what "the connections in Europe" could signify by bringing in the London Rothschilds and the Deutsche Bank of Berlin as participants.[10]

The deal was formally signed by all parties on 15 October 1886. The syndicate managers included Kuhn, Loeb, with half the bonds; and both Brown Brothers & Co., and J. Kennedy Tod & Co., each with a quarter. All three banking firms had associated participants in this transaction, each of whom was allotted a share of the total bonds. Those associated included Kennedy's long-time friends, Robert Lenox Kennedy and John Jacob Astor.

Jacob Schiff, the German Jewish immigrant who never lost his accent, and John Stewart Kennedy, the Scots immigrant who never lost his brogue, had joined forces in a very substantial transaction, the beginning of a long-term relationship between the Manitoba and Kuhn, Loeb. The amount stipulated on the 15th was $4 million at 4^1/$_2$ percent interest, with Kuhn, Loeb receiving an option to float an additional $2 million in bonds, should the Manitoba so desire.

Kennedy—backed by James—had wanted much larger sums, no less than "$6 million *firm*," with an option for an additional $2 million or even $3 million. And those amounts indeed were reached by the 19th, only four days later, when the bond issue was raised sharply, to $5.4 million, with a $2.7 million option. This was of course well above the amounts that Hill, only months before, had presented as necessary and sufficient. But Kennedy, with his well-grounded skepticism regarding Hill's assessments, and his contention that a bigger loan at a reasonable 4^1/$_2$ percent was far wiser than constant scrambling after smaller sums, had prevailed.

With the money in hand, Hill readily accepted the new conditions with good grace: he had, after all, gotten what he needed to drive westward. But he continued his rearguard opposition to the option to which Kennedy and Schiff had agreed, and which would give Kuhn, Loeb priority in all future securities that the Manitoba might sell. This was a long-standing practice in railroad financing, justified in the bankers' eyes by their need to "make a market." That in turn involved, not only organizing a network of banking houses to retail the bonds, but also spending effort and money in recruiting likely bond buyers, thus entailing costs which could be recouped only through future bond sales.[11]

Hill objected nevertheless. The option clause, he contended, damaged the Manitoba's position by granting Kuhn, Loeb the right of first refusal, of discretion in purchasing subsequent Manitoba bond issues. And rejection by Kuhn, Loeb would make it very difficult to gain acceptance elsewhere, for other bankers might be reluctant to buy what Kuhn, Loeb had rejected. Kennedy's counter-argument was that the syndicate would not only tap the European market, but was willing to pay more than the market price for the bonds, and would be more receptive than other bankers to a future issue.[12]

Kennedy remained anxious, in fact, lest still more money would be needed. In writing to Hill on 20 October , he contended that they would have "but $7,400,000 in cash," assuming that the option to sell more bonds was exercised—and it was not. There followed a blunt warning: "You [Hill] will need at least $4,000,000 more, and we must consider and that very soon where it is to come from, for we cannot afford to contract for the work, go on with the expenditures and trust to luck to get the money to meet them."[13] Hill responded equally bluntly on the 22nd. He was opposed to exercising the option to sell more bonds, and pointed out that Kennedy—and Thorne as well—had, having both agreed to the drive into Montana, no cause to raise objections.[14]

But this bickering died down by mid-November 1886, as the bond sale benefited from the Manitoba's high appeal and from the buoyancy of the New York Stock Exchange (whose first million-share day came on 15 December) to achieve a huge success. So great was the demand, Kennedy wrote Hill, that would-be bond purchasers were granted only *half* their requests. The bonds were heavily over-subscribed even in Berlin. Clearly, Kennedy and the other Manitoba men had been right—and Kuhn, Loeb wrong—in predicting that a 4 or a $4^1/_2$ percent interest rate might have sufficed, without depressing the price unduly. The public's response was such that Kennedy gloated: "It will place our credit so high that next time we need not hesitate to float a 4% bond."[15]

At the level of sales, the Manitoba clearly had triumphed. But it could have raised substantially more cash than it actually did from all those would-be investors who found no Manitoba bonds available. Their cash had slipped through the Manitoba's fingers: in deference to Hill's objections, the loan had been kept too small to provide for the substantial construction that lay ahead. The Manitoba was soon to pay a stiff price for this error.

The first hint of trouble came in February 1887. The capital market suddenly lost its optimism, turning cautious, even as Kennedy succeeded in convincing Kuhn, Loeb and the other syndicate managers to exercise their option by taking another $2 million in bonds. He soon realized that they might have to go to fully five percent, but Hill balked, urging Kennedy and the others to wait for better market conditions. To make matters worse, Kennedy feared that Hill had underestimated construction costs for the coming year by more than $1 million. Kennedy was repeating his familiar refrain: it was vital to avoid an eleventh hour scramble for cash.[16]

Yet exactly that happened in April 1887. The growing gap between *estimated* and *actual* costs then forced Kennedy to turn to his old friends and associates to borrow short-term. Though the financial market, providentially, again had turned buoyant, this borrowing was precisely what he had hoped to avoid by working with Kuhn, Loeb.[17]

The continuing financial problem turned personal that summer, with Kennedy acting as peacemaker between those two forceful personalities, Hill and Schiff. In July, with the Manitoba's construction push well underway, Hill had reversed his earlier opposition to borrowing, and now favored having Kuhn, Loeb float a $3,000,000 issue at $4^1/_2$ percent. Kennedy agreed, no doubt muttering "I told you so," for he, James and Thorne doubted that the Manitoba could secure terms as good as those of February. But Hill had objections regarding the terms, including the price of the bonds, the question of options, and a more prominent position for Lee, Higginson & Co., whose good favor Hill thought it was important to retain. These issues brought on strong words with Schiff and John Crosby Brown, a friend of James and a senior partner at Brown Brothers & Co. Kennedy, being anxious lest Schiff and Brown reject the Manitoba, intervened to mollify Schiff. Ironically enough, Hill's objections—which blocked any deal—ultimately *benefited* the bankers. For, as they later told Kennedy, they would have had considerable difficulty in selling the bonds in what had become a worsening market.[18]

All these negotiations involved an unusual amount of carping and highly personal criticism, perhaps due to the realization that the Manitoba's financing problems would have been solved *if* Kennedy's advice of October 1886 regarding a big bond sale had been followed. Instead, there were major difficulties, which seemed to bring out the worst in everyone, briefly threatening the remarkable harmony and cohesion that had contributed to the Manitoba's success.

Not only was Hill being difficult with Brown and the prestigious and powerful Jacob Schiff, but Hill responded peevishly to Kennedy's suggestions that they wait for a change in the market by announcing that his opinion was as good as Kennedy's on such matters. And Stephen and Smith, who still held significant blocks of Manitoba stock, allowed that they agreed with Hill. So, predictably, did Minot, who blamed Kennedy for the Manitoba's troubles, which he incorrectly compared unfavorably to a bond sale recently achieved by the Burlington.

Kennedy nevertheless stood firm in proposing to Hill that they wait for the market to rebound before floating further bonds. There was annoyance in Kennedy's letter in July: "I am personally unwilling to sell more of our bonds now at any such price as has been indicated we could get for them, for I am compelled to believe that three or six months hence should the market improve I would probably be *again submitted to a similar course of treatment.*" [italics added][19]

Talks nevertheless continued that July between Kennedy and Schiff, who agreed in principle to buy several million dollars of Manitoba $4^1/_2$ percent consolidated bonds. Serious negotiations would begin once the Manitoba men fixed their lowest acceptable price. Schiff revived the syndicate with

Brown Brothers & Co. and J. Kennedy Tod & Co., but rejected the idea—emanating from Hill—that Lee, Higginson be included as an equal. Hill was again trying to assist the Bostonians, whose financial resources he respected. Schiff, no doubt feeling that Lee, Higginson could contribute little to sales, would have none of it: the Boston firm could be a mere syndicate participant, but nothing more. Should the Manitoba reject his proposal, Schiff warned, it could take its business to the Bostonians.[20]

After intense negotiations, Kennedy, Schiff and the others reached agreement in early September 1887 on a $2 million bond issue, with the syndicate receiving an option for future sales. Kennedy thought it an "excellent sale." He informed Hill on 1 September that "It is to the same people as before and is the best that can be done." But he warned Hill that, "If this sale is not confirmed, I must decline to undertake the conduct of the finances of the Manitoba any longer." Hill had little choice but to go along, and he did—seconded by Thorne.[21]

The troubled nature of the financing was emphasized yet again in late September, when Hill announced that the cost of the filling and grading required for the Montana Central earthwork had been underestimated: he needed a full million more. This, despite the large amounts raised by the September bond sale, and the cutbacks then being imposed on purchasing. A million was of course no impossible sum to raise with short-term loans, as Kennedy had shown many times over. Nevertheless, he may well have been thankful that so arduous a construction season was closing.[22]

Kennedy did in fact intervene during this September crisis to persuade the Rogers Locomotive Works and the Lackawanna Iron & Coal Co. to accept the Manitoba's notes. His financial connections were of the best: he informed Hill that, "I can always count on getting $300,000-$400,000 more out of the [Manhattan] Bank and [Central] Trust Company for such time as we may need it."[23] Connections also played a part that month when Kennedy approached an acquaintance, Samuel Sloan, the president of the Delaware, Lackawanna & Western, to secure the dock facilities in Buffalo that Hill would need for the Great Lakes fleet he was building to transport iron ore, wheat and various grains from Duluth.[24]

Kennedy surveyed the previous months during a rueful letter to Hill in November 1887. "It is impossible that we can go on as we have been doing, trusting to luck, and we are sure that you yourself would never consent to do so if you knew the dangers we encountered last autumn, and the narrow escape we had from a condition of affairs which, had they occurred, as was for some time anticipated, would have made it absolutely impossible for us either to have sold our bonds or borrowed the money to have tided us through." This, and other admonitions to borrow in good time, did little good: Hill continued to take risks, and Kennedy continued to complain. Nevertheless, they had been through a great deal together, and remained friends, as well as mere associates. Hill was by temperament a great builder and risk-taker; he brought to Kennedy's life the daring and dynamic imagination which the latter could not find in himself.[25]

The winter of 1886-87 saw both men girding, like soldiers for battle, for the summer construction season that lay ahead. There was the purchasing and assembling of materials to consider. "I would accumulate rails, fastenings, ties, bridge timbers etc. during the winter," Kennedy exhorted Hill in October 1886, "and be ready to strike vigorously," when spring arrived.[26] Kennedy reminded Hill that other lines already were buying; spot shortages might develop, raising prices and causing delays in delivery. Hill and Alan Manvel, Minot's replacement as second-in-command in St. Paul, were overburdened; even the twelve-hour or more days that Hill worked—and which he expected from his subordinates—did not suffice. So Hill accepted Kennedy's offer to assist in purchasing. Kennedy drew on his wide experience, constantly suggesting that orders be divided to prevent over-dependency on individual manufacturers—on whose reliability he commented. That Hill understood all this full well didn't inhibit Kennedy's advice.[27]

The key issue, as always, was rails. Work crews could be driven harder, some materials could be improvised, locomotives occasionally could be leased from other lines, but rails were absolutely indispensable. And everyone was buying: buoyed by good economic conditions after the short-lived crisis of 1884, the '80s witnessed an unprecedented railroad expansion.

Yet the iron and steel industry was volatile and still remained archaic, a grab bag of plants, large and small, modern and outmoded, integrated and non-integrated, and costs therefore varied enormously, being—aside from Carnegie's operations—invariably higher than those in Britain. Despite the high tariff (which Kennedy, predictably, opposed), British rails were well worth importing, and largely determined the price. So Kennedy was among those buyers who scouted the foreign as well as the domestic market.

Although the Manitoba had enlarged and systematized its purchasing organization for the great westward drive—over 90,000 tons of rails were bought in some years—there still was a role to be played in small buys by Kennedy, as an experienced former commission merchant with easy access to information and capital. He was, for example, well acquainted with Carnegie, a fellow Scots immigrant whose selling agent Kennedy had been in the late 1870s. Should the Manitoba reject—for price reasons—his offers of rails, Kennedy felt quite free to join a booming, speculative market.[28]

In late September 1885, for example, Kennedy had telegraphed Hill: "Can you use two or three thousand tons of rails to be furnished by the Lackawanna Co.?" Kennedy enlisted Thorne to help convince Hill that a good deal lay ahead. If, however, Hill rejected the proposal, Kennedy intended to speculate elsewhere with the rails for himself and Thorne. But Hill agreed, and in a broad way, authorizing Kennedy to buy no less than 5,000 tons for spring delivery.[29]

In still another transaction, Kennedy notified Hill during February 1886 that "I closed with the Lackawanna Co. for another 5,000 tons of rails in my own name as I was doubtful whether they would sell any more on the same terms as the 10,000 and I made a personal matter of it with Clarke who is under some obligation to me." It appears that some gentlemanly pressure had paid off. That month he telegraphed Hill, "Have closed with Lackawanna Co. but prices strictly confidential. Will have to get 5,000 tons somewhere else."—and that he did.[30] Kennedy also had the expertise to deal in the foreign market, primarily British, but also German, where Krupp steel rails were costly, yet of high quality. He and Hill agreed to secretly buy some Krupp rails, and Kennedy volunteered to negotiate the purchase.[31] Kennedy bought several thousand tons more from the Lackawanna Iron & Coal and from the Troy Iron & Steel Company before the construction season ended that fall.[32]

Fellow Manitoba directors with outside business interests occasionally created difficulties for Kennedy. There was, for example, some tension regarding Thorne, who was for long a director of the Pennsylvania Coal Company, one of the anthracite pioneers, and had various related interests. "I desire to say to you *very privately*" [original underlined], Kennedy confided to Hill in August 1886, "that you must not let your steel purchases be known to Thorne . . . . He is interested in the Lackawanna Iron & Coal Co. at Scranton and does all he can for them, which is all right, but he told them of our probable wants when I was in correspondence with you regarding the 9,000 purchased in July and before I had received your definite instructions, magnified the quantity to 12 c[irca] 15 ,000 tons and when I approached the Lackawanna Iron & Coal Co., . . . to make the purchases I was much embarrassed and placed at a disadvantage by his indiscretion." Here again are hints of what a later generation would call conflict of interest.[33]

A month later, Kennedy's search for steel rails took him into the international market. Working through James, he bought 15,000 tons from the Barrow Company of Barrow-in-Furness, in Lancashire. This brought to fully 40,000 tons the amount ordered in Europe; Kennedy was pleased to be involved in these transactions.[34]

These substantial buys lessened the problem, while not eliminating it. That very month, Hill projected a need for 90,000-95,000 tons of steel rails for the 1887 construction season. He and Kennedy continued to disagree regarding when and how much to buy, with Kennedy consistently urging more, and Hill showing equal consistency in dragging his feet, even after Minot informed Kennedy in November that the Manitoba would soon need no less than 120,000 tons of rails.[35]

Kennedy telegraphed Hill in January 1887 to announce a potential bargain: "Have succeeded in getting an offer of 5,000 tons rails from Lackawanna Iron Co. at $41. . . . If by any chance St. P. M. & M. will require more rails for next year's work than have already been purchased and in view of the strong and rising market here and abroad James and Kennedy strongly advise the above purchase." Hill agreed, and Kennedy closed the deal, noting that unneeded extra rails could be resold, though not without risk.[36]

Hill was hardly the only railroader to risk last-minute rail buys. As the construction season neared its end, railroads everywhere began scouring the market for still more rails. In late August, Kennedy followed Hill's suggestions, managing to buy 3,000 tons from the Troy, and 1,000 more from the Lackawanna. "I hope to be able," he advised Hill, "to squeeze 500 tons more out of the Lackawanna Company though they will not promise positively to let us have them." In early September, Manvel, Hill's principal lieutenant in St. Paul, asked Kennedy to prod the Troy: would the construction season end before the rails arrived?[37]

By late 1887, Kennedy and the Manitoba were, slowly and ruefully, coming to a parting of the ways. As always, Kennedy was anxious, virtually obsessed, with his health and any threat posed by the overwork that was the price of laboring with Hill. Hill's vaulting ambition, his constant drive for more, more and more, were wearing Kennedy out, as he essentially had admitted to Hill in an unusually frank and even poignant letter that past February. His old nemesis—exhaustion—was asserting itself. "I have been quite unwell since the end of last week," he confided,

one of my old turns. I thought I would get over it in a day or two but it hangs on to me and I fear it will take a day or two longer to shake it off. These recurring attacks admonish me to be careful, and to put myself in such shape that I can take the rest and leisure I so much need and have long since earned. I know your views about yourself, that you are determined not to continue in your present position after you have attained your fiftieth year [1888; in actuality, Hill didn't leave until his seventieth year, in 1907], and I think you are right; you also know mine, and I am several years your senior, but what are we doing to accomplish our ends, are we not getting further from them instead of nearer to them all the time? Every time I get unwell as I am now these things flash over me, and in spite of myself, I think what fools we are. You and I have got all we need and a great deal more besides, then what is the use of toiling and laboring night and day to increase?

Kennedy bolstered his insights with some pointed financial facts. "I gave up business [J. S. Kennedy & Co.] more than three years ago in order to have rest and leisure, a business that had been worth to me for many years an average of $200,000-300,000 a year [$5 million in 1995 prices] and I took the vice presidency of the Manitoba Road at a salary of $10,000 a year which for one or two years was reduced to $5,000 without my knowledge or consent."[38]

Here was his valedictory, a farewell touched with a certain sadness—and also with a passing irritability over an old slight that still rankled. Clearly, Kennedy was preparing to bid farewell to a period of risk, activism and accomplishment. It may be that he had not really expected the Manitoba to become the all-consuming Goliath that it became by the late 1880s, when its inevitable drive to the Pacific would entail even more risk. Kennedy felt it was time to go, and he began raising the issue with Hill during 1887, even as James and Thorne also decided to resign as directors.

But Kennedy was no man to burn bridges or cause ill-feeling. When Hill suffered from neuralgia headaches in May 1887, Kennedy faithfully offered to come to St. Paul for a month or two to help lighten Hill's work load.[39] In yet another personal letter that October, Kennedy recapitulated—once again—the *permanent* cost in health that he had paid for his arduous labor on the Manitoba. And Kennedy could cite the stress that was troubling him that very autumn, for the second time in a year. Having fully prepared the ground, Kennedy resigned in January 1888—effective in May—as the Manitoba's vice president. He then followed his doctor's advice by taking a long trip, first to Florida and then to Europe. Kennedy dropped the other shoe in January 1889. Having sold 10,000 of his 25,000 Manitoba shares, he resigned from the board of directors.[40]

Kennedy had by no means retired, however. He remained a mortgage trustee of the Manitoba; the Milwaukee; the International & Great Northern; the Gulf, Colorado & Santa Fe; the Central Railroad of New Jersey; and the New Brunswick, which was associated with the Canadian Pacific. He helped reorganize the Central Railroad of New Jersey; serving as its receiver in 1887 was virtually a full-time position.[41]

The Manitoba—and James Hill—went on from strength to strength. In 1889, poised for the drive to the Pacific, he reached out for further financing by changing the name of the Minneapolis & St. Cloud Railway Company to the

Great Northern Railway Company, which absorbed the St. Paul, Minneapolis
& Manitoba. Having returned from Europe, Kennedy offered advice to Hill in
1890—as he was occasionally to do in later years—on floating Great Northern
bonds. But he now had become more an observer than a player.[42]

▼   ▼   ▼

In an era when so many railroads landed in receivership or were swallowed up by other lines, Kennedy's role in mobilizing capital was absolutely
essential for Hill's great building program. At times, Kennedy served as the
essential anchor, which furnishes stability, although at the cost of speed. The
settlement of western Minnesota, the Dakotas and Montana all depended on
his exertions and willingness to accept risk, as the cost, not only of doing
business, but also of life itself. Hundreds of small towns sprang up along rail
lines so that farmers with wagons could reach rail sidings and return home by
nightfall. Their produce flowed out to the great Eastern urban markets, and
to the European markets as well. City dwellers ate better for less, because this
railroad kept costs down. Similarly, Montana copper could supply the
nascent electrical age more readily. Kennedy, the immigrant whose voice
always rang of Scotland, played a vital part in taming this American frontier
and incorporating it into the international economy.

Notes

1. J. J. Hill to J. S. Kennedy, 23 January, 8 April 1886, James J. Hill Papers, James
   Jerome Hill Reference Library, St. Paul, Minnesota.

2. J. S. Kennedy to J. J. Hill, 20 March 1886; J. J. Hill to J. S. Kennedy, 3 April 1886,
   Hill Papers.

3. J. S. Kennedy to J. J. Hill, 8 April 1886; J. J. Hill to J. S. Kennedy, 10 April, 31
   May 1886, Hill Papers.

4. J. S. Kennedy to J. J. Hill, 1, 8, 12, 14 June 1886; J. J. Hill to J. S. Kennedy, 11 June
   1886, Hill Papers.

5. J. S. Kennedy to J. J. Hill, 20 July 1886; J. S. Kennedy to J. J. Hill, Private, 22 July
   1886, Hill Papers.

6. J. S. Kennedy to J. J. Hill, Private, 27 September 1886; J. S. Kennedy to J. J. Hill,
   20 October 1886, Hill Papers; Vincent Carosso, *Investment Banking in America:
   A History* (Cambridge: Harvard University Press, 1970), 36; Philip Ziegler, *The
   Sixth Great Power: A History of one of the Greatest of all Banking Families, the
   House of Barings, 1762-1929* (New York: Alfred A. Knopf, 1988), 97, 221.

7. Carosso, *Investment Banking in America*, 19.

8. J. S. Kennedy to J. J. Hill, Private, 29 September 1886, Hill Papers.

9. J. S. Kennedy to J. J. Hill, Telegram, October [early] 1886; J. J. Hill to J. S. Kennedy, 9 October 1886; J. S. Kennedy to J. J. Hill, 14 October 1886, Hill Papers.

10. J. S. Kennedy to J. J. Hill, 2 October 1886, Hill Papers.

11. J. S. Kennedy to J. J. Hill, 19 October 1886, Hill Papers.

12. Vincent P. Carosso, *The Morgans: Private International Bankers, 1854-1913* (Cambridge: Harvard University Press, 1987), 248; J. S. Kennedy to J. J. Hill, 14, 15, 16, 19 October 1886; J. J. Hill to J. S. Kennedy, 18 October 1886, Hill Papers.

13. J. S. Kennedy to J. J. Hill, 20 October 1886, Hill Papers.

14. J. J. Hill to J. S. Kennedy, Telegram coded and translated, 22 October 1886, Hill Papers.

15. J. S. Kennedy to J. J. Hill, 12, 13, 16 November 1886, Hill Papers.

16. J. S. Kennedy to J. J. Hill, 11, 16 February, 1 March 1887, Hill Papers.

17. J. S. Kennedy to J. J. Hill, , 11 April 1887, James J. Hill Correspondence, President's Office, Great Northern, Minnesota Historical Society, St. Paul, Minnesota.; J. S. Kennedy to J. J. Hill, 14, 16 April 1887, Hill Papers.

18. J. S. Kennedy to J. J. Hill, Cypher Telegram, 1 September 1887; J. J. Hill to J. S. Kennedy, 7 September 1887, Hill Papers.

19. J. S. Kennedy to J. J. Hill, 14, 16, 22 July 1887; J. J. Hill to J. S. Kennedy, 26 July 1887; H. D. Minot to J. J. Hill, Boston, 26 April 1887, Hill Papers.

20. J. S. Kennedy to J. J. Hill, 26 July 1887; J. J. Hill to J. S. Kennedy, 22 August 1887, Hill Papers.

21. J. S. Kennedy to J. J. Hill, 1 September 1887, Hill Papers.

22. J. J. Hill to J. S. Kennedy, 20 September 1887; J. S. Kennedy to J. J. Hill, 23 September, 1 October 1887, Hill Papers.

23. J. S. Kennedy to J. J. Hill, 8, 23 September 1887, Hill Papers.

24. J. S. Kennedy to J. J. Hill, 3 August, 8 September 1887, Hill Papers.

25. J. S. Kennedy to J. J. Hill, 16 November 1887, James J. Hill Correspondence, President's Office, Great Northern; J. S. Kennedy to J. J. Hill, 4 January, 21 February 1888, Hill Papers.

26. J. S. Kennedy to J. J. Hill, 2 October 1886, Hill Papers.

27. J. S. Kennedy to J. J. Hill, 23 September 1885, 20 October, 17 November 1886, Hill Papers.

28. J. S. Kennedy to J. J. Hill, Private, 22 July 1886; J. S. Kennedy to J. J. Hill, 24, 27, 29 July 1886, Hill Papers; J. S. Kennedy to J. J. Hill, 23 July 1886, J. S. Kennedy to J. J. Hill, Telegram, 24 July 1886, James J. Hill Correspondence, President's Office, Great Northern.

29. J. S. Kennedy to J. J. Hill, Telegram, 25 September 1885; J. S. Kennedy to J. J. Hill, 1, 2, 6 October 1885; J. J. Hill to J. S. Kennedy, Telegram, 25, 30 September, 1 October 1885, Hill Papers.

30. J. S. Kennedy to J. J. Hill, Telegram, 4 February 1886, James J. Hill Correspondence, President's Office, Great Northern; J. S. Kennedy to J. J. Hill, 5, 10 February 1886, Hill Papers.

31. J. S. Kennedy to J. J. Hill, 8, 14 June 1886; J. S. Kennedy to J. J. Hill, Confidential, 11 August 1886; J. J. Hill to J. S. Kennedy, 11 June 1886, Hill Papers.

32. J. S. Kennedy to J. J. Hill, Private, 22 July 1886; J. S. Kennedy to J. J. Hill, 24, 27, 29 July 1886, Hill Papers; J. S. Kennedy to J. J. Hill, 23 July 1886; J. S. Kennedy to J. J. Hill, Telegram, 24 July 1886, James J. Hill Correspondence, President's Office, Great Northern.

33. J. S. Kennedy to J. J. Hill, 11 August 1886, Hill Papers; "Samuel Thorne," *National Cyclopedia of American Biography*, 35: 274.

34. J. S. Kennedy to J. J. Hill, 22, 23 September 1886, Hill Papers.

35. J. S. Kennedy to J. J. Hill, Private, 16 October 1886; J. J. Hill to J. S. Kennedy, 28 September 1886; H. D. Minot to J. S. Kennedy, 26 November 1886, Hill Papers.

36. J. S. Kennedy to J. J. Hill, Telegram, 6 January 1887, James J. Hill Correspondence, President's Office, Great Northern; J. S. Kennedy to J. J. Hill, 8 January 1887, Hill Papers.

37. J. J. Hill to J. S. Kennedy, 24 August 1887; J. S. Kennedy to J. J. Hill, 25 August 1887; A. Manvel to J. S. Kennedy, 8 September 1887, Hill Papers.

38. J. S. Kennedy to J. J. Hill, 11 February 1887, Hill Papers.

39. J. S. Kennedy to J. J. Hill, 12 May 1887, Hill Papers.

40. J. S. Kennedy to J. J. Hill, 29 October 1887, Hill Papers.

41. J. J. Hill to J. S. Kennedy, 13 March 1888; J. S. Kennedy to J. J. Hill, 10 January 1889, Hill Papers.

42. J. S. Kennedy to J. J. Hill, 2, 9 April 1890, Hill Papers.

13 STRATEGY AND RIVALS IN THE GREAT RAILROAD WARS

FROM ITS ORIGINS IN THE 1830s, the railroad industry redefined the conventional wisdom regarding business rivalries and competition. Earlier enterprises—most notably, the great British overseas trading companies—had of course staked out territories and created monopolies which they defended with every means available. But the battling railroad entrepreneurs brought a ruthless, winner-take-all dimension to their rivalries, which Americans watched with fascination as it all unrolled before their eyes, changing their lives in the process.

The language of railroading therefore followed that of armies and war. (Many of the engineers and managers were, in fact, West Point graduates.) There were obvious military analogies in the movable camps whose work gangs, living under canvas and strict commanders, spearheaded the construction. Terms such as "thrust," "attack" and "defense" were widely used; alliances shifted constantly. Lines "advanced" across the plains, following scouts who reconnoitred the best routes to "protect" their interests by "outflanking" other lines. The absence of clear boundaries in the wide open trans-Mississippi West was reminiscent of guerrilla warfare, where defined territories were rare, raids and ambushes were common, and surprise often was the key to victory.

Hence information was carefully guarded, and Kennedy and Hill, for example, used simple codes in their telegrams: with Jay Gould controlling both Western Union and various railroads, prudence was mandatory. There was concern lest ambitious and unscrupulous office staffers exploit inside information, and some may have been open to bribery—though there can only be supposition on this score. (In later years, an argument favoring women office workers was their "inherent" loyalty to their employer.) And the use of rumors, deception, "cover stories" and "snares," tactics straight out of the intelligence realm, were familiar to Kennedy and his contemporaries.

The language of war was reflected in three strategies—construction, consolidation and/or rate-cutting—which the railroad entrepreneurs selected,

173

according to circumstances. Success required anticipation of the rival's reaction and a readiness to meet it. A defensive strategy, i.e., merely defending one's holdings, might invite trouble in an era when attack was supreme. The expansion, even the survival, of a railroad depended on risk-taking and construction, both to link it with junction points and to tap ever more distant markets. It was essential to stake out a territory and then, following the doctrine of "first in time, first in right," aggressively exclude rivals. Yet such decisions required careful judgments, for no line had the resources to expand in all directions without risking a catastrophe.

Consolidation, the merger of two or more lines, was the obvious antidote to the war of all against all that unregulated competition, with its unrestrained shifts in rates and services, could detonate. (Railroads in receivership posed an even greater threat, for they no longer paid interest on bonded debt.) Rate-cutting, be it secret or open, was a form of aggression, a not-so-subtle attempt to entice business away from one line to another. But success required sufficient operating efficiency to keep costs down, making rate cuts bearable. A closely-matched rate war could backfire and lead to mutual destruction, and Kennedy in particular usually favored avoiding battle by making concessions to the aggressor line.

▼   ▼   ▼

By 1879, when Kennedy, Hill and their associates had formed the St. Paul, Minneapolis & Manitoba, consolidation had long since swept the heavily-railroaded territory east of the Mississippi and north of the Ohio. The New York Central, for instance, had moved across Michigan to Chicago, where the Pennsylvania also arrived after swallowing lines in Maryland, Delaware and the Old Northwest. So the Manitoba men knew what the future would likely hold for them, and Kennedy in particular presented inside information to Hill regarding possible acquisitions, and warning about real or anticipated rivals.[1]

First among them were the regional adversaries: the Chicago & North Western; the Chicago, Milwaukee & St. Paul; and the Chicago, Rock Island & Pacific. But always and above all there was the Northern Pacific, which remained for years to come the Manitoba's principal competitor, even its enemy.

There was bad blood on both sides. In theory, neutrality should have prevailed: the Northern Pacific was, after all, an east-west line, while the St. Paul & Pacific moved north and south. But practice was quite different, with both lines grasping whatever opportunities arose, no matter the compass bearing.

The Northern Pacific, tied to a terminus at Duluth, had miscalculated at the outset regarding the geographical direction of the northwest economy—and ultimately suffered for the error. The Manitoba, wisely sited in the Twin Cities, always feared its powerful rival, saw evil intentions in every action from that quarter, and felt justified in unrestrained counterattacks.

In April 1878, for example, Hill complained to Kennedy that the Northern Pacific had failed to inform the Manitoba in advance when changing the rates of its interline business, i.e., freight which originated on one line and transferred to another. The insult rankled, and not merely because it gave the Manitoba no opportunity to adjust: were its leaders being treated as upstarts who could be ignored so lightly? Things changed within months, however, as Jay Cooke—still influential in the Northern Pacific—visited Kennedy to hint that a compromise was in the offing regarding interline rates and other controversies. The Associates, proving themselves as competitors, were being treated respectfully.[2]

But new tensions surfaced that summer. Horace Thompson, a prominent St. Paul businessman and a trustee of the St. Paul & Pacific's First Division, wrote frantically to Kennedy. Thompson understood that railroad trade patterns, once created, were difficult to alter. Hence he urged vigorous action to prevent the Northern Pacific from building a short line down the west bank of the Mississippi River and into Minneapolis, St. Paul's principal rival.

This put Kennedy in a delicate position. He had no intention of becoming involved in defending St. Paul's parochial interests, not least because Minneapolis was growing rapidly and could not indefinitely be denied access to a railroad. Yet he could hardly ignore the pleas of a fellow trustee who was, moreover, a man of influence in the terminus city of the line.

Kennedy's reply was unusually blunt regarding the Northern Pacific and especially Jay Cooke: "He had imbibed all the *prejudices* and *heresies* of the managers of the road and threatened the building of additional lines which were *to ruin* the St. Paul & Pacific."[italics added]. Certainly the Northern Pacific could have all to which it was entitled, Kennedy stated; witness the willingness of the St. Paul & Pacific to enter into an arbitration contract. But he implied to Thompson that he, for one, was quite willing to battle it out, toe to toe, against opponents who seemed fully prepared to build additional lines simply to wreck their competitors. "If they can stand it, I think the St. Paul & Pacific can also . . . and what the St. Paul & Pacific might lose directly it would I think make up largely in other ways through the largely increased development [i.e., settlers] of the country."

Thompson, predictably, failed to block the inevitable. With Kennedy's assent, the Manitoba chose to preempt events by itself building into

Minneapolis. The route followed the west bank of the Mississippi near where the Sauk River joins. The continual skirmishing over traffic interchange charges was resolved later that year, when Kennedy, as trustee of the First Division of the St. Paul & Pacific, signed an arbitration agreement with the Northern Pacific.[3]

But the long-term conflict persisted, and both sides braced for further confrontations as the 1879 building season approached, and the St. Paul & Pacific was reorganized into the St. Paul, Minneapolis & Manitoba. With two decades of experience behind him, Kennedy was well-placed to offer strategic advice—though he never pretended to omniscience—to associates for whom it was all too new: their testing time lay ahead. In April, he urged Stephen to . head off the Northern Pacific in Minnesota and the Dakota Territory by building quickly along the Red River ("make a vigorous demonstration" was one suggestion).[4]

The language of *realpolitik* continued in July, when he told Hill "that with such neighbors as you have in Minnesota the only successful policy will be an aggressive one, i.e., going forward firmly, occupying your own ground, and then, if necessary, negotiating afterwards." Bismarck would doubtless have approved, particularly when Kennedy quite accurately contended that the Northern Pacific—not to mention the Chicago, Milwaukee & St. Paul—were strong at pursuing "their own purposes and talking afterwards."[5] Kennedy continued warning Hill of the dangers ahead: "Where an opening exists some one will step in and fill it unless you frustrate them by occupying the available ground."[6]

Independence, Kennedy insisted, was absolutely essential: this the Manitoba had to retain, no matter how attractive a deal the Northern Pacific might offer. So he warned Hill in July 1879, one month before an agreement dividing their respective territories was signed with the rival line. Hill interpreted the treaty as granting the Manitoba a north-south orientation, while the Northern Pacific was to build from east to west.

But this agreement, meant to impose mutual restraint and thus achieve stability in unregulated and ever-changing situations, soon collapsed—as did virtually all such efforts during the anarchical railroad era. Unanticipated actions by outside lines might upset an inherently fragile set of assumptions. Or irresistible opportunities for profit might arise. Or either side might interpret matters differently, i. e., antagonistically. The railroad "treaties" were mere gentlemen's agreements, not true contracts with legal enforceability, for their attempts to regulate rates and territories violated common law strictures against restraining competition. Thus, it proved impossible to force compliance through court action, as Kennedy and his associates realized full well.

For whatever reason, the agreement rapidly fell apart, and barely six months elapsed before Kennedy was writing to Hill about the need to teach the Northern Pacific a lesson regarding the Manitoba's ability and willingness to defend itself.[7]

But the agreement apparently had an unstated corollary to the effect that J. S. Kennedy & Co. would help in the forthcoming Northern Pacific financing. This involved him in an enormous venture: joining sixteen other banking firms in 1880 to form a huge syndicate that underwrote an unprecedented $40 *million* bond issue with which the Northern Pacific fulfilled its land grant terms by driving from the Dakotas to a Pacific terminus at Portland, Oregon. This meant that, though Kennedy was helping finance a Manitoba rival, he thereby was entering the company of the most eminent American bankers. For the syndicate was co-managed by Drexel, Morgan & Co.; Winslow, Lanier & Co.; and August Belmont & Co.; and it included J. & W. Seligman & Co. and also Kuhn, Loeb & Co., among others.[8]

The struggle against the Northern Pacific resumed in 1880, with Kennedy aggressive as never before. He proposed building a line to within "twenty miles" of the Northern Pacific, or about the distance a settler could cover by wagon in a day round trip from farm to railhead. In effect, Kennedy was considering luring customers away from the Northern Pacific. And if the enemy "interfere with your legitimate business," Kennedy advised one of the Manitoba men, "you will retaliate."[9]

A subsequent letter was still harsher: "I think we are all agreed as to the conduct and course of the Northern Pacific. So long as they dared, they bullied and were unreasonable and when they had to surrender they did it with a bad grace, made as hard terms as they could, and have tried to dictate, bully and browbeat ever since." Kennedy was pressing for a showdown, writing in August to Hill that "I am quite satisfied you have got to have a fight with them, and it may as well come now as any time. They will never respect you till you give them a thorough whipping."[10]

The Northern Pacific's actions increased his alarm. In October 1880, Hill informed Kennedy that the Northern Pacific was seeking an injunction to block the Manitoba's plan to cross both the Red River and the Northern Pacific line. Such a rail intersection ordinarily was worked out quite easily. But this was hardly an ordinary situation, for it involved overlapping land grants, as both lines struggled for the wheat riches of the Red River Valley.

The conflict intensified in February 1881, as Kennedy privately warned Hill that a Canadian front for the Northern Pacific had obtained a charter to build a line from Winnipeg in Manitoba to Casselton in North Dakota. This incursion into the Red River Valley was a direct threat to the north-south orientation which the Manitoba saw as its right and purpose. Behind the construction bonds stood Winslow, Lanier & Co., a powerful house closely associated with the Northern Pacific. Kennedy urged Hill to act aggressively—"We must kill it [the line] if we can"—and to accumulate sufficient tracklaying material "so that at any time you could . . . build fifty or sixty miles of road to head off competition." But the Northern Pacific won this skirmish later that year by buying a controlling interest in the new line.[11]

A hint of peace suddenly appeared in the spring of 1881. As the Manitoba's operating mileage increased—by almost a third that year—so, inevitably, did its contacts and collisions with the Northern Pacific. Henry Villard, the representative of important German investments in the line (of which he soon became president), reacted pacifically, by meeting with Kennedy. "On the whole," Kennedy reported to Hill in June, "he impressed me very favorably." What does this cryptic statement mean? Both sides apparently were fencing, sounding out each other regarding the future, about which Kennedy was guardedly optimistic. Hill held to the key issue: "The original proposition that our lines are north and south and theirs east and west will I think be a proper basis for any adjustment."[12]

There was to be no "adjustment," for the moment. Given the iron law of railroading—"expand or be swallowed"—neither side could back down. From Montreal, George Stephen inquired of Kennedy that August regarding how Henry Villard would react to the Manitoba's continued expansion. Kennedy replied as emotionally as he had concerning Jay Cooke: "Villard has evidently had his mind poisoned against the Manitoba." This was hardly the language of conciliation.[13]

Though the Northern Pacific looked powerful, with its federal land grant, its eminent financial backing (first, Jay Cooke & Co., and then Winslow Lanier & Co., and Drexel Morgan & Co.), its 1,500 miles of track, and its Pacific outlets at Portland and Tacoma after 1883, it suffered from potentially fatal flaws which no amount of managerial skill could overcome. And these defects took their toll, causing default during the crisis year of 1873, as well as 1893. Villard was a bold, well-connected leader, but a plunger rather than a builder, and a financier rather that an operations man. His line had high costs, in part because of his impetuosity and lack of interest in the costly building and operating details which Hill, for one, long since had mastered.

Comparative costs are clarified by examining the details. The Northern Pacific traversed more mountain ranges and operated seventy percent more track in 1884 than did the Manitoba, but had fully 200 percent higher capitalization. In effect, the Northern Pacific had drawn on its excellent financial connections and its extensive land grants to incur—but also to *pay interest on*—far more bonded debt than had the prudently-managed Manitoba, whose undercapitalization complemented a cost-conscious managerial style. Was easy borrowing inducing easy spending by the Northern Pacific?

Moreover, the Manitoba/Great Northern consciously understated profits, thereby countering pressure from stockholders to increase dividends, and reinvesting these retained earnings. Furthermore, the Northern Pacific had an operating ratio ten percent *above* that of the Manitoba, yet ran fewer trains than did the Manitoba, thus raising costs. If the devil is indeed in the details, then they boded ill for the Northern Pacific.[14]

Nevertheless, it was a serious enemy, if only because of its continued access to capital. In offering advice to Hill several years later, Kennedy was cautious and prudent in urging restraint, "I am quite sure you need apprehend no trouble from parties connected with the Northern Pacific Railroad. You have occupied the ground, and it is now too late for them to do so. At the same time I think it would be well to so deal with them, if possible, so as to secure their goodwill, and not have them in a state of chronic hostility towards us."[15]

This caution found expression during 1883, when Hill and Villard signed what can only be defined as a non-aggression pact. Both sides had cogent reasons. The Manitoba was not yet ready for all-out combat. And the Northern Pacific, having spent excessively to reach the Pacific by building across hundreds of miles of empty land, was over-extended, without settlers in place to make its venture profitable. The pact lasted until the summer of 1886, when—as we have seen—the Manitoba breached it by organizing the Montana Central to attack the Northern Pacific's position in that state.[16]

▼   ▼   ▼

The Manitoba's principal adversary on its southern and southwestern flank was the Chicago, Milwaukee & St. Paul, which had emerged during the 1870s and 1880s as a strong regional line. Moving across Iowa in the 1870s, it had reached the Dakotas in 1879, and operated no less than 4,500 miles of track by 1883. Kennedy was of course alert to the possible danger from this quarter, which he understood from first-hand experience. For he, as an agent of the City of Glasgow Bank, had handled a Milwaukee bond issue during 1879 in negotiation with Alexander Mitchell, the Milwaukee's president.[17]

Kennedy's wide circle of inside sources proved itself yet again in early 1880, when David Shepard, a major railroad contractor in the Upper

Midwest, and a friend of Hill, warned Kennedy that the Milwaukee was planning to expand still further by acquiring the Hastings & Dakota Railroad. Could it not be used as a bargaining chip? So Kennedy advised Angus and Hill, but nothing was done—and the Milwaukee did indeed buy the line, later that year.[18]

Kennedy was warning the other Manitoba leaders in the spring of 1880 that a collision—restrained only by the Milwaukee's capacity to borrow—was inevitable, as the rival line threw down the gauntlet by building the Fargo & Southern Railroad into the prosperous Red River Valley. Kennedy's language mixed military metaphors with those of determination, threats, retaliation. "I am quite sure," he wrote to George Stephen in May, "that you have but to maintain a *firm and decided attitude,* such as you have already assumed, and give them [the Milwaukee] to understand that any *hostile* act on their part will immediately be met by *reprisals* on ours, and that done if you go on and *occupy the territory* rightly belonging to you I do not think that any of our rivals will be likely to give you much, if any, trouble" [italics added].[19]

The "inevitable" collision nevertheless was averted, with yet another peace treaty in May 1880, for the Manitoba tried to settle matters with the Milwaukee much as it had with the Northern Pacific. The results were similar: failure. The competition simmered away quietly during the early 1880s, neither disappearing, nor boiling over. This led to different opinions among the Manitoba leaders regarding tactics. During the financial panic of May 1884, for example, Hill proposed that the Manitoba launch a foray into contested territory by organizing a dummy corporation. Kennedy, James and Thorne united in opposing this plan, whose deviousness would quickly become visible to the railroad financial community in New York; they favored building "openly and above board." "We think that whatever we do we should do in the name of and behalf of our Company and do it openly, and in the long run such a course will be most to our credit and also we believe will be beneficial to us in every way." With their connections to a dozen or more rail lines, these men understood that reputation mattered, and that meant playing hard, but also playing fair. Hill's proposal came to naught.[20]

Every poker player knows that there are times to hold 'em, and times to fold 'em. So Kennedy recognized the need for the Manitoba to back off when its rivals acquired reinforcements. And so it was that June of 1884, as William Rockefeller, the liaison between Standard Oil and the New York financial community, entered the board of directors of the Milwaukee line, while Marshall Field, a major Chicago capitalist—and a Manitoba director as well—joined that of the Chicago, Rock Island & Pacific. Led by the ardent expansionist Ransom E. Cable, the Rock Island, whose territory flanked that of the Manitoba to the south, more than doubled its mileage during the 1880s, but abandoned its Pacific ambitions.

Kennedy informed Hill of the bad news, which signified a strengthening in cash and contacts for these rival lines. And though Field's term as a Manitoba director soon ended, thus eliminating a possible conflict of interest, nevertheless he may well have carried an insider's knowledge to his new associates; Kennedy, Hill and the other Manitoba men could not but be displeased. "Until we understand the exact meaning of all these changes," Kennedy wrote Hill, "we think and we are sure you will agree with us that we must act so prudently as not to stir up any hostile feelings on the part of these companies or any other lest they should immediately adopt retaliatory measures for which at the moment we are hardly quite prepared."[21]

Prudence and defensiveness covered one flank, while aggressiveness dominated another. So it was regarding the St. Paul & Duluth, a line whose shortness and limited resources had made it the target of the Milwaukee in 1881. But the Manitoba and the Chicago, St. Paul, Minneapolis & Omaha had intervened to block that annexation, and yet another gentlemen's agreement was reached, whereby the Milwaukee joined these two lines in each buying about a third of the St. Paul & Duluth.

By the summer of 1885, however, Kennedy, James and Thorne apparently began seeing the St. Paul & Duluth as a burden. Perhaps its returns were small; or perhaps there were more attractive investments available. In any case, that August saw them gradually begin selling their shares. Hill, the man on the spot, urged them to halt, which they did. In November, Kennedy assured Hill that, with yet another line, the Rock Island, now buying into the St. Paul & Duluth, he would sell nothing—unless of course Hill agreed. Clearly, the gentlemen's agreement of 1881 was wearing thin, and the Manitoba in fact soon renounced it, selling its holdings the very next year. The Manitoba then took the offensive, building a line between St. Paul and Duluth that brought it to the iron ore of the Mesabi Range and to the Great Lakes, while also paralleling—and thus weakening—the St. Paul & Duluth.[22]

No gentlemen's agreement could settle the rivalry between the Milwaukee and the Manitoba. Hill had tried for peace in a meeting during January 1886 with Philip Armour, the Chicago meatpacker and a Milwaukee director. But Kennedy was as skeptical as ever. "I agree with you," he wrote to Hill that month, "in the opinion that the Chicago, Milwaukee & St. Paul is going on in the old way and we must watch them closely, for before we know it they may make a dash into our territory and we will have to make a move to offset it in some way."[23]

There followed almost immediately a brief episode in which the Milwaukee floated a far-fetched scheme: that it should lease the Manitoba from Hill, Kennedy and the others, guaranteeing them very large, long-term payments in return. In effect, the Manitoba men would give up their line to become mere rentiers, enjoying wealthy lives either in leisure or in other enterprises. Such long-term leases were common enough among the Milwaukee, the Pennsylvania and other lines. But this proposal utterly ignored the temperament of the Manitoba leaders, men who, in active middle age, were experiencing the power, the prestige, the challenge, and of course the risks and dangers of the most dynamic and visible industry on earth.

This naive suggestion was further damaged by the involvement of Thomas Pearsall, the New York stock broker whom Kennedy and Hill had encountered previously—and distrusted as a speculator—as the manager of Manitoba bull pools. Kennedy understood that the leasing proposal might indeed simply be a speculative venture to benefit a Manitoba stock pool organized by Pearsall and others. Should the lease be signed, or even rumored, Manitoba stock would rise, and Pearsall and his associates would make a killing. At the very least, he might well make substantial commissions through the sales of Manitoba stock.

Kennedy also was apprehensive lest the leasing deal would enable a stronger Milwaukee to attack the Burlington line, with whose Boston stockholders the Manitoba recently had allied itself; might not the Bostonians rightly feel betrayed? "We are at least morally committed to do nothing that would be unneighborly towards them," Kennedy told Hill, to whom he gave full freedom to inform Henry Minot, the link between the Manitoba and the Burlington, what was transpiring. Of Minot, Kennedy stated, "His association with us entitles him to know all about it and as he is frank with us we must be entirely frank with him."

Always a man of the long view and the big picture, Kennedy understood full well that a lease which created a *de facto* Milwaukee/Manitoba merger would revolutionize the railroad structure west of the Mississippi, placing the Milwaukee far ahead of the pack: "Should we make a lease to the St. Paul Co. [the Milwaukee], the effect on the whole railroad situation would be terrific, the full consequences of which no one can forsee!"

As Kennedy kept Hill fully informed of events in New York, so he raised the possibility—hypothetical, to be sure—of another lease that might be more attractive. Should they, Kennedy inquired, approach the Burlington, the Chicago & North Western, or the Rock Island, all of which were more appealing than the "aggressive and self asserting" Milwaukee? He intended to discuss the idea with James and Thorne, and tacitly suggested that Hill inform Minot. Kennedy must have understood full well that Hill would absolutely reject "leasing," i.e., liquidating, the Manitoba, and that suggesting it was simply a way of clearing the air, killing the issue once and for all.[24]

And so it did: the Manitoba went on to thrive and prosper, while the Milwaukee gradually lost its expansionist drive after the 1884 panic, stagnating throughout the decade. However, it did reach Kansas City, Missouri, in 1887, and the Pacific Northwest in 1909. The Northern Pacific, encumbered by unhelpful branch lines and financial difficulties, also slid irreversibly downhill.

The Manitoba, by contrast, constantly expanded, gaining capital—thanks to Kennedy—on favorable terms, paying interest and dividends even in 1884, surging westward into North Dakota in 1885 and Montana in 1888, and soon outstripping its rivals, particularly the Northern Pacific. The Manitoba became Kennedy's enduring monument, and, by 1900 or so, one of the half dozen supersystems that controlled about two-thirds of the country's rail network.

NOTES

1. James A. Ward, "Image and Reality: The Corporate-State Metaphor," *Business History Review* 55 (Winter 1981): 494-95, 499, 504, 515; Thomas C. Cochran, *Railroad Leaders 1845-1890* (Cambridge: Harvard University Press, 1953), 128.

2. J. J. Hill to J. S. Kennedy, 11 April 1878; J. J. Hill to D. A. Smith, 12 July 1878; J. J. Hill to J. S. Kennedy & Co., 15, 18 July 1878, James J. Hill Papers, James Jerome Hill Reference Library, St. Paul, Minnesota; Agreement between Northern Pacific and St. Paul & Pacific, 1878, Jay Cooke Papers, Northern Pacific, 13, Baker Library, Harvard University.

3. H. Thompson to J. S. Kennedy, 10 July 1878; J. S. Kennedy to H. Thompson, 16 July 1878, Hill Papers.

4. J. S. Kennedy to G. Stephen, 16 April 1879, Hill Papers.

5. J. S. Kennedy & Co. to J. J. Hill, 14 July 1879, James J. Hill Correspondence, President's Office, Great Northern, Minnesota Historical Society, St. Paul, Minnesota.

6. J. S. Kennedy & Co. to J. J. Hill, 21 July, 10 September 1879, James J. Hill Correspondence, President's Office, Great Northern.

7. J. S. Kennedy & Co. to J. J. Hill, 25 July 1879, James J. Hill Correspondence, President's Office, Great Northern; Robin Winks, *Frederick Billings* (New York: Oxford University Press, 1991), 226; Dolores Greenberg, *Financiers and Railroads: A Study of Morton, Bliss & Company* (Newark: University of Delaware Press, 1980), 139; Vincent P. Carosso, *The Morgans: Private International*

Bankers, 1854-1913 (Cambridge: Harvard University Press, 1987), 249-51, 723n. 133; *Commercial & Financial Chronicle* 31 (4 December 1880): 589; Dietrich G. Buss, *Henry Villard: A Study of Transatlantic Investments and Interests, 1870-1895* (New York: Arno Press, 1978), 116.

8. J. J. Hill to J. S. Kennedy, 26 July 1879, Hill Papers; Albro Martin, *James J. Hill and the Opening of the Northwest* (New York: Oxford University Press, 1976), 224; Ralph W., Muriel E. Hidy, and Roy V. Scott with Don L. Hofsommer, *The Great Northern Railway: A History* (Boston: Harvard Business School Press, 1988), 39.

9. J. S. Kennedy & Co. to J. J. Hill, 2 January 1880; J. S. Kennedy to R. B. Angus, 12 February, 16 March 1880, James J. Hill Correspondence, President's Office, Great Northern.

10. R. B. Angus to J. S. Kennedy & Co., Telegram, 12 April 1880, Hill Papers; J. S. Kennedy to G. Stephen, 10 August 1880, James J. Hill Correspondence, President's Office, Great Northern.

11. J. J. Hill to J. S. Kennedy, 22 October 1880; J. S. Kennedy to J. J. Hill, Private, 21 February 1881; J. S. Kennedy to J. J. Hill, 23 February 1881; Heather Gilbert, *The Life of Lord Mount Stephen* (Aberdeen: Aberdeen University Press, 1976), 1: 85.

12. J. S. Kennedy to J. J. Hill, 7 June 1881; J. S. Kennedy to R. B. Angus, 8 June 1881, James J. Hill Correspondence, President's Office, Great Northern; J. J. Hill to J. S. Kennedy, 10 June 1881, Hill Papers; Cochran, *Railroad Leaders*, 165.

13. G. Stephen to J. S. Kennedy, 8 August 1881; J. S. Kennedy to G. Stephen, 12 August 1881; J. S. Kennedy to R. B. Angus, Private, 12 August 1881, James J. Hill Correspondence, President's Office, Great Northern.

14. N. S. B. Gras and Henrietta M. Larson, *Casebook in American Business History* (New York: Appleton-Century-Crofts, 1939), 409; Buss, *Henry Villard*, 29; Cochran, *Railroad Leaders*, 52.

15. J. S. Kennedy to J. J. Hill, 20 March 1886, Hill Papers.

16. J. S. Kennedy to J. J. Hill, 8 April 1886; J. J. Hill to J. S. Kennedy, Personal, 10 April 1886; H. D. Minot to J. S. Kennedy, 9 August 1886, Hill Papers; Cochran, *Railroad Leaders*, 133; Julius Grodinsky, *Transcontinental Railway Strategy, 1869-1893: A Study of Businessmen* (Philadelphia: University of Pennsylvania Press, 1962), 294.

17. Gras and Larson, *Casebook in American Business History*, 421-23; Greenberg, *Financiers and Railroads*, 165.

18. J. S. Kennedy & Co. to R. B. Angus, 29 January, 11, 12 February 1880; J. S. Kennedy to R. B. Angus, 19, 28 April 1880, James J. Hill Correspondence, President's Office, Great Northern; R. B. Angus to J. S. Kennedy, 6, 7 February 1880, Hill Papers.

19. J. S. Kennedy to G. Stephen, 10 May 1880; J. S. Kennedy & Co. to R. B. Angus, 24 May 1880, James J. Hill Correspondence, President's Office, Great Northern; J. S. Kennedy to J. J. Hill, 15 November 1883, Hill Papers.

20. Rendig Fels, *American Business Cycles 1865-1897* (Chapel Hill: University of North Company, 1950), 63; Grodinsky, *Transcontinental Railway Strategy*, 117, 389. Carolina Press, 1959), 128-30; J. S. Kennedy to J. J. Hill, Private, 29 May 1884, Hill Papers.

21. J. S. Kennedy to J. J. Hill, 6 June 1884, 18 July, 4 November 1885; J. S. Kennedy to J. J. Hill, Private, 26 August 1885, Hill Papers; Grodinsky, *Transcontinental Railway Strategy*, 295; August Derleth, *The Milwaukee Road: Its First Hundred Years* (New York: Creative Age Press, 1948), 142-43.

22. J. S. Kennedy to J. J. Hill, 14 September 1885, Hill Papers.

23. J. S. Kennedy to J. J. Hill, 18 January 1886, Hill Papers; Derleth, *Milwaukee Road*, 142-43; Harper Leech and John Charles Carroll, *Armour and His Times* (New York: Appleton-Century, 1938), 148.

24. J. S. Kennedy to J. J. Hill, Telegram, 26 January 1886; J. S. Kennedy to J. J. Hill, Confidential, 27 January 1886, Hill Papers; Frank P. Donovan, Jr., *Mileposts on the Prairie: The Story of the Minneapolis & St. Louis Railway* (New York: Simmons-Boardman Publishing

14 ENTREPRENEUR TO RENTIER

CONSOLIDATION WAS CENTRAL to railroading from the moment the Baltimore & Ohio began operating in 1830. Railroads developed near each other, which made amalgamation an obvious solution to the constant problem of too many lines competing for too few customers, or of attracting traffic from distant markets.

But consolidation presented managerial problems. Until the mid-1880s, the dictum prevailed among railroad insiders that 500 miles or so of track was the outer limit of control; beyond that, a new organization might be necessary. The well-grounded belief existed that the public—even including private bankers—preferred diversification and therefore might fear investing in a single, massive enterprise.

By the 1890s, these and various other problems had been overcome. The railroads formed part of a great wave of mergers that—in steel, oil and other high fixed cost industries—that swept the American economy during the decades around 1900. Consolidation reduced the number of lines while increasing their size: though more than a thousand existed, only about two dozen were capitalized above $100,000,000. With construction declining as railroads reached virtually every corner of the American landscape, the major systems could grow only by gobbling up lesser lines. Railroads were increasingly separated into divisions, the better to maintain control. Cost accounting had been instituted to deal effectively with management and pricing. And a bigger, more powerful and variegated financial system was successfully coping with the capital requirements of ever-larger and more complex enterprises. The panic of 1893, which brought some railroads down, further impelled consolidation. By the turn of the century, the great railroad wars were reaching a climax, with the public looking on in fascination while headlines announced victory and defeat for the magnates.

All this affected the Great Northern (as successor to the Manitoba), and its adjacent lines. During the 1893 panic, the Northern Pacific defaulted—for the second and last time—and then entered receivership until it was reorganized in 1896, when the Great Northern achieved mastery. The climax arrived in 1901. The Great Northern bought the Chicago, Burlington & Quincy, and E. H. Harriman counterattacked by launching a raid on the Northern Pacific. This precipitated a short-lived stock market panic. Hill and others eked out a narrow victory over Harriman, which they clinched by forming the Northern Securities Company, a gigantic holding company whose sheer size was designed to deter future raids.

Kennedy, as an important investor in the Great Northern, certainly benefited from these successive events. There was, not surprisingly, much mutual congratulation in the letters which he and Hill exchanged throughout the 1890s regarding their successes. Hill exulted in the Pacific expansion, dismissing those who had advised against it. Kennedy replied in kind: "I am sure all your friends and mine whom we induced to be interested in the Great Northern must be highly gratified with the results, and must commend the judgment displayed by you in the management and development of the property and . . . we can afford to take complacently the unjust criticisms which sometimes have been made." Kennedy was wise enough in 1902 to recognize that entrepreneurial skill was not the only factor involved, but also pointed to "the immigration that is going on, and the new settlements that are being made in the Western country."[1]

As of 1890, both he and Hill stood among the 4,000 or so American millionaires; both were, in fact, multi-millionaires. Kennedy's shift from entrepreneur to rentier had become conclusive. He no longer was involved full-time with business, though he continued as a director and trustee of leading financial intermediaries, while devoting himself to a broad range of philanthropies.

Yet he exhibited some ambivalence and nostalgia for the battlefield, with its risks, excitement and rewards. Consider his correspondence—now sporadic and infrequent—with Hill. Fragments of advice and offers of support were interspersed with mention of health problems. In May 1889, for instance, Hill asked for Kennedy's backing in the Great Northern's drive to the Pacific. Kennedy, then in Paris, replied enthusiastically, but also ruefully: "Have not heard from you for over six months." There also was the predictable reference to ill-health: "My judgment approves if my health permits." Kennedy bolstered Hill yet again as the depression deepened in the summer of 1893. Needing collateral to cover a loan, yet trying to avoid selling assets at a loss on a declining market, Hill turned to Kennedy, who provided $500,000 in Manitoba consolidated bonds. There is no evidence that these two men, who had been through so much together, troubled to sign a loan agreement.[2]

As has been noted previously, Kennedy adhered to the practices of private banking in organizing—or reorganizing—properties, adding value, and then selling out to achieve capital gains. Unlike Hill and other more managerially-minded railroad leaders, he was far less interested in operating profits than in capital gains.

So it is hardly surprising that 1883 saw Kennedy propose to Hill and the other insiders that they benefit from the Manitoba's increasingly valuable securities by offering their dominant holdings to the public. In other words, sell out, get out, and go on from there. As Kennedy allegedly put it to Hill, "Now, we have squeezed the lemon, let us give it to the Street." Hill, whose very life pivoted on the Manitoba, opposed adamantly, and that was that.

In 1887, Kennedy provided a variant of this gambit. His purpose remained the same—unloading profitably—and he offered a conventional vehicle to do so. The Manitoba and its subsidiaries would be bought by a hypothetical Dakota Company, which presumably would attract buyers through its component properties. In effect, Kennedy proposed to provide a new wrapper with which to repackage the existing enterprises for the market. Again, Hill's opposition killed the idea. Hill had his own notions regarding his future. With Kennedy, James and Thorne having left as directors by 1889, he felt freer to organize the Great Northern Railway; it absorbed the Manitoba in 1890.[3]

These minor disagreements did not disturb the long-term association between Kennedy and Hill. They retained contact, and participated intermittently in other railroad matters after the 1893 panic and the ensuing depression brought various lines into trouble. The Baltimore & Ohio, for example, entered receivership in 1896. In 1898, Marshall Field, Philip Armour and Jacob Schiff instituted a reorganization. They found associates among some of the most prestigious financiers of that era: Edward H. Harriman, D. Willis James, William Rockefeller, James Stillman and Samuel Thorne, plus Speyer & Co., and Kuhn, Loeb & Co. Needing a major operations consultant, they invited Hill to take command.[4]

Kennedy learned of this from the rumor mill and from the Paris edition of *The New York Herald.* His letter to Hill in October is imploring, slightly wistful. "If I had the opportunity," Kennedy wrote, "I should have liked, and would have been glad, to have joined your syndicate and would be glad to do so still, if not too late. Possibly you may have reserved an interest for me and will yet 'count me in' as Sammy Tilden used to say to me and I shall be pleased . . . to hear that you have done or can do so." Kennedy also mentioned that he knew something about the Baltimore & Ohio, through his former position as a receiver of the Jersey Central, which had had traffic arrangements with the B & O.[5]

Hill already had included his old, reliable associate in this syndicate. As an insider, Hill had bought 12,000 shares at $60, the price at which he offered to sell the stock among Kennedy, George Stephen, and three prominent New York investors: Henry Cannon, John Sterling and James Stillman. Kennedy seized the opportunity, buying fully 4,000 shares from Hill in December, plus another thousand from Speyer & Co. Shortly thereafter, a grateful Kennedy helped arrange a $400,000 loan for Hill from the United States Trust Company, with which Kennedy long had been associated.[6] A similar situation emerged in 1900, two years later, when Kennedy helped Hill and himself by buying half of the stock offered Hill by the reorganizers of the perpetually troubled Erie Railroad, which Hill had been serving since 1895 as an operating consultant.[7]

A puzzling episode during February 1898, in which Kennedy pleaded his case excessively, momentarily shadowed but did not fundamentally trouble the close relationship between the two men. At issue were Manitoba/Great Northern bonds. Who was to have the opportunity to handle them: Kennedy or Jacob Schiff of Kuhn, Loeb? Kennedy, arguing that he had funding available, offered to put up $500,000 or $1,000,000, relatively small sums that would probably not disturb Schiff, who, after all, had been the private banker of the Manitoba/Great Northern since 1886.[8]

But Kennedy went still further: "If any issue you may be making does not exceed $5,000,000 or $6,000,000 I would arrange to take the whole of them and I am sure I can give you at least as good if not a better price than you can get for them elsewhere." Kennedy even submitted a formal offer, and later claimed that it actually had preceded Schiff's. Kennedy kept pressing his case. Within ten days, he wrote to Hill that "I think I should have first chance to buy $5,000,000 or $6,000,000 of the new issue of bonds, as against Schiff, since I made my offer first."[9] Kennedy continued pushing, telegraphing Hill at length on 14 February, when he tried to bolster his case by invoking personal relations: "I desire nothing but what I consider, and I am sure you must admit it, I am fairly and reasonably entitled to, and I lay this matter before you now as all my conversations and negotiations on this subject were with you, and I feel that to you only can I look for a proper adjustment of this matter."[10]

Hill was too aware of the need for good relations with Schiff to go along. He responded with a crisp letter on the following day, the 15th: "As explained to you before you made any offer Kuhn, Loeb had promise that bonds if sold in America would be offered to them. If I had gone direct to hotel, Schiff's offer would have been ahead of yours and under circumstances I asked that you be allowed what you wanted for investment. . . . Trust there will be no misunderstanding."[11] Hill, trying to keep the peace between two touchy associates, had conceded to Kennedy "what you wanted *for investment*," i.e., the one-half million or million that Kennedy now could buy for his own private account, without paying more than did Schiff. Kennedy replied at once, requesting special consideration yet again, and hoping—a bit disingenuously—that Hill would not be "annoyed or embarrassed in any way." Tensions suddenly subsided, as Kennedy and Schiff met and, as Kennedy informed Hill, "everything has been amicably adjusted so please give yourself no further trouble regarding [the bond] matter." Nevertheless, it remains a mystery why Kennedy, ordinarily so concerned about good business behavior, should have pushed things quite so far.[12]

▼   ▼   ▼

These matters, however, were peripheral to Kennedy's principal concern in the mid-1890s, namely, the inexorable antagonism between the Great Northern and the Northern Pacific.

Both faced the problem of all the trans-Mississippi lines: vast distances, few settlers, and relatively little—though increasing—business. These lines were vulnerable to any decline in traffic, with the over-capitalized and inefficiently run Northern Pacific defaulting during the panics of 1873 and 1893. Only the Southern Pacific and—thanks to Hill's brilliant leadership—the Great Northern, avoided this fate during the 1890s depression.

Jay Cooke in the 1870s, and Henry Villard in the 1880s, both tried to make the Northern Pacific profitable. Lacking railroad experience and suitable managerial practices, both failed. The 1890s saw J. P. Morgan involve himself, primarily to protect the bondholders. The key word was "reorganization," both physical and financial. This meant, not only rationalizing the structure and bringing fresh blood into management, but also pushing capitalization down to a level where interest, and perhaps dividends, could be paid. Inevitably, the bondholders of the Northern Pacific, their reasonable expectations of predictable income now disappearing, paid the price.

Despite—or *because* of—the weakness leading to receivership, that line threatened the prosperous Great Northern. As we have seen, receivership freed a line from the obligation to pay interest, which meant it could cut rates, forcing its competitors to follow suit. This meant unpredictability, uncertainty, risk and turmoil, all the forces that threatened profitable business, and that could be eliminated only if the Northern Pacific was brought to heel—as Hill and the Canadian Pacific indeed had tried to do in 1889.

The financial panic struck in the summer of 1893, dragging the Northern Pacific into receivership that August. After the dust had settled, Jacob Schiff urged Hill—in December 1894—to consider reorganizing the line, i.e., to both satisfy the bondholder's needs and to end its recurrent threat to the Great Northern. With both lines now reaching the Pacific, all hope of compromise regarding their routes was eliminated; incessant battling seemed certain, *ad infinitum*. Hill, whose experience, reputation, connections and self-interest as head of the Great Northern made him the obvious leader of reorganization, accepted and began lining up support in the financial and railroad communities. So began what evolved into some half dozen years of pulling-and-tugging between Hill and Morgan over the destiny of the Northern Pacific.

In all this, Kennedy played an essentially marginal role. He was informed of what was happening, not by Hill, but by George Stephen (now Lord Mount Stephen), whom he saw in London during March 1895. Stephen soon wrote Hill that Kennedy—who did, after all, hold $9 million in Great Northern stock—was hurt by being kept in the dark; would it not be wiser to bring him in? This apparently happened by May, when the various parties signed a contract, the famous London Agreement.

This involved Hill, Stephen—who was well connected with British capital and with the Canadian Pacific as well—and representatives of the Northern Pacific's management, its bondholders, and its many German stockholders. There were conflicting goals: to allow the line sufficient income to operate; to prevent it from injuring the Great Northern by cutting rates; and to partially save the investments of the various bondholders by providing them with an assured principal, as well as the maximum sustainable interest. The interests of the bondholders and the viability of the Northern Pacific meant relatively little to Hill and the Great Northern, which—at last!—had gained its goal: control of the Northern Pacific's rates, and thus *de facto* control of the line itself. Kennedy volunteered in June to join Hill's Northern Pacific reorganization syndicate, to exchange new bonds—at a loss, to be sure—against the old ones of the line's bondholders.

But it was essential to test this settlement in the courts, and here Hill and his associates lost. To establish the legality of the Great Northern's control, Thomas Pearsall, a stockholder (and the speculator with whom Kennedy occasionally had crossed swords), brought suit in Minnesota on the grounds that state law banned the consolidation of competing or parallel railroads. The Circuit Court upheld the Great Northern, but the case went to the Supreme Court in Washington, which overturned this decision in March 1896, declaring the joint ownership to be invalid.[13]

Defeated by the court on the question of consolidation, a somewhat similar group of signatories immediately assembled in London to continue the battle. But how? They devised a highly ingenious legal and financial instrument, of interlocking stipulations and requirements, that brought agreement—for the moment.

The formula, as itemized in the new London Agreement of 2 April 1896, mandated subordination of the Northern Pacific to the Hill-Morgan duo. There would be a voting trust and massive stock purchases by Hill and his allies, Kennedy—with his deep pockets and capitalist friends—not least. The Agreement was clarified and amplified in August by the London Memorandum, signed by Hill, J. P. Morgan and Arthur Gwinner, a director of the Deutsche Bank, which represented the line's German stockholders. The stockholders as a whole agreed to transfer their votes to a voting trust for a five-year period, itself a formally-constituted committee which exercised full executive powers to make major policy decisions. Predictably, Morgan headed this voting trust.[14]

Hill's power was—to a degree—heightened by the $20 million in Northern Pacific stock which he, Kennedy and other associates were allotted. This constituted fully a third of the line's total stock, but hardly was a great *financial* prize for a railroad that had done so poorly for so long. But it was significant as a *power* prize, which helped the Hill group choose the board of directors, and certainly would be useful on that distant day when the voting trust would end and control would revert to the stockholders.

In these matters, Kennedy was a staunch loyalist. A third of the Northern Pacific stock was allotted to Hill, Stephen and Gwinner. Kennedy bought half of Hill's portion, and, with fully 40,000 shares in 1901, clearly ranked among the line's largest stockholders. Hill, in fact, had nominated Kennedy as one of the Northern Pacific board of directors.[15]

But Morgan and others, perceiving Kennedy as a Hill loyalist first and last, and perhaps not fully grasping his commitment to the smooth relations that inspired investor confidence, said no—and had their way. Hill returned to the charge in September 1898, however, and Morgan yielded in October, blandly covering his retreat by stating that "Kennedy would . . . be in every way a most acceptable director." Though Kennedy wanted to reduce his directorships, he deferred to Hill's wishes, and was elected to the board in July 1899.[16]

The London Agreement of 1896 eliminated some of the leading problems of the troubled Northern Pacific-Great Northern relationship. Hill had obtained sufficient power over rate-setting to prevent the Northern Pacific from hurting the Great Northern. And Morgan gained *his* priority: protection for the bondholders. But a basic tension remained. Morgan needed a *thriving*, prosperous Northern Pacific that could pay interest to its bondholders. Hill wanted control of a *declining* line that he could subordinate to his Great Northern. The London Agreement could paper over these inherent contradictions, but not resolve them.

Yet the two men had learned to work together—however grudgingly—and Morgan was willing to yield during 1900 to Hill's contention that the voting trust be dissolved. This meant that Hill and his allies had obtained complete control of the Northern Pacific.[17] Kennedy helped Hill consolidate his victory through reconstituting the board of directors after ousting Edward Adams, a financier and American agent of the Deutsche Bank. Kennedy further consented—reluctantly—to remain on the board, and accepted Hill's request in mid-1901 that he serve on the executive committee. Not until 1903, however, were they able to force out Charles Mellen, Morgan's man as the Northern Pacific president since 1897.[18]

▼   ▼   ▼

As we have seen, Kennedy still possessed the financial resources, connections and zest for battle that enabled him to play a peripheral—though meaningful—role in those moments of crisis when Hill needed him. Though Kennedy had turned seventy in 1900, and was devoting himself largely to travel (particularly in Europe) and sundry philanthropies, he still derived great satisfaction from his insider status in the railroad and financial worlds, and was more than delighted to take an occasional hand in the game.

It now pivoted on that "Napoleon of Wall Street," Edward H. Harriman. He had displayed extraordinary talent in rehabilitating the Union Pacific after 1897, but his grandiose ambitions regarding railroad acquisition made his rivals—including Jim Hill—profoundly uneasy. One reason was that the Union Pacific owned—though it lacked anyone on the board of directors—a block of Northern Pacific and Great Northern securities.

The Southern Pacific, left leaderless by the death in 1900 of Collis P. Huntington, its president, seemed next on Harriman's agenda for conquest. Kennedy confidentially reported to Hill in February 1901 that Huntington's Southern Pacific stock just had been sold to a syndicate including Harriman, Jacob Schiff, George Gould, the heir to Jay Gould's empire, and James Stillman, whose presidency of the National City Bank in New York placed him very close to the Rockefellers. This Harriman syndicate had paid $75 million. Moreover, it also had bought Southern Pacific stock from Speyer & Co.

Kennedy perceptively advised Hill "that as Harriman has now got his hands more than full it is just the right time for you and the Northern Pacific to go ahead and build the line on the north side of the Columbia River in to Portland." Here was strategic advice that von Clausewitz would have respected: the term "railroad wars" surely applies.[19]

These developments threatened Hill—and Kennedy, with his sizable holdings in both the Great Northern and the Northern Pacific. After all, where would Harriman stop? Would he be satisfied with control of the Southern Pacific and the Union Pacific? How much more would he want? Ominously enough, the Union Pacific controlled the Oregon Railway & Navigation Company, which offered Harriman an important foothold in the Pacific Northwest. Barely a year earlier, Kennedy had, in fact, transmitted to Hill the press and Wall Street rumors regarding unspecified "friction . . . between the Northern Pacific and the Oregon Railway & Navigation Company."[20]

Harriman indeed was advancing, but not exclusively in the Northwest. His interest had shifted in 1899 toward a private purchase of the Chicago, Burlington & Quincy, which enjoyed high income and a reputation for excellent management. It dominated much of the Midwest and Great Plains area on its way from Chicago to St. Paul, to St. Louis, and to Denver. Above all, a Burlington line from Alliance, Nebraska, connected to the far Northwest via Billings, Montana, offered Harriman the option of competing effectively with the Northern Pacific's Oregon Short Line.[21]

But Harriman could not—or *would* not—meet the Burlington's stiff terms, at a time when his resources and those of his allies were strained. Hill, however, was prepared to meet this high asking price. He intervened and bought the Burlington in April 1901, thus gaining access, through a friendly line, to Chicago and St. Louis. Harriman asked Hill to sell a third of the stock but was firmly rebuffed. Hill divided the Burlington stock equally between the Great Northern and the Northern Pacific. Those selling the Burlington would receive eight percent bonds. The interest rate and great size of the bond issue which the Great Northern and the Northern Pacific issued, primarily for this purchase—$220 million in four percent bonds—reflected both the Burlington's 8,000 miles of track and its impressive efficiency.

As can be imagined, Kennedy, with his major holdings in the two Hill lines, was intensely interested in this, the latest round of railroad wars that were growing in scope and financial size. He faced the customary paradox of most mergers and acquisitions. On the one hand, Hill's latest acquisition had considerable potential, but only if the earnings could be made to exceed eight percent—which, in fact, Hill was to achieve with flying colors by driving costs further down. On the other hand, difficulties were inherent in merging one important line with others, and still greater hazards obtained should Harriman counterattack, as seemed likely.

Kennedy was ill-placed to play any part in these events. He had gone, first to Jekyll Island in south Georgia during February 1901, and then to Europe on 2 April. He was entirely out of touch during Hill's actions, news of which reached him in Constantinople—belatedly—through the international press. Though he quickly contacted Hill to obtain the details, Kennedy was quite satisfied with the terms of the Burlington transaction, and informed Hill in early May that he would accept Hill's terms and share in the syndicate. "I hope," he stated to Hill, "that you had a substantial interest reserved for me."

Meanwhile, Harriman's counterattack began, following the military aphorism, "To strike fast is to strike hard." Unlike the Great Northern, where Hill, Kennedy and their allies held large blocks of stock, there was more than enough Northern Pacific stock in the open market for Harriman—*if* he moved stealthily—to buy a majority of the common stock, thus winning an influential half ownership in the Burlington.

As the price suddenly shot upward, Hill realized what was afoot, and countered with equally frenzied buying. Both men mustered their allies, with James Stillman and William Rockefeller rallying to Harriman, as did Jacob Schiff, both a director of the Great Northern and Hill's long-time banker; his defection was particularly galling. An angry race had begun, a furious, buy-at-any-price campaign that sent the Northern Pacific price soaring and left behind intense ill-feeling.

It was widely misinterpreted by the unknowing as a conventional bull action. Assuming that the stock would decline rapidly, they sold short, were badly hurt, and responded by selling other securities to cover. This led to the Northern Pacific corner on 9 May 1901, i.e., more stock had been sold than was available for sale. The New York Stock Exchange, which had experienced its very first 2,000,000 share day in early January, gyrated wildly as 3,200,000 shares were sold on the 9th, when the corner was completed: what became known as the Northern Pacific panic was in full swing.

▼   ▼   ▼

Kennedy, far off in the French Alpine spa of Aix-les-Bains, encountered J. P. Morgan, who was troubled and indeed furious at these events. Morgan's concern for the Northern Pacific's bondholders, his belief in stability and community of interest, and especially his position as the symbol of a responsible American high finance: all were being threatened, and by whom? Inevitably, Harriman's name was being bruited about. Morgan was—as Kennedy put it to Hill on 13 May—"much annoyed and disturbed by the course of events in New York during the last 8 or 10 days and I do not wonder at it. *We must stand by him to the end be the outcome what it may."*

Clearly, a grand alliance was assembling against Harriman and his cohort. Kennedy was exhilarated: "These are most exciting times but I hope all the same," he wrote Hill on the 13th, "that you will not lose control of either Northern Pacific or Great Northern. I am sorry to have been absent at such a time. I should like to have been on hand to have stood by and assisted you."[22]

The facts had become all too clear by now. Hill, who had rushed to New York and had confronted Schiff, had learned the extent of the Harriman/Schiff plan, which nearly succeeded, had its leaders not slowed their buying drive at the critical moment.

Hill, Kennedy and their associates had won, though not by much. Harriman had indeed acquired a majority of the Northern Pacific's combined voting stock, though Hill's continued control of the common stock checkmated him. Predictably, the Northern Pacific authorized redemption of the preferred as of 1 January 1902, thus nullifying Harriman's voting power.

Moreover, Hill and his allies blocked the recurrence of a threat by creating the Northern Securities Company, which was designed to hold the stock of *all* three railroads, thus requiring any raider seeking a majority to have enormous resources at his disposal. Finally, this holding company would eliminate competition. Kennedy was to be the second largest stockholder in the new company, having held no less than 96,000 shares in the Great Northern and 30,000 in the Northern Pacific. He was joined by such likely long-term investors as George Stephen and Donald Smith in exchanging their stock, and helped recruit similar investors like D. Willis James. Kennedy offered some wise advice. "I am glad," he declared to Hill in July, "that you are proceeding with the organization of the Holding Co. I think the sooner we get it into operation the better."[23]

But Hill had delayed instructing his counsel, and the actual drafting of the articles of incorporation lagged. With summer, Kennedy left New York; only in early October did he begin prodding Hill, who submitted the articles a month later. Hill became the president, with Kennedy and James as vice presidents.[24]

The Northern Securities Company never had a chance to demonstrate its business mettle. For its formation sparked a major political/judicial struggle, lasting until 1904 and making headlines everywhere, as President Theodore Roosevelt pounced on this target to launch an antitrust suit that went all the way to the Supreme Court before bringing him victory by a five to four vote. That the law could be used to regulate business practices shocked a business community for which laissez faire had been the paramount rule for many generations. The result was a landmark battle between the Progressive movement, whose suspicions of big business enjoyed widespread support, and the world of finance of which Kennedy was very much a part. As a vice president and director of the company, Kennedy, inevitably, became involved. This supremely private man testified publicly, entering an unwanted limelight for the first and last time in his life.[25]

Roosevelt, with both the law, i.e., the Sherman Antitrust Act of 1890, and much of popular opinion on his side, had a strong case. The formation of the Northern Securities Company had conclusively ended the "healthy"—or so the public saw it—competition between the Great Northern and the Northern Pacific, thus bringing under one management virtually *all* railroading from the Twin Cities, through the Dakotas and the northern Rockies, to the Pacific Ocean. To Roosevelt and others, this was a monopoly: were such immense aggregations of economic power desirable? So Roosevelt argued, from his message to Congress in December 1901, through the filing of the antitrust suit in Minnesota on 10 March 1902.

Hill reacted angrily to this attack on his brainchild by a man whom only the accident of the assassin's bullet had elevated to the presidency. Kennedy was less condemnatory. He had, after all, known the Roosevelt family— including the young Theodore—as neighbors and friends for many years. "I was surprised," Kennedy commented to Hill that month, "but not alarmed by the action taken by President Roosevelt. I have no fear as to the final outcome." Kennedy's optimism was misplaced, but not unwarranted, in light of the near-tie in the Supreme Court during 1904. Kennedy was called on to testify in the spring of 1902. Much of his eighteen pages of testimony was disingenuous, as he stated—accurately enough—that he had not been present when others devised the company. All that he revealed was a bland skill at parrying questions.[26]

Having read press accounts in October 1902 of Hill's testimony, Kennedy pointed out an omission that he felt a later witness must rectify: that Schiff, even as he had joined Harriman in raiding the Northern Pacific, had been simultaneously a Great Northern director and a close associate of Jim Hill. Kennedy may well have been concerned about the rumors then circulating of a *rapprochement* between Hill and Schiff, rumors that would certainly provide some segments of the public with new "proof" to bolster polemics against "malefactors of great wealth."[27]

We can trace the evolution of Kennedy's thinking on the case as it developed day by day, in scattered remarks. Like so many others in that period of changing and frequently ambiguous court decisions, he was often insensitive to the leading issue of the Progressive era, the relationship between government and big business. He discerned, for example, in Judge Peter Grosscup's rather mild decision against the meatpackers some hope for the future.

Writing to Hill in February 1903, Kennedy outlined a possible compromise with the government. He discounted the likelihood of an outright dissolution of the Northern Securities Company, a virtually unprecedented legal action. The government, he speculated, "might compel us to modify our organization in such a way as to eliminate any features . . . that contain the element, or the possibility, of 'restraint of trade' or 'combination' as has already been construed by the Supreme Court under the Sherman Antitrust Law." Although the federal Circuit Court of Minnesota had decided against Northern Securities, he was heartened by Judge William Lochren's decision in the parallel antitrust case filed by the State of Minnesota. "I think," he wrote Hill in August, that "he makes out a very clear case for us."[28]

During the summer of 1903, Kennedy joined D. Willis James and others close to Hill in helping select the counsel to represent Northern Securities before the Supreme Court. Their nominee (who accepted) was John G. Johnson, a prestigious Philadelphia lawyer, highly experienced before the Court in antitrust cases, but very much a man of an older generation, with minimal sympathies for the economic and political forces of the Progressive era.

By October, while waiting for the Supreme Court to digest the testimony and pleadings, Kennedy presented Hill with an assessment both relaxed and realistic. "Some eminent lawyers say it will be for us and others equally eminent say it will be against us, that shows how uncertain the law is and how necessary it is to have an authoritative interpretation from which there is no appeal. We must just wait patiently for the decision and live up to it as soon as it is announced."[29]

Roosevelt's oft-impassioned denunciations of "the lords of creation" did not extend to close personal relations. So Kennedy and his wife attended a Cabinet dinner with the President in December. "We had a pleasant time," he reported to Hill in early January 1904, "and met a good many friends. The following day I lunched alone with the President and had a frank and pleasant talk with him." Several times thereafter, Kennedy caught and sent Roosevelt some excellent Atlantic salmon, including a remarkable 34-pounder.[30]

Their relationship easily survived the Supreme Court's dissolution of the Northern Securities Company. Kennedy then wrote the President, denying press charges that the company would evade the decision. To the contrary: there would be full compliance. Roosevelt's reply offered a tribute to

Kennedy's integrity: "Such a letter as that from you naturally gives me pleasure, but, my dear sir, it was not necessary for you to tell me what you would do. I could have told it in advance."[31]

The economic effect of the Court decision of 14 March 1904 was trivial, amounting essentially to the restoration of the *status quo ante bellum.* Thus, it allowed the Northern Securities Company to either distribute the stocks to its stockholders, or to return the stocks to the Great Northern and Northern Pacific holders. Hill and Kennedy chose the former option. Harriman responded by suing, but lost in 1905. The Great Northern and Northern Pacific were restored as independent entities, with the passageway that had connected the two lines in their headquarters building in St. Paul being bricked up. Their stock was distributed on a *pro rata* basis among the shareholders of the now-defunct Northern Securities Company. In early 1904, this meant that Kennedy, who once again had retreated to the sidelines, held 78,500 shares of the Great Northern, and 103,000 in the Northern Pacific. The key question for both Kennedy and Hill remained control, not earnings. So August 1905 saw Kennedy inquiring from Hill whether he should use some available funds to either purchase shares of a proprietary road, or to equalize his holdings in the two lines by buying additional shares in the Great Northern.[32]

Notwithstanding the furor over the Northern Securities case, its dissolution had purely limited financial consequences. The economy was booming and, with Hill's hand on the tiller, so were the Burlington, Great Northern and Northern Pacific. Kennedy exulted to Hill in July 1906, "The earnings of the 3 Roads . . . show a wonderful increase. How long is this increase going to last?" Hill still consulted him occasionally, for example, as to a new mortgage instrument, in which Kennedy found features unknown to him from an earlier day. The key, he responded, was selecting a trustee, perhaps from the United States Trust Company, where Kennedy himself held important positions.[33]

▼   ▼   ▼

Kennedy entered the autumn of his life in the 1890s, as he moved into semi-retirement, left major business responsibilities behind, traveled for months at a time in North America and Europe, and focused on supporting Jim Hill, who was dueling with Morgan, Harriman and others. Kennedy was a passionately interested observer, who participated only marginally in these intense battles.

Though these struggles gave Theodore Roosevelt the opportunity to mobilize public opinion in the Northern Securities case, neither Kennedy nor his peers understood the essential problem. They had spent decades in a business world in which entrepreneurial and market forces meant a great deal, political decisions relatively little.

Now circumstances were changing. The public and Congress, increasingly fearful of great concentrations of wealth and power, were prepared to intervene: witness the Northern Securities case. Kennedy saw the specific event, but not necessarily the long-term trends. Nor did his peers: it was tempting to blame it all on Roosevelt personally and condescend to a public which could not—or *would* not—understand the transcendent economic forces at work. But a new generation of business leaders would learn to take that public seriously, and to meet its objections half way.

NOTES

1. J. S. Kennedy to J. J. Hill, 27 July 1898, 1 August 1902, 8 August 1905, Hill Papers.
2. J. S. Kennedy to J. J. Hill, Paris, 8 May 1889; J. J. Hill to J. S. Kennedy, 15 August 1893, Hill Papers.
3. J. J. Hill to Lord Mount [George] Stephen, 15 June 1904, Hill Papers.
4. Stuart Daggett, *Railroad Reorganization* (Boston: Houghton, Mifflin, 1908), 31-32; Harold U. Faulkner, *The Decline of Laissez Faire, 1897-1917* (New York: Rinehart, 1951), 192; Lloyd J. Mercer, *E. H. Harriman: Master Railroader* (Boston: Twayne, 1985), 135-36; John F. Stover, *History of the Baltimore & Ohio Railroad* (West Lafayette, Ind.: Purdue University Press, 1987), 190; J. J. Hill to Mount Stephen, 9 October 1898, Hill Papers.
5. J. S. Kennedy to J. J. Hill, Paris, 3 October 1898, Hill Papers.
6. J. S. Kennedy to J. J. Hill, 3 November, 2 December 1898; J. J. Hill to E. T. Nichols, 26 November 1898, Hill Papers.
7. Edward Harold Mott, *The Story of the Erie: Between the Ocean and the Lakes* (New York: Ticker Publishing, 1908), 515; Vincent P. Carosso, *Investment Banking in America: A History* (Cambridge: Harvard University Press, 1970), 101; Vincent P. Carosso, *The Morgans: Private International Bankers, 1854-1913* (Cambridge: Harvard University Press, 1987), 372-78; J. S. Kennedy to J. J. Hill, Confidential, 27 December 1900, Hill Papers.
8. J. S. Kennedy to J. J. Hill, 4 February 1898, Hill Papers.
9. J. S. Kennedy to J. J. Hill, 14 February 1898, Hill Papers.
10. J. S. Kennedy to J. J. Hill, Telegram, 14 February 1898, Hill Papers.
11. J. J. Hill to J. S. Kennedy, 15 February 1898, Hill Papers.
12. J. S. Kennedy to J. J. Hill, Telegram, 16, 17 February 1898; J. S. Kennedy to J. J. Hill, Telegram, 17 February 1898, Hill Papers.

13. Joseph Gilpin Pyle, *The Life of James J. Hill* (Garden City: Doubleday, Page & Co., 1917), 2: 16, 18-19; Don L. Hofsommer, "Hill's Dream Realized: The Burlington Northern's Eight-Decade Gestation," *Pacific Northwest Quarterly* 79 (October 1988): 138 citing Jacob Schiff to J. J. Hill, 28 December 1894; G. Stephen to J. J. Hill, 16 March 1895; J. S. Kennedy to J. J. Hill, 5 June 1895; J. S. Kennedy to J. J. Hill, Bar Harbor, 6 July 1895, Hill Papers.

14. Carosso, *The Morgans*, 383-85.

15. Pyle, *The Life of James J. Hill*, 2: 24-25; J. S. Kennedy to J. J. Hill, 10 February 1897, Hill Papers.

16. J. P. Morgan & Co. to J. J. Hill, 8 October 1898, Hill Papers.

17. J. S. Kennedy to J. J. Hill, 21 July 1899, Hill Papers.

18. J. S. Kennedy to J. J. Hill, 4, 22 July 1901, Hill Papers; Mira Wilkins, *The History of Foreign Investment in the United States to 1914* (Cambridge: Harvard University Press, 1989), 221.

19. J. S. Kennedy to J. J. Hill, 6 February 1901, Hill Papers.

20. J. S. Kennedy to J. J. Hill, 2 December 1898, Hill Papers.

21. Richard C. Overton, *Burlington Route: A History of the Burlington Lines* (New York: Alfred A. Knopf, 1965), chap. 14; Mercer, *E. H. Harriman*, chap. 6; Carosso, *The Morgans*, 474-77; Albro Martin, *James J. Hill and the Opening of the Northwest* (New York: Oxford University Press, 1976), chaps. 15, 16, 17; Ralph W. Hidy, Muriel E. Hidy, and Roy V. Scott with Don L. Hofsommer, *The Great Northern Railway: A History* (Boston: Harvard Business School Press, 1988), chap. 12; Maury Klein, *Union Pacific: The Rebirth, 1894-1969* (New York: Doubleday, 1989), chaps. 5 and 6.

22. J. S. Kennedy to J. J. Hill, Constantinople, 23 April 1901, J. J. Hill to Lord Mount [George] Stephen, 8 May 1901; J. S. Kennedy to J. J. Hill, Aix-les-Bains, 9 May 1901, Hill Papers; Kennedy testimony, Northern Securities Record, 1: 187; J. S. Kennedy to J. J. Hill, Aix-les-Bains, 13 May 1901; J. J. Hill to J. S. Kennedy, 16 May 1901, Hill Papers.

23. J. S. Kennedy to J. J. Hill, 22 July, 12 August 1901; D. W. James to J. J. Hill, 14 August 1901; J. J. Hill to J. S. Kennedy, 14 August 1901; List of stockholders in Northern Securities Co., and amount of stock held by them [1 January] 1904, Hill Papers.

24. J. J. Hill to J. S. Kennedy, 10 October 1901; A. Carnegie to J. J. Hill, December 1901 [n.d.], Hill Papers; Carosso, *The Morgans*, 529.

25. J. S. Kennedy to J. J. Hill, 16 September 1901, Hill Papers; W. Thomas White, "A Gilded Age Businessman in Politics: James J. Hill, the Northwest and the American Presidency, 1884-1912," *Pacific Historical Review* 57 (November 1988): 529.

26. *Northern Securities Company v United States*, Kennedy testimony, Record, 1: 180-98; J. S. Kennedy to J. J. Hill, 1 March 1902, Hill Papers.

27. J. S. Kennedy to J. J. Hill, 23 October 1902, Hill Papers.

28. J. S. Kennedy to J. J. Hill, 21 February, 5 August 1903, Hill Papers.

29. J. S. Kennedy to J. J. Hill, 13 June, 28 October 1903, Hill Papers.

30. J. S. Kennedy to J. J. Hill, 1 January 1904, Hill Papers; J. S. Kennedy to "My Dear Mr. Roosevelt," 20 June 1907, Theodore Roosevelt Papers, Library of Congress.

31. David McCullough, *Mornings on Horseback* (New York: Simon and Schuster, 1981), 19, 22, 24, 27, 141; J. S. Kennedy to T. Roosevelt, 21 March 1904; T. Roosevelt to J. S. Kennedy, 22 March 1904, Theodore Roosevelt Papers, Library of Congress.

32. J. S. Kennedy to J. J. Hill, 1 January 1904, 25 July 1904, 8 August 1905, Hill Papers.

33. J. S. Kennedy to J. J. Hill, 8 August 1905, 13 April, 5 May, 25 July 1906, 2 November 1907, 20 July 1908, Hill Papers; J. S. Kennedy to G. Washburn, 4 February, 13 December 1907, Papers of Cyrus Hamlin and George Washburn, Houghton Library, Harvard University.

15 PHILANTHROPY AND CIVIC-MINDEDNESS

As a leading railroad financier, Kennedy of necessity took a broad view and a national perspective. How could it be otherwise for a man whose interests stretched from Chicago to the Twin Cities, and on to the Pacific Northwest, with occasional tangents reaching New Jersey, Iowa and Texas?

Nevertheless, Kennedy remained very much a New Yorker, an adopted son of the largest, most exuberant and dynamic American city of his day. New York's position as the country's social, cultural and economic capital lent national significance to events there. This city of mass migration gradually outstripped its cultural and social infrastructure, even as it spawned a new elite of wealthy, self-made men, who were more attuned to philanthropy than were the inheritors of wealth.

Kennedy, a classic self-made man, became part of that elite. His migration was both lateral and vertical, first from Scotland to the United States, and then from near the bottom of society to near its top. In both cases, he succeeded remarkably in integrating himself into his new position, and gained the respect and trust of his peers.

Philanthropy was part of the process. Such longtime friends and associates of Kennedy as Robert de Forest, D. Willis James, Morris Jesup, the elder Theodore Roosevelt and much of his clan, and William E. Dodge and *his* family, all were deeply involved in various New York philanthropies. Although there were, of course, some wealthy men who kept their fortunes within their families, other American millionaires gave in different ways. Andrew Carnegie may well have been motivated by the Homestead Strike of 1894 and the ensuing public vilification, when he chose to give millions to create the Carnegie Foundation and some 3,000 libraries. The $63 million estate that Russell Sage accumulated from railroads, banking and stock speculation was turned by his widow into the Russell Sage Foundation. Philanthropy became a social imperative to which Kennedy brought a staunch Presbyterian conscience. Having benefited so richly from the Lord's largesse, Kennedy felt a strong moral obligation to bestow much of his wealth on a society whose needs were all too apparent.[1]

Though he devoted increasing time and energy to philanthropy as he entered semi-retirement in the late 1880s, Kennedy also followed his peers in traveling frequently to the wealthy enclaves of North America and Western Europe. His regular summer visits to Europe now extended into other seasons and places. On the advice of physicians, he rested and recuperated, first in Florida and then in Switzerland, for more than a year after leaving the Manitoba in 1888-89. In May 1888, Kennedy and his wife traveled to Constantinople, where an association ensued with the influential Robert College that brought him back to the city in later years. Kennedy became somewhat ill in the spring of 1904 and 1905, but not sufficiently to curtail the frequent travel—generally with friends or family—that filled his later years. So he and his party were in San Francisco in the spring of 1906, where they narrowly missed the earthquake.[2]

With travel came residences. Unlike many elite New Yorkers, Kennedy apparently never had a second home, typically a week-end or seasonal place in the nearby countryside. But his retirement at age fifty-eight in 1888 brought major changes. The emigrant from Glasgow returned to the Scots Highlands that year to enjoy his success by buying a hunting and salmon fishing estate. The seller withdrew, however, even after signing the purchase agreement, accusing Kennedy of taking unfair advantage. Kennedy brought suit to clear his name; having been sustained by the courts, he went no further.[3]

By the 1890s, he had established seasonal homes in fashionable sites far to the north and south of his home base at 6 West 57th Street and his office at 45-47 Wall Street. In 1892, he built Kenarden Lodge in Bar Harbor, Maine. This 250-foot long, forty-five room stone "cottage" was designed by his nephew, James Barnes Baker, and cost some $300,000, including furnishings and twenty acres of grounds. Baker, of the New York architectural firm of Rowe & Baker, later gained substantial recognition by designing commercial and public buildings. "Kenarden" not only had its own steam and electric plant, but an Italian garden, planned by Beatrix Jones Farrand, a pioneer landscape architect. (The house, by then no longer in the Kennedy family, survived the great fire of 1947, but was torn down in 1960.)[4]

Kennedy later joined other summer residents in helping preserve the remarkable beauty of Mount Desert island, laying the foundations for what became the Acadia National Park in 1929. They began organizing in August 1901 to buy land at risk of desecration, and Kennedy became one of the original incorporators of the Hancock County Trustees of Public Reservations, created in 1903 to hold lands for public use. These holdings were donated to the federal government in 1916. In 1907, Kennedy and others countered a railroad project with a conservation-minded plan of their own, for which he provided much of the money. And in 1908, he bought a hundred acres—transferred to a preservation trust upon his death—at the summit of what later was renamed Cadillac Mountain.[5]

With this summer retreat in hand, Kennedy became a habitue after 1898 of south Georgia's Jekyll Island Club, then well into its fame as a winter colony of the very rich. At first a renter, he bought an apartment in 1902. During the pleasantly warm months from January to late March, northern magnates enjoyed the fishing, hunting and sociability of a private and semi-tropical paradise made accessible by the railroad. This planned community offered beauty and conviviality under lavish conditions to a limited number of millionaires, often from New York, whom Kennedy had known or known *of,* for many years: George Baker, Cornelius Bliss, Robert de Forest, James Hill, Morris Jesup, Charles Lanier, J. P. Morgan, William Rockefeller, James Scrymser and Samuel Spencer. Kennedy's acceptance into the club by this inner circle of American wealth symbolized the ultimate testimonial to his upward climb.[6]

Yet Kennedy never forgot his own countrymen, the far-flung Scots diaspora, many of them members of the St. Andrew's Society of the State of New York, which he had joined upon emigrating permanently in 1857. In this charitable and burial organization he held various offices, including the presidency no fewer than six times: 1879-82 and 1884-87. His work for fellow Scots and their descendants strengthened his ties to Andrew Carnegie, who sent Kennedy copies of his books, and who joined him both in honoring various officers of the Society, and in subscribing to the cost of a statue of John Witherspoon, a Scots-born signer of the Declaration of Independence. Carnegie was just five years younger than Kennedy, who felt free to warn him in 1907 of the dangers of overwork and the need for rest as they both experienced their seventies.[7]

Kennedy's primary concern in his later years were the philanthropies needed by a booming New York. Aside from his long and generous involvement with Robert College, a conservation commitment to Bar Harbor, and various bequests in his will to distant educational institutions, he reached beyond the city only once, and even then the conduit was a relief fund established by New York's mayor. The occasion was a donation in September 1894 to the victims of a forest fire which devastated the Wisconsin/Minnesota lumbering regions—where Kennedy was involved in railroading—that centered on Hinckley, Minnesota. Fires were common enough after hot, dry summers, but this one struck on a grand and horrifying scale: 260,000 acres were lost, as were some 500 lives.[8]

It was, nevertheless, New York to which he was primarily devoted. Like his fellow Scots, Andrew Carnegie and George Stephen, he gave during his lifetime, and not merely in his will. Unlike most donors, he showed an extraordinary discretion and modesty, rejecting the norm by having virtually nothing named after him. Witness his $1 million gift to the New York Presbyterian Hospital in 1908: "I had, and still have a great reluctance to have the building or any other named after me as it might give the impression that I had it erected for the purpose of magnifying myself, which I have certainly not wished to do; the object in my mind in all such cases is simply to honor the Master by doing our duty and not have it proclaimed ostentatiously before our fellowmen." For Kennedy strongly believed in "stewardship of wealth." Wealthy men, having succeeded through God's grace, owed good works in return, and therefore should serve as stewards or trustees for the public as a whole.[9]

So he gave to institutions both financially, *and* through service on their boards of trustees. As he put it to Hill in June 1895, "I never come down town on Saturdays, as I reserve that day for my charitable and other work in the upper part of the city." In practice, this meant a major involvement with Columbia University, the New York Public Library, the New York Presbyterian Hospital, the Metropolitan Museum of Art, and the Charity Organization Society. There were lesser associations with the New-York Historical Society, and also Robert College, whose overall leadership resided in the city.[10]

▼   ▼   ▼

It is worth addressing Kennedy's involvement in the complex and protracted gestation of the New York Public Library. So large a city of course had possessed a variety of libraries for some decades: the Astor Library, for example, had opened in 1854 with a bequest from John Jacob Astor that provided impressive strength in classics, history and the humanities. There also was the Lenox Library, which had been founded in 1870 by James Lenox, and through which Kennedy entered the library realm in the 1880s: he became a trustee in 1885 and president in 1887 (following the death of Robert Lenox Kennedy, a long-standing associate, but no relative). Lenox had contributed 20,000 books to this library, including manuscripts and portraits.

The Astor, Lenox and virtually all the other "name" private libraries were essentially reference, non-circulating institutions for scholarly use, with the inevitable restrictions this entailed. These, however, were loosened by Kennedy and the other trustees at the Lenox in 1894. The prospective borrower seeking general books could always join—at a price—one of the many subscription libraries. With but a single notable exception, there was no free, circulating public library, even as visions were spreading of the book as a civilizing force for the great mass of new immigrants. Boston and Chicago had shown the way by creating public libraries, i.e., publicly financed and controlled; how would New York respond?

Matters began crystallizing in 1886, with the death of Samuel Tilden, a prominent statesman, railroad lawyer and millionaire. Tilden had been a fervent bibliophile, with some 15,000 books, a law library and railroad-related materials. His will provided some $5 million for the Tilden Trust, to create another library.

Tilden's plan ran afoul, however, of his heirs who, not content with the million he left them, contested the will and won in court—at first. An outraged public opinion, plus second thoughts by one heir, yielded a compromise during 1891-92, in which the Trust regained some $2,500,000, and Tilden's books and pamphlets. This sum, however, proved insufficient for the full-scale library that he had envisaged, but sufficed to prompt marriage proposals from various cultural leaders who sought to strengthen their own institutions by gaining Tilden's splendid dowry. And the Trust's three trustees were spurred onward by public pressures to—at last!—create a reference and circulating library on a scale worthy of the greatest city in the country.

In a situation that broadly paralleled the great railroad rivalries, Kennedy, as head of the Lenox Library and a firm believer in the benefits of reorganization and consolidation, felt impelled to take a hand. Never a traditionalistic supporter of existing institutions *per se,* he showed great practicality in favoring a consolidation that brought together the large Astor general collection, the Lenox rare books and manuscripts, and the Tilden financing.

The Tilden trustees were considering merger proposals from Columbia University, New York University, the Astor Library and the Scientific Alliance of New York. But opinion was gelling in the early 1890s for a large-scale free library *system,* with a central reference collection and neighborhood branches for circulation. So the Tilden trustees, the Astor Library, and Kennedy and his Lenox associates, all came together. The result was the 1895 agreement that created the New York Public Library—whose full title still refers to its Astor, Lenox and Tilden antecedents.

Kennedy was elected a trustee of the new library—whose first director he helped select—and also to its executive committee. In 1901, the library crowned its achievements by absorbing the twenty-one-year-old New York Free Circulating Library, acquiring the neighborhood branches that Kennedy, for one, had advocated. This new merger was facilitated by

Kennedy's connection with James Loeb, a trustee of the merged institution, and both a partner in Kuhn, Loeb, and a brother-in-law of Jacob Schiff. As so often in Kennedy's life, personal relations helped smooth decision-making.

A great library merited a building both grand and large, and Kennedy—who knew the reform mayor, William Strong—played a part during 1896 in acquiring, free, the present site at Fifth Avenue and 42nd Street. Kennedy also set an example for other trustees by making substantial library purchases even during his lifetime. In 1896, for example, he spent $150,000 for the extensive Thomas Addis Emmet collection of American Revolution manuscripts. He helped persuade Jacob Schiff to provide for the purchase of Semitic literature. In his will, Kennedy bequeathed no less than $2.5 million to the library, which honored him with a bust by Herbert Adams, just inside the main entrance.[11]

Though New York was slow to build a broad-based library system, it was a leader in presenting art to the urban populace, through the establishment in 1870 of the Metropolitan Museum of Art, which became the flagship of the museums emerging subsequently in a dozen or so major cities. The growing business elite, waxing rich in a booming America, and expanding its cultural horizons through European travel, provided the necessary funding. In this, Kennedy—who had been collecting personally since at least the 1870s—played an active role, serving as a trustee of the Metropolitan from 1889 onward, and as a member of its executive committee from 1905. He donated liberally but unobtrusively, and gave $2.5 million to the museum on his death in 1909.

By far his most popular gift occurred in 1897, with *Washington Crossing the Delaware*, painted in 1851 by Emmanuel Leutze of the Dusseldorf School. After consulting a fellow trustee who also was an art dealer, Kennedy bought this work at auction for $16,100, with the Metropolitan as its intended destination. It is perhaps no coincidence that a Scots immigrant should give his adopted country this picture, which overcame its banality to represent a guiding myth of American patriotism. Similar qualities also appeared in *Niagara Falls, from the American Side*, a huge panorama by Frederic Church, a painter for the mass audience; an admission, in fact, had been charged to view this work. Kennedy bought it at auction from the renowned Alexander Stewart collection for $7,050 in 1887, and donated it that year to Edinburgh's National Gallery. Here it was his homeland that was being granted a glimpse of the natural splendors of his adopted land.

Being a Metropolitan trustee could involve controversy. Kennedy was on the losing side of a dispute in 1891 regarding opening the museum on Sundays. As a good Presbyterian, he followed church doctrine regarding the sanctity of the sabbath. But a majority of the trustees disagreed. Another battle erupted in 1895. The "Impressionist gang," led by Kennedy's friend, de Forest, and including Kennedy himself, contended that contemporary works deserved inclusion, and that Louis (Luigi) Palma di Cesnola, the director, should be replaced. Such traditionalists as J. P. Morgan, however, visualized the Museum as a repository for past treasures, particularly those of the Renaissance and post-Renaissance. The traditionalists had a majority; di Cesnola retained power until his death in 1904.

Notwithstanding his support for the Impressionists, Kennedy's own collecting appears to have been both moderate and quite conventional. He corresponded occasionally with Hill on art matters. In October 1883, for example, he sent Hill some photographs of pictures available from a German dealer. "I am not myself going to buy any more pictures at present as I have no place to put them," Kennedy declared, "but even were I ready to do so the only ones I would care to have out of the present lot would be *The Promenade* by Bordenmuller, and *A Study of a Head* by Max and perhaps *Preparing for Church* by Luebey."—all artists who long since have been forgotten. In February 1886, Kennedy suggested to Hill, then building a substantial collection of Barbizon paintings, that he visit New York to consider a collection then up for auction.[12]

Kennedy also was involved with the New-York Historical Society, a private institution that dated to 1804, and which therefore attracted a phalanx of old-line New Yorkers among whom he made a place for himself. He became a life member in 1883, one of the executive committee during 1885-1901, and second vice president during 1889-1901. A growing collection required construction of the present building at 77th Street and Central Park West. Kennedy assisted by helping obtain a challenge grant of $300,000 from Mrs. Robert L. Stuart, the widow of a New York merchant who, like Kennedy, was part of the Scots overseas community. Kennedy bolstered the matching process with a substantial gift of his own.[13]

The public library issue showed Kennedy at his best as a consolidator, a builder of new institutions from the bits and pieces of the old. But he also was involved in relatively simple, straightforward philanthropy: witness his frequent gifts to the Presbyterian Hospital in the upper reaches of Manhattan, a tax-exempt, not-for-profit institution whose wealthy and active trustees created an excellent physical plant and facilities. Admissions were strictly nondenominational; hence the credo: "For the poor of New York without regard to race, creed, or color."

Kennedy began an association with the hospital some years after its founding in 1868. He served on its lay board of trustees from 1876 onward, and as president from 1884 until his death in 1909; in 1911, the hospital merged with the Columbia University College of Physicians and Surgeons. In 1890, he funded the Presbyterian's new nursing school, which emphasized practical, rather than educational, training. And in 1908, anticipating his will, and also celebrating his fiftieth wedding anniversary, he gave it $1 million to build both an administration building and a residence hall for nurses.[14]

Kennedy also was involved in other Presbyterian causes, most notably as a member and trustee, first of the Fifth Avenue Presbyterian Church, and then of the Madison Square Presbyterian Church, where he was closely associated with its civic-minded minister, Charles H. Parkhurst. Kennedy gave over $2,703,000 upon his death to build churches and residences for ministers. All told, his will provided fully $10 million for various Presbyterian-related institutions.[15]

Kennedy's social welfare interests extended to the secular and, predictably, to the political. Though never politically active, he was a low-tariff, anti-imperialist Democrat who opposed the war with Spain in 1898, but whose fear of Bryan's silver crusade had led him to back McKinley in 1896. "We have been saved from a revolution," he wrote Hill upon McKinley's victory. In 1897, Kennedy joined Morgan in helping fund the Indianapolis Monetary Commission, which prepared the way for the Gold Standard Act of 1900.[16]

Kennedy stood among the high-minded, good government, anti-Tammany Hall, upper class reformers who provided the indispensable moral and financial backing for the humanitarian activists of the 1890s. A sense existed that their city confronted unprecedented problems, and that something had to be done.

There were, for example, the exorbitant interest rates charged by pawnshops, the only lending institutions accessible to the poor. Led by James Speyer, of Speyer & Company, and driven onward by the 1893 crash, Kennedy, de Forest, Morgan, Schiff and others in the charitable community formed the Provident Loan Society, a semi-philanthropic pawnshop that covered its costs while maintaining a maximum interest of six percent, about half the market rate. The organizers supplied $100,000 in working capital, with Kennedy contributing generously. A trustee until his death in 1909, he also served on the executive committee during 1894-99.[17]

Vice was a more visible, more serious issue. Unlike those who advocated legalized, or at least tolerated prostitution, Kennedy took a staunchly moral line. In 1892, he joined those who supported the anti-vice crusade of Parkhurst, the Madison Square minister, in arguing that crime victimized the poor and threw their daughters into prostitution, even as a grafting police force looked aside. Parkhurst's efforts were sponsored by the Chamber of Commerce of the State of New York, to which Kennedy had belonged since

1887, becoming a vice president during 1903-1907, and again in 1909. (His fellow financiers, Dodge and Jesup, also were leading members.) In 1894, Kennedy further served on the Committee of Seventy, i.e., the Lexow Committee, which extended and substantiated Parkhurst's accusations. Kennedy and others applauded his reform efforts with a public letter of commendation in that year; Parkhurst later became the Jekyll Island Club's sole honorary member.

But graft and vice are obstinate, and the reformers returned to the charge in 1899. Police-protected prostitution and its corollary, a quasi-tolerated red light district, continued unabated, and Kennedy joined Jacob Schiff, Abram Hewitt—a philanthropist and former mayor—and others in calling a public meeting in 1900 that formed a citizen's Committee of Fifteen to combat these evils; the Chamber of Commerce also applied pressure on City Hall. So did Kennedy's personal attorney, de Forest, who led the reform-minded Charity Organization Society for many years, and who used the bully pulpit provided by its Tenement House Committee to denounce tenements as a social evil. He demanded building code changes: improved fireproofing, ventilation and sanitation. In 1901, The Committee of Fifteen, with its elite reformers who despised slumlords, also threw its weight behind change, and this culminated in the Tenement House Act of 1901 that broke new ground in New York and nationally by regulating tenement housing.[18]

Underlining Kennedy's participation lay his service as vice president in the Charity Organization Society from 1893 onward. Beyond this bland title lay goals that closely fitted his experience and outlook in eliminating waste and increasing efficiency by rationalizing and coordinating railroads and other enterprises. Could not similar techniques be applied to the charities that had proliferated in troubled cities? Here was the precursor of the Community Chest and the United Fund.

The concept of an umbrella charity organization had originated in England in 1869, and had been brought to New York in 1882 by influential public benefactors; it spread to no less than twenty-five American cities within a year. The focus was on "the deserving poor," those victimized by such circumstances as the 1893 depression, rather than by alcohol, gambling and other moral transgressions. Cooperation among the charities would rationalize solicitation, reduce administrative costs and—more importantly—opportunities for fraud if administrators were in sufficiently close proximity to routinely discuss policies and clients.

The logical solution was a building large enough to bring under one roof a broad spectrum of nominally non-sectarian but essentially upper class Protestant charities. Jewish, Catholic and immigrant organizations generally were, not so much deliberately excluded, as unconsciously ignored or over-looked. The idea for a building originated with Abram Hewitt, and de Forest prevailed upon Kennedy in 1891 to provide the total cost of $1 million for the United Charities Building, at Fourth Avenue and 22nd Street. There it remains today, still performing its original charitable function, having been well enough designed by Kennedy's architect nephew, James Barnes Baker, to gain a place during 1985 in the National Register of Historic Places.

Though we can only speculate about Kennedy's specific motivation, he was surrounded by business and family friends who were deeply involved in various charities. D. Willis James, for example, had been a trustee of the Children's Aid Society for nearly thirty years; J. Kennedy Tod, Kennedy's nephew, also was a trustee; and Adolph Frederick Schauffler, Kennedy's brother-in-law, headed the New York Mission and Tract Society. Much as he did in business, Kennedy could draw on inside information before deciding how best to deploy his capital.

Discussions began among the various participants. Kennedy outlined his plans on 8 March 1891, to de Forest, Schauffler, William A. Booth, the wealthy president of the Children's Aid Society, and to John Paton, a Scots-born banker and head of the Association for Improving the Condition of the Poor; Paton's life had touched Kennedy's in myriad ways. These two organizations, plus the Mission and Tract Society, and the Charity Organization Society, would pay no rent, each receiving a quarter share in ownership of the building; other charity agency tenants would get a twenty percent discount on comparable rents elsewhere.

As the sole benefactor, Kennedy was in a powerful position. His gifts to the Charity Organization Society continued throughout his lifetime, outstripping those of any other benefactor, but he chose neither to influence policies nor to affix his name to the building. Kennedy's dedicatory remarks in 1893 bore an ecumenical and non-sectarian spirit, a sense of "need" rather than "creed," that was unusual indeed for a city still dominated by old-line Protestants. Though Jews and Catholics doubtless were granted charity as needy individuals, their charitable organizations nevertheless were not represented in the building, and were being formed largely because they felt excluded from the larger society. In 1909, Kennedy's will provided $1.5 million to enlarge the building for the United Charities of the State of New York, the corporate entity holding the title.

From Kennedy's support of charity for the needy, it was a logical step to that for social work, whose professionalization was growing during the 1890s and after. The belief spread that benevolence was not enough, but that training and special skills were required to achieve the good of the recipient. In

November 1904, he gave $750,000 to the Charity Organization Society to help transform its existing training school into the New York School of Philanthropy, which later became Columbia University's School of Social Work. In a letter to the Society, Kennedy insisted: "This school shall give a training in the practice of that broad charity which is free of any limitation of creed or nationality." In 1905, the school recognized his generosity by establishing the Kennedy Lectureship, which he funded.[19]

It is hardly surprising that Kennedy, an heir to the Scots tradition of basic education for all, donated generously to higher education. So did many business leaders of his day, but no more than five percent gave over $100,000: Kennedy went well beyond that. Having been elected a trustee of Columbia University in 1903, he gave it a $500,000 gift during 1905—"provided I can do it without letting anybody know about it"—which Columbia chose to use for the construction of Hamilton Hall, a classroom building. Though Kennedy's name did surface in 1908, his spectacular generosity to Columbia continued, and he left it fully $2.5 million in his will, double any gift the university ever had received. And, unlike many donors, his gifts were unrestricted; Kennedy gave both money and complete freedom in using it. His will included gifts to various colleges and universities in the Northeast, plus $100,000 to the University of Glasgow. The Tuskegee and Hampton institutes also received $100,000 apiece, as Kennedy followed a pattern of Northern philanthropic grants to black colleges.[20]

Kennedy's generosity to higher education reached its zenith with a long and intimate involvement in the complex affairs of Robert College in Constantinople. Here was an American enclave in a decaying Ottoman Empire under assault, from without by the Balkan states and such great powers as chose to back them, and from within by modernization and conflicting nationalisms. And the traditional Ottoman bureaucracy, with its relative tolerance and easy-going corruption, was being superseded by an aggressively nationalist and xenophobic elite. All this boded ill for a Western college, virtually all of whose students were not only Christians, but also were drawn primarily from those Balkan nationalities whom the Turks most feared.

Robert College clearly needed political influence as well as financial support, and Kennedy, with his wealth, elite connections and propensity for travel, was well placed to serve as a patron. As we have shown, he and his wife first visited the college while traveling during 1888. There was a distant family connection: the older brother of Kennedy's brother-in-law had taught there some twenty years earlier. Kennedy fell ill while in Constantinople, and this led to contact with George Washburn, the college president.

With his belief in progress and improvement, Kennedy soon became not only a very large benefactor, but also head of the board of trustees from 1895 to his death in 1909. The Robert facilities improved greatly during his tenure. He became close to Washburn, and paid for a presidential house, Kennedy Lodge—the only occasion when his name was linked to a building. After Washburn retired in 1903, Kennedy helped pick Caleb Frank Gates as the new president.

Kennedy partially funded an academic building in 1891; housing for six professors followed a decade later. He occasionally met the operating deficit, which was over $10,000 during 1902 and 1903. In 1906, he discussed the endowment with Cleveland Dodge of Phelps, Dodge, who was on the trustees' executive committee. They also agreed to a new appointment, that of a professor of English, whose salary Kennedy was prepared to provide in hope of getting a "first class man," though normal faculty salary scales had to be respected. Not only did Kennedy give outright $100,000 in 1907, but he advanced $8,000 to settle urgent debts, and probably facilitated a collateralized loan of $12,000 from Bank of the Manhattan Company, of which he long had been a director. All this was capped by the bequest in his will of $1.5 million, which helped finance the engineering school that opened in 1912.

Kennedy also prevailed upon his friends and associates to be supportive. D. Willis James, for example, gave $25,000 in 1907, while Kennedy and de Forest encouraged Mrs. Russell Sage, the widow of the prominent railroad financier, to donate $50,000 in 1908. De Forest was a trustee for a decade around the turn of the century, while John Sloane, a long-time friend and fellow Scots immigrant, served on the board from 1896 to 1905. Kennedy had a definite method. Consider his letter to Washburn in 1907: "I am trying all the time to get people interested, but I find it very difficult to get people to take an interest in the College who have never been in the East. Whenever I hear of any people going on . . . an excursion [to Constantinople] I always beg them to go and see the College, and I hope some of these excursionists may become so interested in it that they will be led to do something for it."

Neither "the excursionists" nor Kennedy himself had the background or interest to understand the deeper causes behind the increasingly ominous situation in Constantinople, where a Turkish backlash was building against all things foreign. In April 1901, Kennedy wrote Hill that "the laws and customs here are so very peculiar. The Bosporus where I am now is one of the most beautiful places in the world, but the people and their laws are intolerable."

With Robert College under an official cloud, and with the American embassy unwilling or unable to do much for it, Kennedy invoked his long friendship with President Roosevelt. In November 1901, for example,

Kennedy forwarded a letter to the president from Washburn, who complained that the American charge d'affaires was inept in dealing with the authorities regarding difficulties faced by Americans. In 1906, Kennedy informed Washburn that J. G. Leishman, the American ambassador in Constantinople (and a former Carnegie partner), actually spent much of his time in Paris, far from the Ottoman officials. If Washburn agreed, Kennedy was willing to protest in Washington, first with Assistant Secretary of State Robert Bacon (a former Morgan partner), and then with the president, if need be. Within a year, things changed, however, as Kennedy and Washburn praised Leishman's efforts with Sultan Abdul Hamid. Kennedy also had complained about Consul General Dickinson, passing on to Washburn the kind of political tidbit that flowed easily in his circle: "I understand he is a protégé of Senator [Thomas] Platt but whose influence has long been on the wane, and I think it would not be difficult to have him recalled in spite of Platt should you think such a course desirable."[21]

By the turn of the century, Kennedy's oldest friends, men with whom he often shared both business and philanthropic interests, were falling away. James A. Roosevelt, a neighbor on West 57th Street, died in 1898. John Sloane, a fellow Scots immigrant just four years younger than Kennedy, died in 1905. Kennedy was saddened: "He was one of my oldest and best friends," he wrote to Hill. "I have been acquainted with him and his family for about fifty years and I will miss him greatly."

D. Willis James died in 1907, leaving Kennedy to express his sadness to Hill. "He was a good man, a true and loyal friend and on whom you could always rely and I know you valued his friendship as I did, and had done for well nigh fifty years. He was one of the oldest and most valued friends I had and I mourn his loss as I do that of Mr. Sloane. . . . I cannot tell you how lonely I feel when he and other friends like him are called away to join the great majority."[22]

Kennedy himself was called away on 31 October 1909, a few months shy of his eightieth birthday. Late that month, he had become ill with whooping cough, whose victims in those days were not children alone. Hill was informed, but, not realizing the end was so near, simply expressed his concern to Mrs. Kennedy: "I have heard Kennedy confined to his room. Hope he is improving. Kindly advise me." Kennedy died two days later.

His funeral brought out the New York financial community in force. The eleven financiers designated by the Chamber of Commerce as its representatives included Morgan, Schiff and Hill—though he was unable to come from St. Paul. Among the honorary pallbearers were Stephen Baker, Cleveland Dodge, John A. Stewart and still others from the Wall Street elite. Carnegie and Charles Schwab also attended, and a memorial meeting was held at Kennedy's brainchild, the United Charities Building.[23]

The will, drawn up by de Forest and signed just six months before Kennedy's death, revealed him to be one of America's richest men, with an estate of $67 million. His major holdings fully reflected his career: $23 million in the Northern Pacific, and $14 million in the Great Northern. With fully fifty-five percent of the estate in these two lines, the remaining forty-five percent was split many ways, of which $2 million in Standard Oil and $1 million in real estate comprised the largest portions. With Kennedy, Hill and a few other very large stockholders controlling the two lines, there was less need for the diversification by which prudent investors protected themselves against dangerous and unpredictable fluctuations.[24]

Kennedy's fortune compared very favorably with that of his peers. D. Willis James had left $40 million in 1907. E. H. Harriman also died in 1909, leaving about $70 million; J. P. Morgan left about $80 million (of which he had inherited some $12 million from his father in 1890) upon his death in 1913; while Hill's estate stood at $63 million when he died in 1916.

The Kennedy fortune was dispersed among many persons and institutions. His widow received $16 million, and continued his philanthropic work in a minor way, touring the Mediterranean by yacht in the spring of 1914 to visit places and institutions that had been aided by her husband. She removed from the 57th Street townhouse to a Park Avenue residence. She died in 1930 at age ninety-seven.

Another $15 million of his estate went to his American relatives. As we have seen, very large bequests—roughly half his fortune—were given to a wide range of educational and philanthropic institutions. There were modest sums for his two brothers and other relatives in Scotland. Conspicuous by their omission were Andrew and James Tod, his black sheep nephews, who were drifters with no known addresses. Two reliable and successful Tod nephews, William Stewart and Robert Elliott, joined de Forest as executors of this complex will.

Kennedy's front-page obituaries in the New York press gave much attention to his will, which they applauded for so greatly benefiting so many of the city's institutions. The *New York Times* went further, pointing out "that Kennedy made no provision for the attachment of his name to any of the works he elected to aid." The complexities of his career, the long climb upward, the difficulties and hazards along the route: these were not easily understood, and so were largely ignored.[25]

NOTES

1. *New York Times*, 15 October 1908, 3: 3; Heather Gilbert, *The Life of Lord Mount Stephen* (Aberdeen: Aberdeen University Press, 1977), 2: 162; Harold C. Livesay, *Andrew Carnegie and the Rise of Big Business* (Boston: Little, Brown and Co., 1975), 128, 188; Winifred E. Howe, *A History of the Metropolitan Museum of Art* (New York: Metropolitan Museum of Art, 1913), 2: 316; Frederick Cople Jaher, "Nineteenth-Century Elites in Boston and New York," *Journal of Social History* 6 (Fall 1972): 63-65; Merle Curti, "Anatomy of Giving in Millionaires in the Late 19th Century," *American Quarterly* 15 (Fall 1963): 416-35, *passim*.

2. J. S. Kennedy to J. J. Hill, 13 April, 5 May, 25 July 1906.

3. J. K. Tod to J. J. Hill, 20 November 1888; E. T. Nichols to J. J. Hill, 17 April 1889, Hill Papers; *New York Times*, 9 December 1888, 20: 3, 20 February 1893, 3: 5.

4. *Belfast [Maine] Republican Journal*, 15 August 1895, based on the *New York Herald*; G. W. Helfrich and Gladys O'Neil, *Lost Bar Harbor* (Camden, Maine: Down East Books, 1982), 58; *Bar Harbor [Maine] Record*, 14 April 1892, 4 August 1909; *Who Was Who in America*, 1897-1942; Henry F. and Elsie R. Withey, *Biographical Dictionary of American Architects* (Los Angeles: New Age Publishing Co., 1956); John Milnes Baker, *The Baker Family and the Edgar Family of Rahway, N.J. and New York City* (Middletown, N.Y.: Trumbull Publishing, 1972), 345; "Beatrix Jones Farrand," *Dictionary of American Biography*, Supplement 5: 221-22; Roger G. Reed to SE, 6 March 1989; "The Garden of Mr. J. P. Kennedy at Bar Harbor, Maine," *Country Life in America* 29 (November 1915): 44-45 (the initial P is incorrect); Mac Griswold and Eleanor Weller, *The Golden Age of American Gardens* (New York: Harry N. Abrams, 1991), 34.

5. George B. Dorr, *Acadia National Park: Its Origin and Background* (Bangor, Maine: Burr Printing Co., 1942), 5-7, 13; George B. Dorr, *Acadia National Park: Its Growth and Development* (Bangor, Maine: Burr Printing Co., 1948), 5-6.

6. William B. McCash to SE, 17 November 1988, 26 January, 13, 16, 23 June 1989; William Barton and June Hall McCash, *The Jekyll Island Club: Southern Haven for America's Millionaires* (Athens: University of Georgia Press, 1989), *passim*, 97, 99.

7. *New York Times*, 20 February 1893; George Austin Morrison, "John Stewart Kennedy," *New York Genealogical and Biographical Record* 41 (July 1910): 166; Morrison, *Two Hundredth Anniversary 1756-1956 of St. Andrew's Society*, 133, 135, 194; J. S. Kennedy to J. J. Hill, 8 November 1884, Hill Papers; J. S. Kennedy to A. Carnegie, 4 May 1907, Andrew Carnegie Papers, Library of Congress.

8. J. S. Kennedy to J. J. Hill, 8 September 1894, Hill Papers.

9. Eleanor Lee, *History of the School of Nursing of the Presbyterian Hospital, New York, 1892-1942* (New York: G. P. Putnam's Sons, 1942), 51-52.

10. J. S. Kennedy to J. J. Hill, 21 February 1888, 15 August 1893, 5 June 1895, James J. Hill Papers, James Jerome Hill Reference Library, St. Paul, Minn.

11. Henry Miller Lydenberg, *History of the New York Public Library* (New York: New York Public Library, 1923), 117, 120, 125, 142, 312, 322, 337, 340, 349, 367, 392-93, 442, 522; Henry Miller Lydenberg, *John Shaw Billings* (Chicago: American Library Association, 1924), 57-58, 72; *New York Times*, 9 August 1896, 20: 1, 7 November 1909, 1: 7; "Robert Lenox Kennedy," *National Cyclopedia of American Biography*, 5: 537; "Samuel J. Tilden," *Dictionary of American Biography*, 18: 541; Fielding H. Garrison, *John Shaw Billings* (New York: G. P. Putnam's Sons, 1915), 289; Patricia Albjerg Graham, *Community and Class in American Education, 1865-1918* (New York: John Wiley & Sons, 1974), 175; David C. Hammack, *Power and Society: Greater New York at the Turn of the Century* (New York: Russell Sage Foundation, 1982), 149; Phyllis Dain, *The New York Public Library: A History of the Founding and Early Years* (New York: New York Public Library, 1972), 3, 5, 11, 13, 47, 60-61, 67, 86, 116, 130-31, 133, 148, 194, 352, 373n. 40; "Herbert Adams," *Dictionary of American Biography*, 23:1-2; Robert Sink, New York Public Library, to SE, 20 March 1990; Wilberforce Eames, "The Library of Hon. Samuel J. Tilden," *Bulletin of the New York Public Library*, January 1899, 5.

12. W. G. Constable, *Art Collecting in America* (London: Thomas Nelson and Sons Ltd., 1964), 42-43, 50, 71-73, 76, 97, 105, 109, 111, 145; "John Taylor Johnston," *National Cyclopedia of American Biography*, 23:156; "John Taylor Johnston," *Dictionary of American Biography*, 10:143-44; *New York Times*, 24 March 1887, 5:4; 19 February 9:4; 1 March, 1:7; 3 March, 1:7; 5 March 1895, 8:1; 23 January 1897, 5:2 Supplement; 7 November 1909, 1:7; Oliver W. Larkin, *Art and Life in America* (New York: Rinehart & Company, 1949), 212, 242, 295, 361; Robert L. Herbert, *Barbizon Revisited* (New York: Clarke & Way, 1962), 10, 13, 75-82; Germaine Bazin, *The Museum Age* (New York: Universe Books, 1967), 249; Robert W. de Forest, "Address," *Sixtieth Founding of the Museum, Bulletin of the Metropolitan Museum of Art*, 25 (May 1930): sect. 2:4; "Joseph H. Choate," *Dictionary of American Biography*, 4:83-86; "Samuel P. Avery," *National Cyclopedia of American Biography*, 1:157; "Samuel P. Avery," *Dictionary of American Biography*, 1:445; "John Stewart Kennedy," *Bulletin of the Metropolitan Museum of Art* 4 (December 1909): 216; Howe, *A History of the Metropolitan Museum of Art*, 1:318, 2:8, 72, 232; "Luigi Palma di Cesnola," *Dictionary of American Biography*, 3:584; "Henry Gurdon Marquand," *Dictionary of American Biography*, 12:292-93; Elizabeth McFadden, *The Glitter and the Gold: A Spirited Account of the Metropolitan Museum of Art's First Director . . . Luigi Palma di*

Cesnola (New York: Dial Press, 1971), 242, 244; Karl E. Meyer, *The Art Museum: Power, Money, Ethics* (New York: William Morrow & Company, 1979), 28; Calvin Tomkins, *Merchants and Masterpieces: The Story of the Metropolitan Museum of Art* (New York: E. P. Dutton & Co., 1970), 75-76, 78, 81-82, 86, 165, 363-65; J. S. Kennedy to J. J. Hill, 30 October 1883, 10 February 1886, Hill Papers; Michael Clarke, National Gallery of Scotland, Edinburgh, to SE, 3 August 1989; J. S. Kennedy to G. Steel, National Gallery of Scotland, Edinburgh, 22 April 1887; John K. Howat, "Washington Crossing the Delaware," *Bulletin of the Metropolitan Museum of Art* 26 (March 1968): 289-99.

13. "Robert Leighton Stuart," *Dictionary of American Biography*, 18:176-77; "Robert L. Stuart," *National Cyclopedia of American Biography*, 10:24; *New York Times*, 13 July 1988; Robert Hendre Kelby, *New-York Historical Society, 1804-1904* (New York: Published for the Society, 1905), 64, 84, 90, 106, 113, 123; R. W. G. Vail, *Knickerbocker Birthday: A Sesqui-Centennial History of the New-York Historical Society, 1804-1954* (New York: New-York Historical Society, 1954), 159, 165, 477, 483.

14. David Bryson Delavan, *Early Days of the Presbyterian Hospital in the City of New York* (East Orange, N.J.: Published Privately, 1926), 107; Albert R. Lamb, *The Presbyterian Hospital and the Columbia-Presbyterian Medical Center, 1868-1943* (New York: Columbia University Press, 1955), 32, 40, 42, 44, 57-58, 61-62, 467, 469, 475-76; Albert R. Lamb, "The Story of the Founding of the Columbia University Medical Center," *American Journal of Medicine* 15 (December 1953): 755, 757; Lee, *History of the School of Nursing of the Presbyterian Hospital, New York, 1892-1942*, 10, 13, 51-52; Charles E. Rosenberg, *The Care of Strangers: The Rise of America's Hospital System* (New York: Basic Books, 1987), 109, 118, 232-33, 238, 240-41, 243, 264, 278, 337; Charles Rosenberg to SE, 3 January 1988; Paul Barth, Medical Librarian, St. Luke's Roosevelt Hospital Center, to SE, 16 June 1988; *New York Times*, 15 October 1908, 3:3.

15. *New York Times*, 6 November, 1:7; 7 November 1909, 1:7; 24 July 1930, 21:1; *New York Post*, 6 February 1909; Clifford Merrill Drury, *Presbyterian Panorama: One Hundred and Fifty Years of National Missions History* (Philadelphia: Board of Christian Education Presbyterian Church in the United States of America, 1952), 196; Charles H. Parkhurst, *A Brief History of the Madison Square Presbyterian Church* (New York: n.p., 1906), 32-33, 58, 69.

16. J. S. Kennedy to J. J. Hill, 3 September 1896, 10 March, 27 July 1898; J. S. Kennedy to J. J. Hill, Confidential, 4 November 1896, Hill Papers; James Livingston, *Origins of the Federal Reserve System: Money, Class, and Corporate Capitalism* (Ithaca: Cornell University Press, 1986), 107; W. Thomas White, "A Gilded Age Businessman in Politics: James J. Hill, the Northwest, and the American Presidency, 1884-1912," *Pacific Historical Review* 57 (November 1988),

441, 444; Margaret G. Myers, *A Financial History of the United States* (New York: Columbia University Press, 1970), 220-21.

17. Cyrus Adler, *Jacob H. Schiff* (Garden City, N.Y.: Doubleday, Doran and Co., 1928), 1:365; Gordon Atkins, *Health, Housing, and Poverty in New York City, 1865-1898* (n.p.: n.p., 1947), 142; Provident Loan Society of New York, *Twenty-Fifth Anniversary, 1894-1919* (New York: Provident Loan Society, 1919), 11; Provident Loan Society of New York, *Fifty Years of Remedial Lending, 1894-1944* (New York: n.p., 1944), 1, 3-4, 6, 8-10, 46; Peter Schwed, *God Bless Pawnbrokers* (New York: Dodd, Mead & Co., 1975), 22-35; John M. Glenn, Lilian Brandt and F. Emerson Andrews, *Russell Sage Foundation* (New York: Russell Sage Foundation, 1947), 66.

18. Joseph Bucklin Bishop, *A Chronicle of One Hundred & Fifty Years of the Chamber of Commerce of the State of New York, 1768-1918* (New York: Charles Scribner's Sons, 1918), 162, 263-64; Julia Waldron to SE, 10 May 1989; Hammack, *Power and Society*, 121, 141, 144, 147-48, 154, 283, 285, 313; Jeremy P. Felt, "Vice Reform as a Political Technique: The Committee of Fifteen in New York, 1900-1901," *New York History* 54 (1973): 28-29, 31, 39, 49, 51; James A. Scrymser, *Personal Reminiscences of James A. Scrymser* (n.p.: n.p., 1915), 110; *New York Times*, 25 March 1901, 2:3, 1 November 1909; *Harper's Weekly* 44 (15 December 1900), 1207; "William Henry Baldwin, Jr.," *Dictionary of American Biography*, 1:548-49; John Graham Brooks, *An American Citizen: The Life of William Henry Baldwin, Jr.* (Boston: Houghton Mifflin Company, 1910), 255; McCash, *The Jekyll Island Club*, 50, 72.

19. "Anson Phelps Stokes," *Dictionary of American Biography*, 18:66-67; Allen F. Davis, *Spearheads for Reform: The Social Settlements and the Progressive Movement, 1890-1914* (New York: Oxford University Press, 1967), 18-19, 25; "Daniel Willis James," *Dictionary of American Biography*, 9:573; Charles Loch Mowat, *The Charity Organization Society, 1869-1913* (London: Methuen, 1961), 110; William Rhinelander Stewart, *The Philanthropic Work of Josephine Lowell* (New York: Macmillan, 1911), 140; *The United Charities: Act of Incorporation and Amendments* (New York: United Charities, 1939); Robert W. de Forest, *The Story of the United Charities Building: Mr. John S. Kennedy's Relation to the Building and His Policies Regarding It* (New York: United Charities [1931]), 1-7; John S. Kennedy, *Address of John S. Kennedy at the Opening of the United Charities Building March 6, 1893*, 4, *passim*; Lilian Brandt, *The Charity Organization Society of the City of New York, 1882-1907* (New York: Charity Organization Society, 1907), 17, 20-21, 28, 44-45; Rachel B. Marks, "Educationin Social Work," in Harry L. Lurie, ed., *Encyclopedia of Social Work* (New York: National Association of Social Work, 1965), 277; Sally Herman Lunt, "The Professionalization of Social Work," Ed.D. diss. (Cambridge: Harvard

University, 1974), 49, 67, 121, 141-43; Hammack, *Power and Society*, 77-78, 115, 117, 151; "Robert W. de Forest," *National Cyclopedia of American Biography*, 42:16, B:61-62; "James Alexander Scrymser," *National Cyclopedia of American Biography*, 18:315; *New York Times*, 10 March, 8:1; 11 March 1891, 4:1; 1 April 1901, 7: 4; 23 November 1904, 6: 5; 7 November 1909, 1: 7; Scrymser, *Personal Reminiscences of James A. Scrymser*, 137-38; *Charity Organization Society of New York Annual Report*, 1903-1904, 22-24; 1909-1910, 24; David Baillie Morrison, ed., *Two Hundredth Anniversary 1756-1956 of the St. Andrew's Society of the State of New York* (New York: St. Andrew's Society of the State of New York, 1956), 56; Daniel M. Fox, "Editor's Introduction," in Simon Patten, *The New Basis of Civilization* (Cambridge: Harvard University Press, 1968), xxxiii-xxxiv; Paul Boyer, *Urban Masses and Moral Order in America, 1820-1920* (Cambridge: Harvard University Press, 1978), 147, 158, 223; "In Memory of John S. Kennedy," *Survey* 23 (27 November 1909): 277; Robert H. Bremner to SE, 19 November 1984; J. S. Kennedy to J. J. Hill, 4 February 1887; J. S. Kennedy to J. J. Hill, Telegram, 24 December 1891, James J. Hill Papers, James Jerome Hill Reference Library, St. Paul, Minnesota.; J. S. Kennedy to J. J. Hill, 14 December 1891, James J. Hill Correspondence, President's Office, Great Northern, Minnesota Historical Society, St. Paul, Minnesota.; Edward T. Devine, *When Social Work Was Young* (New York: Macmillan, 1939), 130; Alexander Johnson, *Adventures in Social Welfare* (Fort Wayne, Ind.: Fort Wayne Printing Co., 1923), 372, 378; Elizabeth G. Meier, *A History of the New York School of Social Work* (New York: Columbia University Press, 1954), 21-22, 37, 41, 141; *Harper's Weekly* 35 (26 September 1891): 736-37; 37 (18 March 1893): 262; Miriam Z. Langsam, *Children West: A History of the Placing-Out System of the New York Children's Aid Society* (Madison: State Historical Society of Wisconsin, 1964), 31, 33; "William A. Booth," *National Cyclopedia of American Biography*, 10: 382; J. S. Kennedy to William A. Booth, 9 March 1891, copy from Children's Aid Society; "A History," United Charities Building, copy from Children's Aid Society; Ethel J. Sambert to SE, 28 April 1989; "Adolph Frederick Schauffler," *National Cyclopedia of American Biography*, 18: 281.

20. Merle Curti and Roderick Nash, *Philanthropy in the Shaping of American Higher Education* (New Brunswick: Rutgers University Press, 1965), 144; *New York Times*, 11 March, 6:5; 7 November 1909, 1:7; Edward C. Elliott, ed., *The Rise of a University* (New York: Columbia University Press, 1937), 2:48; Nicholas Murray Butler, "How to Civilize New York," *Review of Reviews* 40 (December 1909): 64-65; *A History of Columbia College on Morningside* (New York: Columbia University Press, 1954), 239; Theodore Francis Jones, ed., *New York University, 1832-1932* (New York: New York University Press, 1933), 190; Frederick Paul Keppel, *Columbia* (New York: Oxford University Press, 1914), 67; New York

Chamber of Commerce, *Fifty-Second Annual Report of the Chamber of Commerce of the State of New York for the Year 1909-1910*, 78; Edwin E. Slosson, *Great American Universities* (New York: Macmillan, 1910), 472; Daniel A. Wren, "American Business Philanthropy and Higher Education in the Nineteenth Century," *Business History Review* 57 (Autumn 1983): 324, 328, 336, 342-43.

21. "Caleb Frank Gates," *Dictionary of American Biography*, 24:319; J. S. Kennedy to J. J. Hill, Constantinople, 23 April 1901, Hill Papers; Caleb Frank Gates, *Not to Me Only* (Princeton: Princeton University Press, 1940), 154-55, 169-70, 174-75, 197; Keith M. Greenwood, "Robert College: The American Founders," Ph.D. diss. (Baltimore: Johns Hopkins University, 1965), 1, 35-36, 51-55, 99, 102-3, 106, 111-114, 136, 154, 182, 214-16, 230, 240, 245, 266-67, 285, 289, 293, 295, 308; *New York Times*, 7 November 1909, 1:7; George Washburn, *Fifty Years in Constantinople and Recollections of Robert College* (Boston: Houghton Mifflin, 1909), 195, 235, 266, 291; "Cleveland H. Dodge," *National Cyclopedia of American Biography*, 26:407; Herbert Lane, "The Story of Robert College," manuscript history in the possession of Robert College of Istanbul, Turkey, undated, 108-9, 112-13, 117-18, 131-32, 133-34, 136; "William Gottlieb Schauffler," *Dictionary of American Biography*, 16:420-21; "Henry Albert Schauffler," *Dictionary of American Biography*, 16:420; "Christopher Rhinelander Robert," *Dictionary of American Biography*, 16:1; "Christopher Rhinelander Robert," *National Cyclopedia of American Biography*, 10:492; "George Washburn," *Dictionary of American Biography*, 19:500-1; "George Washburn," *National Cyclopedia of American Biography*, 10:492-93; "Cyrus Hamlin," *Dictionary of American Biography*, 8:195; Richard Lowitt, *A Merchant Prince of the Nineteenth Century: William E. Dodge* (New York: Columbia University Press, 1954), 176; "William Gottlieb Schauffler," *National Cyclopedia of American Biography*, 18:280-81; "John G. A. Leishman," *National Cyclopedia of American Biography*, 13:598; "John G. A. Leishman," *Dictionary of American Biography*, 11:155-56; Henry V. Poor, *History of the Railroads and Canals of the United States of America* (New York: John H. Schultz & Co., 1860), 435; Joseph S. Szyliowicz, *Education and Modernization in the Middle East* (Ithaca: Cornell University Press, 1973), 150; Merle Curti, *American Philanthropy Abroad: A History* (New Brunswick, N.J.: Rutgers University Press, 1963), 148; Sydney N. Fisher, "Two Centuries of American Interest in Turkey," in David H. Pinkney and Theodore Ropp, eds., *Festschrift for Friedrich Artz* (Durham, N.C.: Duke University Press, 1964), 119-20, 137; Daniel Hodas, *The Business Career of Moses Taylor* (New York: New York University Press, 1976), 98; Harold van B. Cleveland and Thomas F. Huertas, *Citibank, 1812-1970* (Cambridge: Harvard University Press, 1985), 17, 20; Thomas C. Cochran, *Railroad Leaders, 1845-1890* (Cambridge: Harvard University Press, 1953), 31; Roderic H. Davison, "Westernized Education in

Ottoman Turkey," *Middle East Journal* 15 (Summer 1961): 292, 294; Stanford J. Shaw and Ezel Kural, *History of the Ottoman Empire and Modern Turkey* (Cambridge: Cambridge University Press, 1977), 2:110, 250; J. S. Kennedy to G. Washburn, 11 July, 29 August, 9 November 1906, 4 January, 4 February, 3 June, 22 July, 3 October, 26 November, 13 December 1907, 31 January, 18 February 1908, Papers of Cyrus Hamlin and George Washburn, Houghton Library, Harvard University; "Adolph Frederick Schauffler," *National Cyclopedia of American Biography*, 18:281; J. S. Kennedy to T. Roosevelt, 19 November 1901; T. Roosevelt to J. S. Kennedy, 22 November 1901, 25 April 1902, Theodore Roosevelt Papers, Library of Congress; "William A. Booth," *National Cyclopedia of American Biography*, 10:382.

22. *New York Times*, 14 February 1895, 1:1, 16 July, 7:6, 28 July 1898, 12:4, 10 December 1905, 7:6, 14 September 1907, 9:5; "John Sloane," *National Cyclopedia of American Biography*, 37:268-69; J. S. Kennedy to J. J. Hill, 19 July 1900, 25 December 1905, 13 September 1907, Hill Papers; J. S. Kennedy to G. Washburn, 15 September, 3 October 1907, Papers of Cyrus Hamlin and George Washburn, Houghton Library, Harvard University.

23. *New York Times*, 1 November, 11:3, 2 November, 9:4, 4 November, 9:4, 23 November, 7:4, 1909; J. J. Hill to Mrs. John S. Kennedy, 29 October 1909, Hill Papers; *Bar Harbor Record*, 10 November 1909.

24. *New York Times*, 6 November, 1:7; 7 November 1909, 1:7; 2:1; 1 January 1911, 4:3, 21 April 1914, 10:8; 24 July 1930, 24:1; Printed will of John Stewart Kennedy, 26 March 1909.

25. *New York Times*, 1 November, 6 November, 1:7, 2:1, 7 November 1909, 2:1, 12:1; Glenn, Brandt, and Andrews, *Russell Sage Foundation*, 4; "Robert W. de Forest," *National Cyclopedia of American Biography*, 42:15, B:64; "Mr. Kennedy's Munificent Bequests," *Review of Reviews* 40 (December 1909): 656; Butler, "How to Civilize New York," *Review of Reviews* 40 (December 1909): 680; Edward T. Devine, "Mr. Kennedy's Will," *Survey* 23 (13 November 1909): 217-18; *Outlook* 93 (13 November 1909): 569 (20 November 1909): 619; *Independent* 67 (11 November 1909): 1097-98; Nicholas Murray Butler, "John Stewart Kennedy," *Columbia University Quarterly* 12 (December 1909): 64, 66; *Commercial & Financial Chronicle* 89 (6 November 1909): 1197-98, (13 November 1909): 1246, 1258; Undated memorandum, Hill Papers; Lloyd J. Mercer, *E. H. Harriman: Master Railroader* (Boston: Twayne Publishers, 1985), 23; Vincent P. Carosso, *The Morgans: Private International Bankers, 1854-1913* (Cambridge: Harvard University Press, 1987), 276, 644, 869n. 69.

AFTERWORD

CLEARLY, THE TRANSPORTATION revolution of the nineteenth century dramatically altered the face of the globe, conquering distance, transforming concepts of time and space, vastly extending the market, and facilitating both peaceful migration and armed expansion.

Railroad captains did not do the job unaided—though it is tempting to think so if we accept the tradition of heroic biography. They had assistants, lieutenants, specialists, all those who helped convert grandiose dreams into marketable realities. John Stewart Kennedy possessed those indispensable skills. He mobilized capital, bolstered its safety in an intensely competitive and unregulated industry, facilitated its movement from Western Europe to the United States, and helped men with economic vision convince those with wealth to invest. In an industry whose high stakes, immense prestige and national prominence attracted a full complement of gamblers and adventurers. Kennedy stood out for his uncharacteristic honesty.

He did so during the second stage of American railroading, the decades from approximately 1850 to around 1914. In the first stage, the generation after 1830 learned the necessary truths about railroad financing through trial and error, success and failure. Kennedy distinguished himself during a later stage, one of defining parameters and clarifying patterns of addressing and resolving problems. An example was his private opposition to speculators, who not only could threaten normal business, but would stir the anxiety of the relatively unsophisticated investors who trusted Kennedy but nevertheless feared getting in beyond their depth.

That trust was his greatest strength. In an era of confused and ambiguous business ethics, Kennedy demonstrated a concern for integrity that evoked confidence among potential investors. Nor was it a matter of business alone, but of charitable involvement that showed an acute sensitivity to the public good. No doubt realizing how much his reputation mattered, he defended himself against the criticism of benefiting improperly during the final stages of the formation of the Manitoba. Reputation was literally priceless with

227

those individuals who plucked up the courage to invest in a railroad in, say, far-off Minnesota. Poor by background, Kennedy understood full well what mattered to such investors.

Both gifted and lucky, he allied himself with winners, with men on the make whose triumphs aided his own success. Witness both James Hill and—to a much lesser extent—William Menzies, whose victories Kennedy was shrewd enough to anticipate. In sagely associating himself with them, Kennedy also recognized his own limitations, those of the lieutenant seeking a forceful leader from whom he could benefit. For Kennedy was far less comfortable in the public eye than he was in a quiet back room, where he could analyze the pros and cons, and join other quiet men in negotiating the agreements that enabled the railroad to spread itself across the continent.

He became a seminal figure in American banking and in the New York business community. As the quintessential intermediary linking those needing financial services (including advice and information) with those ready to provide them, Kennedy helped both sides profit by reducing transaction costs. Whether as a commission merchant, private banker, or director and trustee of several of the most potent financial institutions of his day, Kennedy played an influential part in quickening the growth of the American economy, particularly in the all-important transportation sector.

BIBLIOGRAPHY

Manuscript Collections

Barnes, John Sanford, "My Egotistigraphy," (1910), typescript MS, New-York Historical Society, New York.

Carnegie, Andrew, Library of Congress, Washington, D.C.

Chase Manhattan Bank Archives, New York, New York.

Cooke, Jay, Baker Library, Harvard Business School.

Great Northern Railway Company Records, Minnesota Historical Society, St. Paul, Minnesota.

Hamlin, Cyrus, Houghton Library, Harvard University.

Heartman Collection, New-York Historical Society, New York, New York.

Hill, James Jerome, James Jerome Hill Reference Library, St. Paul, Minnesota.

Illinois Central Papers, Newberry Library, Chicago, Illinois.

Manufacturers Hanover Bank Archives, New York, New York.

R. G. Dun Credit Ledgers, Baker Library, Harvard Business School.

Robb, James, Historic New Orleans Collection, New Orleans, Louisiana.

Roosevelt, Theodore, Library of Congress, Washington, D.C.

Scottish American Investment Company, Edinburgh, Scotland.

Washburn, George, Houghton Library, Harvard University.

Books, Articles, and Newspapers

Abdill, George B. *Rails West.* Seattle, Wash.: Superior Publishing Company, 1960.

Adler, Cyrus. *Jacob H. Schiff.* 2 vols. Garden City, N.Y.: Doubleday, Doran and Co., 1938.

Adler, Dorothy R. *British Investment in American Railways 1834-1898.* Edited by Muriel E. Hidy. Charlottesville, Va.: University Press of Virginia, 1970.

Alexis, Karin M. E. "Russell Sturgis: A Search for the Modern Aesthetic—Going Beyond Ruskin." *Athanor*, 3: 31-40. 1992.

229

Alexis, Karin M. E. "Russell Sturgis: Crittic and Architect." Ph.D doss., University of Virginia, 1986.

American Iron and Steel Institute Bulletin. 1878, 1882, 1896.

Atack, Jeremy, and Jan K. Brueckner. "Steel Rails and American Railroads, 1867-1880." *Explorations in Economic History* 20 (July 1983): 258-62.

Atkins, Gordon. *Health, Housing, and Poverty in New York City 1865-1898.* n.p.: n.p., 1947.

Baker, John Milnes. *The Baker Family and the Edgar Family of Rahway, N.J. and New York City.* Middletown, N.Y.: Trumbull Publishing, 1972.

Bankers' Magazine, 1860.

Bar Harbor [Maine] Record, 1892, 1909.

Baring, Alexander. *My Recollections 1848-1931.* Santa Barbara, Calif.: Schauer Printing Studio, 1933.

Baughman, James P. *Charles Morgan and the Development of Southern Transportation.* Nashville, Tenn.: Vanderbilt University Press, 1968.

Bazin, Germaine. *The Museum Age.* New York: Universe Books, 1967.

Belfast [Maine] Republican Journal, 1895.

Berton, Pierre. *The Impossible Railway: The Building of the Canadian Pacific*, 2 vols. New York: Alfred A. Knopf, 1970, 1972.

Bethlehem Steel Corp. "History of the Bethlehem Steel Corp.," unpublished manuscript, circa 1950, Charles M. Schwab Memorial Library, Bethlehem, Pa..

_____. "History of the Cambria Plant of the Bethlehem Steel Corp.," unpublished manuscript, circa 1950, Charles M. Schwab Memorial Library, Bethlehem, Pa.

_____. "History of the Cambria Plant, Bethlehem Steel Company, 1852-1935," unpublished manuscript, 1935, Charles M. Schwab Memorial Library, Bethlehem, Pa.

Biographical Directory of the Railway Officials of America. Chicago: Railway Age, 1887.

Birch, Alan. *The Economic History of the British Iron and Steel Industry, 1784-1879.* London: Frank Cass and Company Ltd., 1967.

Bishop, Joseph Bucklin. *A Chronicle of One Hundred & Fifty Years of the Chamber of Commerce of the State of New York 1768-1918.* New York: Charles Scribner's Sons, 1918.

Bogen, Jules I. *The Anthracite Railroads.* New York: Ronald Press, 1927.

Boston Transcript, 1890.

Boyer, Paul, *Urban Masses and Moral Order in America, 1820-1920.* Cambridge: Harvard University Press, 1978.

Brandt, Lilian. *The Charity Organization Society of the City of New York, 1882-1907*. New York: Charity Organization Society, 1907.

Brewer, H. Peers. "The Emergence of the Trust Company in New York City: 1870-1900." Ph.D. diss., New York University Graduate School of Business Administration, 1974.

Brooks, John Graham. *An American Citizen: The Life of William Henry Baldwin, Jr*. Boston: Houghton Mifflin, 1910.

Brown, William Adams. *Morris Ketchum Jesup*. New York: Charles Scribner's Sons, 1910.

Bruce, Robert V. *The Launching of American Science 1846-1876*. New York: Alfred A. Knopf, 1987.

Buley, R. Carlyle. *Equitable Life Assurance Society of the United States 1859-1964*. 2 vols. New York: Appleton-Century-Crofts, 1967.

Burkert, Richard A. "Iron and Steelmaking in the Conemaugh Valley." In *Johnstown—The Story of a Unique Valley*, edited by Karl Berger. Johnstown, Pa: Johnstown Flood Museum, 1985.

Burton, James C., ed. *Arthur Young and the Business He Founded*. New York: Privately Printed, 1948.

Buss, Dietrich G. *Henry Villard: A Study of Transatlantic Investments and Interests, 1870-1895*. New York: Arno Press, 1978.

Butler, Nicholas Murray. "How to Civilize New York." *Review of Reviews* 40 (December 1909): 679-80.

_____. "John Stewart Kennedy." *Columbia University Quarterly* 12 (December 1909): 64-65.

Campbell, E.G. *The Reorganization of the American Railroad System, 1893-1900*. New York: Columbia University Press, 1938.

Campbell, R. H. *Scotland Since 1707: The Rise of an Industrial Society*. New York: Barnes & Noble, 1965.

Carosso, Vincent. *Investment Banking in America: A History*. Cambridge: Harvard University Press, 1970.

_____. *The Morgans: Private International Bankers 1854-1913*. Cambridge: Harvard University Press, 1987.

Carosso, Vincent P., and Richard Sylla. "U.S. Banks in International Finance." In *International Banking 1870-1914*, edited by Rondo Cameron and V. I. Bovykin. New York: Oxford University Press, 1991.

Cary, John W. *The Organization and History of the Chicago, Milwaukee & St. Paul Railway Company*. New York: Arno Press, 1981.

Casson, Herbert N. *The Romance of Steel*. New York: A. S. Barnes & Company, 1907.

Caudle, Robert E. *History of the Missouri Pacific Lines Gulf Coast Lines and Subsidiaries International—Great Northern.* n.p.: n.p., 1949.

Chapman, Stanley. *The Rise of Merchant Banking.* London: George Allen & Unwin, 1984.

Charity Organization Society of New York. *Annual Reports, 1903-1910.*

Checkland, S. G. *Scottish Banking: A History: 1695-1973.* Glasgow: Collins, 1975.

Clark, Ira G. *Then Came the Railroads: The Century from Steam to Diesel in the Southwest.* Norman: University of Oklahoma Press, 1958.

Clark, Victor S. *History of Manufactures in the United States, 1860-1914.* Washington, D.C.: Carnegie Institution, 1928.

Cleland, Robert Glass. *A History of Phelps Dodge 1834-1950.* New York: Alfred A. Knopf, 1952.

Cleveland, Harold van B., and Thomas F. Huertas. *Citibank 1812-1970.* Cambridge: Harvard University Press, 1985.

Cochran, Thomas C. *Railroad Leaders 1845-1890.* Cambridge: Harvard University Press, 1953.

Coleman, Charles H. *The Election of 1868.* New York: Columbia University Press, 1933.

Corliss, Carlton J. *Main Line of Mid-America: The Story of the Illinois Central.* New York: Creative Age Press, 1950.

Commercial and Financial Chronicle, 1871-1909.

Constable, W. G. *Art Collecting in the United States of America.* London: Thomas Nelson and Sons Ltd., 1964.

Corrins, R. D. "William Baird and Company, Coal and Iron Masters 1830-1914." Ph.D. thesis, University of Strathclyde, 1974.

Cottman, George S. *Centennial History and Handbook of Indiana.* Indianapolis, Ind.: Max R. Hyman, 1915.

Curti, Merle. *American Philanthropy Abroad: A History.* New Brunswick, N.J.: Rutgers University Press, 1963.

_____. "Anatomy of Giving in Millionaires in the Late 19th Century." *American Quarterly* 15 (Fall 1963): 416-35.

Curti, Merle, and Roderick Nash. *Philanthropy in the Shaping of American Higher Education.* New Brunswick, N.J.: Rutgers University Press, 1965.

Daggett, Stuart. *Railroad Reorganization.* Boston: Houghton Mifflin, 1908.

Dain, Phyllis. *The New York Public Library: A History of the Founding and Early Years.* New York: New York Public Library, 1972.

Davis, Allen F. *Spearheads for Reform: The Social Settlements and the Progressive Movement 1890-1914.* New York: Oxford University Press, 1967.

Davis, Burke. *The Southern Railway.* Chapel Hill: University of North Carolina Press, 1985.

Davison, Roderic H. "Westernized Education in Ottoman Turkey." *Middle East Journal* 15 (Summer 1961): 289-301.

de Forest, Robert W. "Address," Sixtieth Founding of the Museum. *Bulletin of the Metropolitan Museum of Art* 25 (May 1930) sec. II: 4-7.

_____. *The Story of the United Charities Building: Mr. John S. Kennedy's Relation to the Building and His Policies Regarding It.* New York: United Charities [1931].

Delevan, David Bryson. *Early Days of the Presbyterian Hospital in the City of New York.* East Orange, N.J.: Published Privately, 1926.

Denison, Merrill. *Canada's First Bank: A History of the Bank of Montreal.* Toronto: McClelland & Stewart, 1967.

Derleth, August. *The Milwaukee Road.* New York: Creative Age Press, 1948.

Devine, Edward T. "Mr. Kennedy's Will." *Survey* 23 (13 November 1909): 217-18.

_____. *When Social Work Was Young.* New York: Macmillan, 1939.

Donovan, Frank P. "The Illinois Central Railroad in Iowa." *Palimpsest* 43 (June 1962): 265-85.

_____. *Mileposts on the Prairie: The Story of the Minneapolis & St. Louis Railway.* New York: Simmons-Boardman Publishing Company, 1950.

Dorr, George B. *Acadia National Park: Its Origin and Background.* Bangor, Maine: Burr Printing Co., 1942.

_____. *Acadia National Park: Its Growth and Development.* Bangor, Maine: Burr Printing Co., 1948.

Drury, Clifford Merrill. *Presbyterian Panorama: One Hundred and Fifty Years of National Missions History.* Philadelphia: Board of Christian Education, Presbyterian Church in the United States of America, 1952.

Dunaway, Wayland Fuller. *A History of Pennsylvania.* New York: Prentice-Hall, 1935.

Eames, Wilberforce. "The Library of Hon. Samuel J. Tilden." *Bulletin of the New York Public Library* (January 1899): 4-8.

Edson, William D. *Railroad Names: A Directory of Common Carrier Railroads Operating in the United States, 1826-1982.* Potomac, Md.: William D. Edson, 1984.

Elliott, Edward C. ed. *The Rise of a University.* New York: Columbia University Press, 1937.

Farley, Jesse Kelso, Jr. *Twelve Generations of Farleys.* Evanston, Ill.: Privately Printed, 1943.

Faulkner, Harold U. *The Decline of Laissez Faire 1897-1917*. New York: Rinehart, 1951.

Fels, Rendig. *American Business Cycles, 1865-1897*. Chapel Hill: University of North Carolina Press, 1959.

Felt, Jeremy P. "Vice Reform as a Political Technique: The Committee of Fifteen in New York, 1900-1901." *New York History* 54 (1973): 24-51.

Fisher, Sydney N. "Two Centuries of American Interest in Turkey." In *Festschrift for Frederick Artz*, edited by David H. Pinkney and Theodore Ropp. Durham, N.C.: Duke University Press, 1964.

Folsom, Burton W. Jr. *Urban Capitalists: Entrepreneurs and City Growth in Pennsylvania's Lackawanna and Lehigh Regions, 1800-1920*. Baltimore: Johns Hopkins University Press, 1981.

Folwell, William Watts. *A History of Minnesota*. 4 vols. 1926. Reprint, St. Paul: Minnesota Historical Society, 1969.

Foner, Eric. *Reconstruction: America's Unfinished Revolution, 1863-1877*. New York: Harper & Row, 1988.

Fox, Daniel M. Introduction to *The New Basis of Civilization*, by Simon Patten. [c. 1907], Cambridge: Harvard University Press, 1968.

"The Garden of Mr. J. P. Kennedy at Bar Harbor, Maine." *Country Life in America* 29 (November 1915): 44-45.

Garrison, Fielding H. *John Shaw Billings*. New York: G. P. Putnam's Sons, 1915.

Gates, Caleb Frank. *Not to Me Only*. Princeton: Princeton University Press, 1940.

Gates, Paul Wallace. *The Illinois Central Railroad and Its Colonization Work*. Cambridge: Harvard University Press, 1934.

Gilbert, Heather. *The Life of Lord Mount Stephen*. 2 vols. Aberdeen: Aberdeen University Press, 1976, 1977.

_____. "The Unaccountable Fifth: Solution of a Great Northern Enigma." *Minnesota History* 42 (Spring 1971): 175-77.

Glasgow, George. *The Scottish Investment Trust Companies*. London: Eyre and Spottiswoode, 1932.

Glazebrook, George P. de T. *History of Transportation in Canada*. New Haven: Yale University Press, 1938.

Glenn, John M., Lilian Brandt and F. Emerson Andrews, *Russell Sage Foundation, 1907-1946*. New York: Russell Sage Foundation, 1947.

Graham, Patricia Albjerg. *Community and Class in American Education, 1865-1918*. New York: John Wiley & Sons, 1974.

Grant, H. Roger. *The Corn Belt Route: A History of the Chicago Great Western Railroad Company*. De Kalb: Northern Illinois University Press, 1984.

Gras, N. S. B., and Henrietta M. Larson. *Casebook in American Business History.* New York: Appleton-Century-Crofts, 1939.

Greenberg, Dolores. *Financiers and Railroads 1869-1889: A Study of Morton, Bliss & Company.* Newark: University of Delaware Press, 1980.

_____. "A Study of Capital Alliances: The St. Paul & Pacific." *Canadian Historical Review* 57 (March 1976): 25-39.

Greenwood, Keith M. "Robert College: The American Founders." Ph.D. diss., Johns Hopkins University, 1965.

Griswold, Mac, and Eleanor Weller. *The Golden Age of American Gardens.* New York: Harry N. Abrams, 1991.

Grodinsky, Julius. *Transcontinental Railway Strategy, 1869-1893: A Study of Businessmen.* Philadelphia: University of Pennsylvania Press, 1962.

Hacker, Louis M. *The World of Andrew Carnegie 1865-1901.* Philadelphia: J. B. Lippincott Company, 1968.

Hamilton, Henry. *The Industrial Revolution in Scotland.* Oxford: Oxford University Press, 1932.

Hammack, David C. *Power and Society: Greater New York at the Turn of the Century.* New York: Russell Sage Foundation, 1982.

Harlow, Alvin F. *The Road of the Century: The Story of the New York Central.* New York: Creative Age Press, 1947.

Harnsberger, John L. *Jay Cooke and Minnesota: The Formative Years of the Northern Pacific Railroad, 1868-1873.* New York: Arno Press, 1981.

Harnsberger, John, and Robert P. Wilkins. "Transportation on the Northern Plains." *North Dakota Quarterly* 29 (Summer 1961): 83-92 and (Autumn 1961): 97-112.

Harper's Weekly, 1891, 1893, 1900.

Hayes, John D. "The Battle of Port Royal, S.C. From the Journal of John Sanford Barnes." *New-York Historical Society Quarterly* 45 (October 1961): 365-95.

Helfrich, G. W., and Gladys O'Neil. *Lost Bar Harbor.* Camden, Maine: Down East Books, 1982.

Herbert, Robert L. *Barbizon Revisited.* New York: Clarke & Way, 1962.

Heslin, James J. "John Sanford Barnes (1836-1911): Naval Officer, Financier, Collector." *New-York Historical Society Quarterly* 47 (January 1963): 41-65.

Hidy, Ralph W., and Muriel E. Hidy. "Great Northern History Manuscript." Archives, Baker Library, Harvard Business School.

Hidy, Muriel Emmie. *George Peabody Merchant and Financier, 1829-1854.* New York: Arno Press, 1978.

Hidy, Ralph W., Muriel E. Hidy, and Roy V. Scott, with Don L. Hofsommer, *The Great Northern Railway: A History.* Boston: Harvard Business School Press, 1988.

A History of Columbia College on Morningside. New York: Columbia University Press, 1954.

Hodas, Daniel. *The Business Career of Moses Taylor: Merchant, Finance Capitalist, and Industrialist.* New York: New York University Press, 1976.

Hofsommer, Donovan L. "'The Grandest Railroad Project of the Age'." *Annals of Iowa* 44 (Fall 1977): 118-36.

_____. "Hill's Dream Realized: The Burlington Northern's Eight-Decade Gestation." *Pacific Northwest Quarterly* 79 (October 1988): 138-46.

_____. *The Southern Pacific, 1901-1985.* College Station: Texas A & M University Press, 1986.

Hogan, William T. *Economic History of the Iron and Steel Industry in the United States.* 4 vols. Lexington, Mass.: Lexington Books, D.C. Heath and Company, 1971.

Howat, John K. "Washington Crossing the Delaware." *Bulletin of the Metropolitan Museum of Art* 26 (March 1968): 289-99.

Howe, Winifred E. *A History of the Metropolitan Museum of Art.* New York: Metropolitan Museum of Art, 1913.

Hughes, Jonathan. *The Vital Few.* New York: Oxford University Press, 1965.

Hungerford, Edward. *Men and Iron: The Story of the New York Central.* New York: Thomas Y. Crowell Company, 1938.

Hutchinson, William K. "Import Substitution, Structural Change, and Regional Economic Growth in the United States: The Northeast, 1870-1910." *Journal of Economic History* 45 (June 1985): 319-25.

"In Memory of John S. Kennedy." *Survey* 23 (27 November 1909): 276-78.

Innis, Harold A. *A History of the Canadian Pacific Railway.* London: P. S. King, 1923.

Iron Age, 1875, 1879.

Jackson, W. Turrentine. *The Enterprising Scot: Investors in the American West After 1873.* Edinburgh: Edinburgh University Press, 1968.

Jaher, Frederick Cople. "Nineteenth-Century Elites in Boston and New York." *Journal of Social History* 6 (Fall 1972): 32-77.

Jeal, Tim. *Livingstone.* New York: G. P. Putnam's Sons, 1973.

Johnson, Alexander. *Adventures in Social Welfare.* Fort Wayne, Ind.: Fort Wayne Printing Company, 1923.

Jones, Theodore Frances, ed. *New York University, 1837-1932.* New York: New York University Press, 1933.

Kelby, Robert Hendre. *New-York Historical Society, 1804-1904.* New York: Published for the Society, 1905.

Kennedy, John S., "Address of John S. Kennedy at the Opening of the United Charities Building," 6 March 1893.

"John Stewart Kennedy." *Bulletin of the Metropolitan Museum of Art* 4 (December 1909): 216-17.

"John S. Kennedy's Bequests." *Independent* 67 (11 November 1909): 1097-98.

"John S. Kennedy." *Outlook* 93 (13 November 1909): 569.

Keppel, Frederick Paul. *Columbia.* New York: Oxford University Press, 1914.

Kerr, William G. *Scottish Capital on the American Credit Frontier.* Austin: Texas State Historical Association, 1976.

Kirkland, Edward C. *Industry Comes of Age 1860-1897.* New York: Holt, Rinehart and Winston, 1961.

_____. *Men Cities and Transportation: A Study in New England History, 1820-1900,* 2 vols. Cambridge: Harvard University Press, 1948.

Klein, Maury. *The Great Railroad Terminal.* Charlottesville: University of Virginia Press, 1970.

_____. *The Life and Legend of Jay Gould.* Baltimore: Johns Hopkins University Press, 1986.

_____. *Union Pacific: The Rebirth 1894-1969.* New York: Doubleday, 1989.

Korn, Bernhard C. "Eber Brock Ward." Ph.D. diss., Marquette University, 1942.

Lamb, Albert R. *The Presbyterian Hospital and the Columbia-Presbyterian Medical Center, 1868-1943.* New York: Columbia University Press, 1955.

_____. "The Story of the Founding of the Columbia-Presbyterian Medical Center." *American Journal of Medicine* 15 (December 1953): 754-60.

Lamb, W. Kaye. *History of the Canadian Pacific Railway.* New York: Macmillan, 1977.

Lane, Herbert. "The Story of Robert College." Manuscript history in the possession of Robert College of Istanbul, Turkey, undated.

Lane, Wheaton J. *From Indian Trail to Iron Horse: Travel and Transportation in New Jersey, 1620-1860.* Princeton: Princeton University Press, 1939.

Langsam, Miriam Z. *Children West: A History of the Placing-Out System of the New York Children's Aid Society.* Madison: State Historical Society of Wisconsin, 1964.

Larkin, Oliver W. *Art and Life in America.* New York: Rinehart & Company, 1949.

Larson, Henrietta M. *Jay Cooke: Private Banker.* Cambridge: Harvard University Press, 1936.

Lee, Eleanor. *History of the School of Nursing of the Presbyterian Hospital, New York, 1892-1942*. New York: G. Putnam's Sons, 1942.

Leech, Harper, and John Charles Carroll. *Armour and His Times*. New York: Appleton-Century, 1938.

"The Lesson of a Great Generosity." *Outlook* 93 (20 November 1909): 618-20.

Livesay, Harold C. *Andrew Carnegie and the Rise of Big Business*. Boston: Little, Brown and Co., 1975.

_____. "Marketing Patterns in the Antebellum American Iron Industry." *Business History Review* 45 (Autumn 1971): 269-95.

Livesay, Harold C., and Glenn Porter. "The Financial Role of Merchants in the Development of U.S. Manufacturing, 1815-1860." *Explorations in Economic History* 9 (Fall 1971): 63-87.

Livingston, James C. *Origins of the Federal Reserve System: Money, Class, and Corporate Capitalism, 1890-1913*. Ithaca: Cornell University Press, 1986.

Lowitt, Richard. *A Merchant Prince of the Nineteenth Century: William E. Dodge*. New York: Columbia University Press, 1954.

Lunt, Sally Herman. "The Professionalization of Social Work," Ed.D. diss., Harvard University, 1974.

Lydenberg, Harry Miller. *History of the New York Public Library*. New York: New York Public Library, 1923.

_____. *John Shaw Billings*. Chicago: American Library Association, 1924.

McCash, William Barton, and June Hall McCash. *The Jekyll Island Club*. Athens: University of Georgia Press, 1989.

McComb, David G. *Houston: A History*. Austin: University of Texas Press, 1981.

McCullough, David. *Mornings on Horseback*. New York: Simon and Schuster, 1981.

MacDougall, J. Lorne. *Canadian Pacific*. Montreal: McGill University Press, 1968.

McFadden, Elizabeth. *The Glitter and the Gold: . . . the Metropolitan Museum of Art's First Director . . . Luigi Palma di Cesnola*. New York: Dial Press, 1971.

Mallach, Stanley. "Robert Weeks de Forest." In *Biographical Dictionary of Social Welfare*, edited by Walter Trattner. Westport, Conn.: Greenwood Press, 1986.

Marks, Rachel B. "Education in Social Work," In *Encyclopedia of Social Work*, edited by Harry L. Lurie. New York: National Association of Social Workers, 1965.

Martin, Albro. "Crisis of Rugged Individualism: The West Shore-South Pennsylvania Railroad Affair, 1880-1885." *Pennsylvania Magazine of History and Biography* 93 (April 1969): 218-43.

_____. *James J. Hill and the Opening of the Northwest.* New York: Oxford University Press, 1976.

Masters, Judge Joseph. "Brief History of the Early Iron and Steel Industry of the Wood, Morrell & Co., and the Cambria Iron Co. at Johnstown, Pa." Official Souvenir Program. 11th Department Encampment, United Spanish War Veterans, Johnstown, Pa., 1915.

Meier, Elizabeth G. *A History of the New York School of Social Work.* New York: Columbia University Press, 1954.

Mercer, Lloyd J. *E. H. Harriman: Master Railroader.* Boston: Twayne Publishers, 1985.

Merk, Frederick. *Economic History of Wisconsin During the Civil War Decade.* Madison: State Historical Society of Wisconsin, 1916.

Meyer, Karl E. *The Art Museum: Power, Money, Ethics.* New York: William Morrow and Company, 1979.

Moehlman, Arthur H., "The Red River of the North," Ph.D. diss., University of Michigan, 1932.

Moore, Powell A. *The Calumet Region: Indiana's Last Frontier.* n.p.: Indiana Historical Bureau, 1959.

Morris, Edmund. *The Rise of Theodore Roosevelt.* New York: Coward, McCann & Geoghegan, 1979.

Morrison, David Baillie, ed. *Two Hundredth Anniversary 1756-1956 of St. Andrew's Society of the State of New York.* New York: St. Andrew's Society of the State of New York, 1956.

Morrison, George Austin. "John Stewart Kennedy." *New York Genealogical and Biographical Record* 41 (July 1910): 163-68.

Mott, Edward Harold. *The Story of Erie: Between the Ocean and the Lakes.* New York: Ticker Publishing, 1908.

Mowat, Charles Loch. *The Charity Organization Society, 1869-1913.* London: Methuen & Co., 1961.

"Mr. Kennedy's Munificent Bequests." *Review of Reviews* 40 (December 1909): 656.

"Mr. Kennedy's Will." *Survey* 23 (13 November 1909): 217-18.

Murphy, Ared Maurice. "Big Four Railroad in Indiana." *Indiana Magazine of History* 21 (June and September 1925): 109-273.

Myers, Margaret G. *Financial History of the United States.* New York: Columbia University Press, 1970.

New York Chamber of Commerce. *Fifty-Second Annual Report of the Chamber of Commerce of the State of New York for the Year 1909-1910.* 1910.

New York Post, 1909.

New York Times, 1878, 1895, 1909.

Nugent, Walter T. K. *Money and American Society, 1865-1880.* New York: Free Press, 1968.

Oberholtzer, Ellis P. *Jay Cooke.* Philadelphia: George W. Jacobs & Co., 1907.

Oliver, John W. *History of American Technology.* New York: Ronald Press, 1956.

Overton, Richard C. *Burlington Route: A History of the Burlington Lines.* New York: Alfred A. Knopf, 1965.

Parkhurst, Charles H. *A Brief History of the Madison Square Presbyterian Church.* New York: n.p., 1906.

Payne, Peter L. *Colvilles and the Scottish Steel Industry.* Oxford: Clarendon Press, 1979.

Perine, Edward Ten Broeck. *The Story of the Trust Companies.* New York: G. P. Putnam's Sons, 1916.

Peters, Richard, Jr. *Two Centuries of Iron Smelting in Pennsylvania.* Philadelphia: Pulaski Iron Company, 1921.

Pierce, Harry H. "Foreign Investment in American Enterprise." In *Economic Change in the Civil War Era,* edited by David T. Gilchrist and W. David Lewis. Greenville, Del.: Eleutherian Mills-Hagley Foundation, 1965.

Pomfret, Richard. *Economic Development of Canada.* Toronto: Methuen & Co., 1981.

Poor, Henry V. *History of the Railroads and Canals of the United States of America.* New York: John H. Schultz & Co., 1860.

Porter, Glenn, and Harold C. Livesay. *Merchants and Manufacturers.* Baltimore: Johns Hopkins University Press, 1971.

Potts, Charles S. *Railroad Transportation in Texas.* Bulletin of the University of Texas No. 119. Austin: University of Texas, 1909.

Prosser, Richard S. *Rails to the North Star.* Minneapolis: Dillon Press, 1966.

Provident Loan Society of New York. *Twenty-Fifth Anniversary, 1894-1919.* New York: Provident Loan Society, 1919.

_____. *Fifty Years of Remedial Lending, 1894-1944.* New York: n.p., 1944.

Pyle, Joseph Gilpin. *The Life of James J. Hill.* 2 vols. Garden City, N.Y.: Doubleday, Page & Co., 1917.

Rae, John B. "The Great Northern Land Grant." *Journal of Economic History* 12 (Spring 1952): 140-45.

Railroad Gazette, 1870-1887.

Redlich, Fritz. *History of American Business Leaders.* Ann Arbor, Mich.: Edwards Brothers, 1940.

Reed, S. G. *A History of Texas Railroads.* Houston: St. Clair Publishing Co., 1941.

Ringwalt, J. L. *Development of Transportation Systems in the United States.* 1888. Reprint, New York: Johnson Reprint Corporation, 1968.

Rosenberg, Charles E. *The Care of Strangers: The Rise of America's Hospital System.* New York: Basic Books, 1987.

Russell, Charles Edward. *Stories of the Great Railroads.* Chicago: Charles H. Kerr & Company, 1912.

"Russell Sturgis's Architecture." *Architectural Record* 25 (June 1909): 404-10.

Sage, Leland L. *A History of Iowa.* Ames: Iowa State University Press, 1974.

Sarnoff, Paul. *Russell Sage.* New York: Ivan Obolensky, Inc., 1965.

Scanlon, Ann M. "The Building of the New York Central: A Study in the Development of the International Iron Trade." In *An Emerging Independent American Economy, 1815-1875,* edited by Joseph R. Frese and Jacob Judd. Tarrytown, N.Y.: Sleepy Hollow Press, 1980.

Schauffler, A. F. "John S. Kennedy." *Charities Review* 1 (March 1892): 228-31.

Schwed, Peter. *God Bless Pawnbrokers.* New York: Dodd, Mead & Company, 1975.

Scotland, James. *The History of Scottish Education.* 2 vols. London: University of London Press, 1969.

Scrymser, James A. *Personal Reminiscences of James A. Scrymser.* n.p.: n.p., 1915.

Seaver, George. *David Livingstone.* London: Lutterworth Press, 1957.

Sharkey, Robert P. *Money, Class, and Party: An Economic Study of the Civil War and Reconstruction.* Baltimore: Johns Hopkins University Press, 1959.

Shaw, Stanford J., and Ezel Kural. *History of the Ottoman Empire and Modern Turkey.* Cambridge: Cambridge University Press, 1977.

Slaven, Anthony. *The Development of the West of Scotland: 1750-1960.* London: Routledge & Kegan Paul, 1975.

Slosson, Edwin E. *Great American Universities.* New York: Macmillan, 1910.

Smalley, Eugene V. *History of the Northern Pacific Railroad.* 1883. Reprint, New York: Arno Press, 1975.

Smith, Willard H. *Schuyler Colfax.* Indianapolis: Indiana Historical Bureau, 1952.

Sobel, Robert. *The Big Board: A History of the New York Stock Exchange.* New York: Free Press, 1965.

Smout, T. C. *A History of the Scottish People 1830-1950.* New Haven: Yale University Press, 1986.

Stewart, William Rhinelander. *The Philanthropic Work of Josephine Shaw Lowell.* New York: Macmillan, 1911.

Stover, John F. *History of the Baltimore & Ohio Railroad.* West Lafayette, Ind.: Purdue University Press, 1987.

_____. *History of the Illinois Central Railroad.* New York: Macmillan, 1975.

_____. *The Railroads of the South 1865-1900.* Chapel Hill: University of North Carolina Press, 1955.

Swank, James M. *History of the Manufacture of Iron in All Ages*. Philadelphia: American Iron and Steel Association, 1892.

Szyliowicz, Joseph S. *Education for Modernization in the Middle East*. Ithaca: Cornell University Press, 1973.

Taylor, George Rogers. *The Transportation Revolution 1815-1860*. New York: Holt, Rinehart and Winston, 1951.

Temin, Peter. *Iron and Steel in Nineteenth-Century America*. Cambridge: MIT Press, 1964.

Thomas, Maurice Walton. *The Early Factory Legislation*. Leigh-on-Sea, Essex: Thames Bank Publishing, 1948.

Tomkins, Calvin. *Merchants and Masterpieces: The Story of the Metropolitan Museum of Art*. New York: E. P. Dutton & Co., 1970.

Trumbull, L. R. *A History of Industrial Paterson*. Paterson, N.J.: Carleton M. Herrick, 1882.

Tyson, R. E. "Scottish Investment in American Railways: The Case of the City of Glasgow Bank, 1856-1881." In *Studies in Scottish Business History*, edited by Peter L. Payne. London: Frank Cass, 1967.

The United Charities Act of Incorporation and Amendments. New York: United Charities, 1939.

United States Trust Company of New York. *Promise Fulfilled: A Story of the Growth of a Good Idea, 1853-1953*. New York: United States Trust Company of New York, 1953.

Vail, R. W. G. *Knickerbocker Birthday: A Sesqui-Centennial History of the New-York Historical Society 1804-1954*. New York: New-York Historical Society, 1954.

Veenendaal, Augustus, J., Jr. "An Example of 'Other People's Money': Dutch Capital in American Railroads." *Business and Economic History* 21 (1992): 147-58.

_____. "The Kansas City Southern Railway and the Dutch Connection." *Business History Review* 61 (Summer 1987): 291-316.

Wall, Joseph Frazier. *Andrew Carnegie*. New York: Oxford University Press, 1970.

Wallace, William, ed. *Trial of the City of Glasgow Bank Directors*. Glasgow: William Hodge & Co., 1905.

Ward, James A. "Image and Reality: The Railway Corporate-State Metaphor." *Business History Review* 55 (Winter 1981): 491-516.

Warren, Kenneth. *The American Steel Industry, 1850-1970*. Oxford: Clarendon Press, 1973.

Washburn, George. *Fifty Years in Constantinople and Recollections of Robert College*. Boston: Houghton Mifflin, 1909.

Wasson, R. Gordon, *The Hall Carbine Affair.* New York: Pandick Press, 1948.

Weir, Ronald B. *A History of the Scottish American Investment Company Limited, 1873-1973.* Edinburgh: Scottish American Investment Company, 1973.

_____. "William John Menzies." *Dictionary of Scottish Business Biography 1860-1960.* Aberdeen: Aberdeen University Press, 1990, 2:414-15.

White, John H., Jr. *American Locomotives: An Engineering History, 1830-1880.* Baltimore: Johns Hopkins University Press, 1968.

_____. *A Short History of American Locomotive Builders in the Steam Era.* Washington, D.C.: Bass, 1982,

White, W. Thomas. "A Gilded Age Businessman in Politics: James J. Hill, the Northwest, and the American Presidency, 1884-1912." *Pacific Historical Review* 57 (November 1988): 439-56.

Wilgus, William J. *The Railway Interrelations of the United States and Canada.* New Haven: Yale University Press, 1937.

Wilkins, Mira. *The History of Foreign Investment in the United States to 1914.* Cambridge: Harvard University Press, 1989.

Winks, Robin. *Frederick Billings.* New York: Oxford University Press, 1991.

Withey, Henry F., and Elsie R. Withey. *Biographical Dictionary of American Architects.* Los Angeles: New Age Publishing Co., 1956.

Wren, Daniel A. "American Business Philanthropy and Higher Education in the Nineteenth Century." *Business History Review* 57 (Autumn 1983): 321-46.

Ziegler, Philip. *The Sixth Great Power: A History of One of the Greatest of all Banking Families, the House of Barings, 1762-1929.* New York: Alfred A. Knopf, 1988.

COURT CASES

Liquidators of the City of Glasgow Bank v William Mackinnon (1881), Glasgow, Scotland.

Jesse P. Farley v James J. Hill, et al., 39 F. Rep. 513 (1889).

Jesse P. Farley v James J. Hill, et al. (1888). Transcript of the Record, St. Paul Public Library, St. Paul, Minnesota.

John S. Kennedy & Co. v St. Paul & Pacific Railroad Co., 1873 Federal Cases, 7,706.

Sahlgaard v J. S. Kennedy, et al., 2 Fed. R. 295 (1880).

Sahlgaard v J. S. Kennedy, et al., 13 Fed. R. 242 (1882).

U.S. v Northern Securities Co., 193 US 197 (1909) Transcript of the Record.

INDEX

77, 78, 118, 120, 141-42, 146, 148;
and the Chicago, Burlington &
Quincy Railroad, 78; and Henry
Villard, 178; and James J. Hill, 164;
and Jesse Farley, 68; and John
Stewart Kennedy, 72, 78, 192; and
the Northern Pacific Railroad, 78,
192, 193; and the Northern
Securities Company, 197; and the
"outstanders," 69; and the St. Paul &
Pacific Railroad, 55, 56, 58, 59, 62,
63; and the St. Paul, Minneapolis &
Manitoba Railway, ownership of
stock in, 71, 72, 73, 76, 77, 118, 141-
42, 143, 148, 150; and the St. Paul,
Minneapolis & Manitoba Railway,
resignation from board of, 77; resig-
nation as president, 120
Sterling, John, 190
Stewart, John A., 23, 29, 30, 34, 217
Stickney, A. B., 153-54
Stillman, James, 189, 190, 194, 196
Strong, William, 210
Sturgis, Russell, 103

T

Taylor, Moses, 16, 17
Tenement House Act of 1901, 213
Texas & New Orleans Railroad, 16
Thompson, Horace, 175
Thorne, Samuel: and the Baltimore &
Ohio Railroad, 189; and the Central
Trust Company of New York, 108;
and the Lackawanna Iron & Coal
Co., 167; and the Mason City & Fort
Dodge Railroad, 151, 154; and the
Montana Central Railroad, 159; and
the Pennsylvania Coal Company,
121, 167; and the St. Paul & Duluth
Railroad, 181; and the St. Paul,
Minneapolis & Manitoba Railway,

board of directors of, 121; and the
St. Paul, Minneapolis & Manitoba
Railway, expansion tactics of, 180,
189; and the St. Paul, Minneapolis &
Manitoba Railway, rail purchase of,
167; and the St. Paul, Minneapolis &
Manitoba Railway, resignation from,
159, 169; and the St. Paul,
Minneapolis & Manitoba Railway,
second mortgage bond issue of, 67-
68, 118, 124
Tilden, Samuel, 44, 45-46, 47, 209
Tilden Trust, 209
Tod, Andrew, 105-6, 218
Tod, James, 105, 218
Tod, John Kennedy: and the Canadian
Pacific Railway, 101; and the
Children's Aid Society, 214; and J.
Kennedy Tod & Co., 104; and J. S.
Kennedy & Co., 101; and the
Montana Central Railroad, 104, 159;
and the Scottish American
Investment Company, 23
Tod, Mary, 101
Tod, Robert Elliott, 104-5, 135, 218
Tod, William Stewart, 104, 105, 218
Torrence, Joseph Thatcher, 135
Touzalin, Albert E., 147, 148
Troy Iron & Steel Company, 167

U

Union Depot Company, 122
Union Pacific Railroad, 1, 7, 43, 194,
195
United Charities Building, 214
United States Trust Company of New
York, 23, 190

V

Villard, Henry, 178, 179, 191

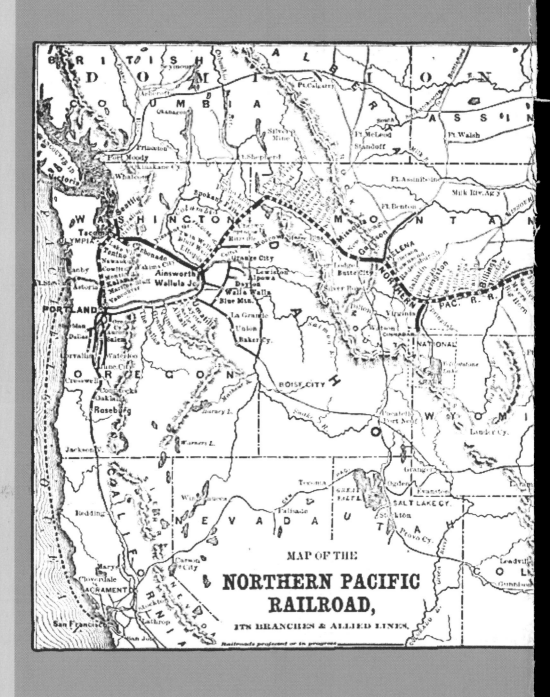

MAP OF THE

NORTHERN PACIFIC RAILROAD,

ITS BRANCHES & ALLIED LINES.

Railroads projected or in progress